T0317453

How to Calculate Options Prices and Their Greeks

WILEY

How to Calculate Options Prices and Their Greeks: Exploring the Black Scholes Model from Delta to Vega

PIERINO URSONE

WILEY

This edition first published 2015
© 2015 Pierino Ursone

Registered office
John Wiley & Sons Ltd, The Atrium, Southern Gate, Chichester, West Sussex, PO19 8SQ, United
Kingdom

For details of our global editorial offices, for customer services and for information about how to apply
for permission to reuse the copyright material in this book please see our website at www.wiley.com.

Wiley publishes in a variety of print and electronic formats and by print-on-demand. Some material
included with standard print versions of this book may not be included in e-books or in print-on-
demand. If this book refers to media such as a CD or DVD that is not included in the version you
purchased, you may download this material at http://booksupport.wiley.com. For more information
about Wiley products, visit www.wiley.com.

Library of Congress Cataloging-in-Publication Data is available

ISBN 978-1-118-96200-8 (hardback)
ISBN 978-1-118-96198-8 (ebk)
ISBN 978-1-118-96199-5 (ebk)

Cover Design: Wiley
Cover image: ©Cessna152/shutterstock

Set in 10/12pt Times by Laserwords Private Limited, Chennai, India
Printed in Great Britain by TJ International Ltd, Padstow, Cornwall, UK

Table of contents

Preface

In September 1992 I joined a renowned and highly successful market-making company at the Amsterdam Options Exchange. The company early recognised the need for hiring option traders having had an academic education and being very strong in mental calculation. Option trading those days more and more professionalised and shifted away from "survival of the loudest and toughest guy" towards a more intellectual approach. Trading was a matter of speed, being the first in a deal. Strength in mental arithmetic gave one an edge. For instance, when trading option combinations, adding prices and subtracting prices – one at the bid price, the other for instance at the asking price – being the quickest brought high rewards.

After a thorough test of my mental maths skills, I was one of only two, of the many people tested, to be employed. There I stood, in my first few days in the open outcry pit, just briefly after September 16th 1992 (Black Wednesday). On that day the UK withdrew from the European EMS system (the forerunner of the Euro), the British pound collapsed, the FX market in general became heavily volatile – all around the time the management of the company had decided to let me start trading Dollar options.

With my mentor behind me, I stood in the Dollar pit (training on the job) trying to compete with a bunch of experienced guys. My mentor jabbed my back each time when a trade, being brought to the pit by the floorbrokers, seemed interesting. In the meantime he was teaching me put–call parity, reversals and conversions, horizontal and time spreads, and whereabouts the value of at the money options should be (just a ballpark figure). There was one large distinction between us and the other traders; we were the only ones not using a computer printout with options prices. My mentor was certain that one should be able to trade off the top of the head; I was his guinea pig.

In those days, every trader on the floor was using a print of the Black Scholes model, indicating fair value for a large set of options at a specific level in the underlying asset. These printouts were produced at several levels of the underlying, so that a trader did not need to leave the pit to produce a new printout when new levels were met. Some days, however, markets could be so volatile that prices would "run off" the sheet. As a result the trader would have to leave the pit to print a new price sheet. It was exactly these moments when trading in the pit was the busiest: not having to leave the pit was an advantage as there were fewer traders to compete with. So, not having to rely on the printouts would create an edge while liquidity in trading would be booming at those times.

All the time we kept thinking of how to outsmart the others, how to value options at specific volatility levels and how, for instance, volatility spreads would behave in changing market circumstances. Soon we were able, when looking at option prices in other trading pits, to come up with fairly good estimates on the prevailing volatilities. We figured out how the delta of in the money options relate to the at the money options, how the at the moneys have to be priced and how to value butterflies on the back of the delta of spreads and more. Next to that we had our weekly company calculation and strategy sessions. There was a steady accumulation of knowledge on options pricing and valuing some of the Greeks.

After having run my own company from 1996 to 2001 at the Amsterdam exchange, I entered the energy options market, a whole different league. There was no exchange to trade on, no clearing of trades (hence counterparty risk), the volumes were much larger and it was professional against professional. As a market maker on the exchange one was in general used to earning a living on the back of the margins stemming from the differences in bid and asking prices (obviously we were running some strategies at the same time as well). Now however, with everyone knowing exactly where prices should be, all margins had evaporated. As a result, the only way to earn money was to have a proper assessment of the market and have the right position to optimise the potential profits. So I moved from an environment where superior pricing was a guarantee for success to an area where only the right strategy and the right execution of this strategy would reap rewards. It truly was a challenge how to think of the best strategy as there is a plethora of possible option combinations.

It has been the combination of these two worlds which has matured me in understanding how option trading really works. Without knowing how to price an option and its Greeks it would be onerous to find the right strategy. Without having the right market assessment it is impossible to generate profits from options trading.

In this book I have written down what I have learned in almost 20 years of options trading. It will greatly contribute to a full understanding of how to price options and their Greeks, how they are distributed and how strategies work out under changing circumstances. As mentioned before, when setting up a strategy one can choose from many possible option combinations. This book will help the reader to ponder options and strategies in such a way that one can fully understand how changes in underlying levels, in market volatility and in time impact the profitability of a strategy.

I wish to express my gratitude to my friends Bram van der Lee and Matt Daen for reviewing this book, for their support, enthusiasm and suggestions on how to further improve its quality.

Pierino Ursone

CHAPTER 1

Introduction

The most widely used option model is the Black and Scholes model. Although there are some shortcomings, the model is appreciated by many professional option traders and investors because of its simplicity, but also because, in many circumstances, it does generate a fair value for option prices in all kinds of markets.

The main shortcomings, most of which will be discussed later, are:
the model assumes a geometric Brownian motion where the market might deviate from that assumption (jumps); it assumes a normal distribution of daily (logarithmic) returns of an asset or Future while quite often there is a tendency towards a distribution with high peaks around the mean and fat tails; it assumes stable volatility while the market is characterised by changing (stochastic) volatility regimes; it also assumes all strikes of the options have the same volatility; it doesn't apply skew (adjustment of option prices) in the volatility smile/surface, and so on.

So in principle there may be a lot of caveats on the Black and Scholes model. However, because of its use by many market participants (with adjustments to make up for the shortcomings) in combination with its accuracy on many occasions, it may remain the basis option model for pricing options for quite some time.

This book aims to explore and explain the ins and outs of the Black and Scholes model (to be precise, the Black '76 model on Futures, minimising the impact of interest rates and leaving out dividends). It has been written for any person active in buying or selling options, involved in options from a business perspective or just interested in learning the background of options pricing, which is quite often seen as a black box. Although this is not an academic work, it could be worthwhile for academics to understand how options and their derivatives perform in practice, rather than in theory.

The book has a very practical approach and an emphasis on the distribution of the Greeks; these measure the sensitivity of the value of an option with regards to changes in parameters such as the strike, the underlying (Future), volatility (a measurement of the variation of the underlying), time to expiry or maturity, and the interest rate. It further emphasises the implications of the Greeks and understanding them with regards to the impact they will/might have on the P&L of an options portfolio. The aim is to give the reader a full understanding of the multidimensional aspects of trading options.

When measuring the sensitivity of the value of an option with regards to changes in the parameters one can discern many Greeks, but the most important ones are:

Delta: the price change of an option in relation to the change of the underlying;

Vega: the price change of an option in relation to volatility;

Theta (time decay): the price change of an option in relation to time;

Rho: the price change of an option in relation to interest rate.

These Greeks are called the first order Greeks. Next to that there are also second order Greeks, which are derivatives of the first order Greeks – gamma, vanna, vomma, etcetera – and third order Greeks, being derivatives of the second order Greeks – colour, speed, etcetera.

The most important of the higher order Greeks is gamma which measures the change of delta.

TABLE 1.1

Parameters	First order Greeks	Second order Greeks	Third order Greeks
Strike	Delta	Gamma	Colour
Underlying	Vega	Vanna	Speed
Volatility	Theta	Vomma	Ultima
Time to maturity	Rho	Charm	Zomma
Interest rate		Veta	
		Vera	

When Greeks are mentioned throughout the book, the term usually relates to delta, vega, theta and gamma, for they are the most important ones.

The book will also teach how to value at the money options, their surrounding strikes and their main Greeks, without applying the option model. Although much is based on rules of thumb and approximation, valuations without the model can be very accurate. Being able to value/approximate option prices and their Greeks off the top of the head is not the main objective; however, being able to do so must imply that one fully understands how pricing works and how the Greeks are distributed. This will enable the reader to consider and calculate how an option strategy might develop in a four dimensional way. The reader will learn about the consequences of options pricing with regards to changes in time, volatility, underlying and strike, all at the same time.

People on the verge of entering into an option strategy quite often prepare themselves by checking books or the internet. Too often they find explanations of a certain strategy which is only based on the payoff of an option at time of maturity – a

Short the 40 put at $1.50 (at inception: Future at 50, volatility 28%, maturity 1 year)

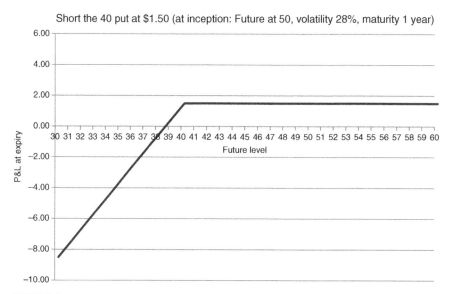

CHART 1.1   P&L distribution of a short 40 put position at expiry

two-dimensional interpretation (underlying price versus profit loss). This can be quite misleading since there is so much to say about options during their lifetime, something some people might already have experienced when confronted with adverse market moves while running an option strategy with associated losses. A change in any one of the aforementioned parameters will result in a change in the value of an option. In a two-dimensional approach (i.e. looking at P&L distribution at expiry) most of the Greeks are disregarded, while during the lifetime of the option they can make or break the strategy.

Throughout the book, any actor who is active in buying or selling options – i.e. a private investor, trader, hedger, portfolio manager, etcetera – will be called a trader.

Many people understand losses deriving from bad investment decisions when buying options or the potentially unlimited losses of short options. However, quite often they fail to see the potentially devastating effects of misinterpretation of the Greeks.

For example, as shown in chart 1.1, a trader who sold a 40 put at $1.50 when the Future was trading at 50 (volatility at 28%, maturity 1 year), had the right view. During the lifetime of the option, the market never came below 40, the put expired worthless, and the trader consequently ended up with a profit of $1.50.

The problem the trader may have experienced, however, is that shortly after inception of the trade, the market came off rapidly towards the 42 level. As a result of the sharp drop in the underlying, the volatility may have jumped from 28% to 40%. The 40 put he sold at $1.50 suddenly had a value of $5.50, an unrealised loss of $4. It would have at least made the trader nervous, but most probably he would have bought back the option because it hit his stop loss level or he was forced by

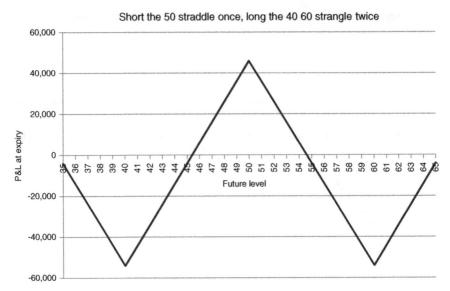

CHART 1.2   P&L distribution of the combination trade at expiry

his broker, bank or clearing institution to deposit more margin; or even worse, the trade was stopped out by one of these institutions (at a bad price) when not adhering to the margin call.

So an adverse market move could have caused the trader to end up with a loss while being right in his strategy/view of the market. If he had anticipated the possibility of such a market move he might have sold less options or kept some cash for additional margin calls. Consequently, at expiry, he would have ended up with the $1.50 profit. Anticipation obviously can only be applied when understanding the consequences of changing option parameters with regards to the price of an option.

A far more complex strategy, with a striking difference in P&L distribution at expiry compared to the P&L distribution during its lifetime, is a combination where the trader is short the 50 call once (10,000 lots) and long the 60 call twice (20,000 lots) and at the same time short the 50 put once (10,000 lots) and long the 40 put twice (20,000 lots). He received around $45,000 when entering into the strategy. The P&L distribution of the combination trade at expiry is shown above in Chart 1.2.

The combination trade will perform best when the market is at 50 (around $45,000 profit) and will have its worst performance when the market is either at 40 or at 60 at expiry (around $55,000 loss).

The strategy has been set up with 1 year to maturity; a lot can happen in the time between inception of the trade and its expiry. In an environment where the Future will rapidly change and where as a result of the fast move in the market the volatility might increase, the P&L distribution of the strategy could look, in a three dimensional way, as follows (P&L versus time to maturity versus underlying level):

Chart 1.3 shows the P&L distribution of the combination trade in relation to time. When looking at expiry, at the axis "Days to expiry" at 0, the P&L distribution

P&L Chart

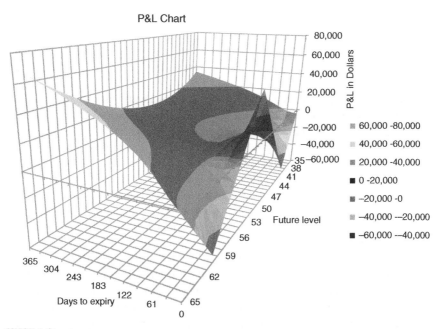

CHART 1.3 Combination trade, long 20,000 40 puts and 60 calls, short 10,000 50 puts and 50 calls

is the same as the distribution depicted in the two-dimensional chart 1.2. The best performance is at 50 in the Future, resulting in a P&L of around $45,000 and the worst case scenario is when the Future is at 40 or at 60, when the loss will mount up to around $55,000. However, when the maturity is 365 "days to expiry" and the market starts moving and consequently the volatility will, for instance, increase, the performance will overall be positive, there will be some profit at the 50 level in the Future. This is the smallest amount, but still a few thousand up: a profit of around $35,000 when the Future is at 60 and around $10,000 when the Future is at 40. These P&L numbers keep changing during the lifetime of the strategy. For instance, the $35,000 profit at 60 in the Future (at 365 days to expiry) will turn into a $55,000 loss at expiry when the market stays at that level – losses in time, called the time decay or theta. Also, when the trade has been set up, the P&L of the portfolio increases with higher levels in the Future, so there must be some sort of delta active (change of value of the portfolio in relation to the change of the Future). Next to that, the P&L distribution displays a convex line between 50 and 65 at 365 days to expiry, which means that the delta will change as well; changes in the delta are called the gamma.

So the P&L distribution of this structure is heavily influenced by its Greeks: the delta, gamma, vega and theta – a very dynamic distribution. Thus, without an understanding of the Greeks this structure would not be understandable when looking at the P&L distribution from a more dimensional perspective.

It is of utmost importance that one realises that changing market conditions can make an option portfolio with a profitable outlook change into a position with an almost certainly negative P&L; or the other way around, as shown in the example above. Therefore it is a prerequisite that when trading/investing in options one understands the Greeks.

This book will, in the first chapters, discuss probability distribution, volatility and put call parity, then the main Greeks: delta, gamma, vega and theta. The first order Greeks, together with gamma (a second order Greek), are the most important and will thus be discussed at length. As the other Greeks are derived from these, they will be discussed only briefly, if at all. Once the regular Greeks are understood one can easily ponder the second and third order Greeks and understand how they work.

In the introduction of a chapter on a Greek, the formula of this Greek will be shown as well. The intention is not to write about mathematics, its purpose is to show how parameters like underlying, volatility and time will influence that specific Greek. So a mathematical equation like the one for gamma, $\gamma = \frac{\varphi(d1)}{F\sigma\sqrt{T}}$, should not bring despair. In the chapter itself it will be fully explained.

In the last chapter, trading strategies will be discussed, from simple strategies towards complex structures. The main importance, though, is that the trader must have a view about the market; without this it is hard to determine which strategy is appropriate to become a potential winner. An option strategy should be the result of careful consideration of the market circumstances. How well the option strategy performs is fully related to the trader making the right assessment on the market's direction or market circumstances. A potential winning option strategy could end up disastrously with an unanticipated adverse market move. Each strategy could be a winner, but at the same time a loser as well.

The terms "in", "at" or "out" of the money will be mentioned throughout the book. "At the money" refers to an option which strike is situated at precisely the level of the underlying. When not meant to be precisely at the money, the term "around the at the money" will be applied. "Out of the money" options are calls with higher strikes and puts with lower strikes compared to the at the money strike; "in the money" options are calls with lower strikes and puts with higher strikes compared to the at the money strike.

The options in the book are treated as European options, hence there will be no early exercise possible (exercising the right entailed by the option before maturity date), as opposed to American options. Obviously, American option prices might differ from European (in relation to dividends and the interest rate level), however discussing this falls beyond the scope of the book. When applying European style there will be no effect on option pricing with regards to dividend.

For the asset/underlying, a Future has been chosen; it already has a future dividend pay out and the interest rate component incorporated in its value.

For reasons of simplicity and also for making a better representation of the effect of the Greeks, 10,000 units has been applied as the basis volume for at the money options where each option represents the right to buy (i.e. a call) or sell (i.e. a put) one Future. The 10,000 basis volume could represent a fairly large private investor or a fairly small trader in the real world. For out of the money options, larger quantities will be applied, depending on the face value of the portfolio/position.

CHAPTER 2

The Normal Probability Distribution

The "Bell" curve or Gaussian distribution, called the normal standard distribution, displays how data/observations will be distributed in a specific range with a certain probability. Think of the height of a population; let's assume a group of people where 95% of all the persons are between 1.10 m and 1.90 m, implying a mean of 1.50 m ($\frac{1.9+1.1}{2}$). Looking at Chart 2.1, one can see that 95% of the observations are within 2 standard deviations on either side of

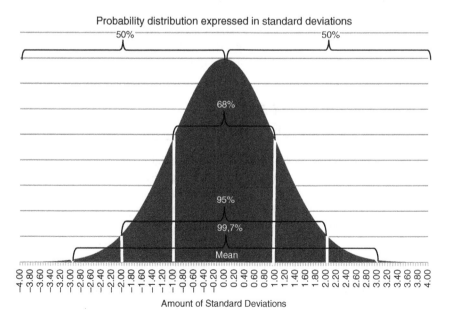

Probability distribution expressed in standard deviations

CHART 2.1   Normal probability distribution

the mean (on the chart at 0.00), totalling 4 standard deviations. So 0.80 m (the difference between 1.90 and 1.10) represents 4 standard deviations, resulting in a standard deviation of 0.20 m.

With a mean of 1.50 m and a standard deviation of 0.20 m one could say that there is a likelihood of 68% for the people to have a height between 1.30 and 1.70 m, a high likelihood of 95% for people to have a height between 1.10 and 1.90 m and almost certainty, around 99.7%, for people to have a height between 0.90 and 2.10 m. Or to say it differently; hardly any person is taller than 2.10 m or smaller than 0.90 m.

STANDARD DEVIATION IN A FINANCIAL MARKET

The same could be applied to the daily returns of a Future in a financial market. According to its volatility it will have a certain standard deviation. When, for instance, a Future which is trading at 50 with a daily standard deviation of 1%, one could say that with 256 trading days in a year (365 days minus the weekends and some holidays), in 68% of these days, being 174 days, the Future will move during each trading day between 0 and 50 cents up or down. Twenty-seven per cent (95% minus 68%) of the days (69 days) it will shift between 50 cents and a dollar up or down. There will be around 13 days where the Future will move more than 1 dollar during the day.

In the financial markets where a Future trades at 50 (hence a mean of 50), a standard deviation of $\sigma \times \sqrt{T}$ (or simply $\sigma\sqrt{T}$) will be applied, where σ stands for volatility and $\sqrt{T}$ stands for the square root of time to maturity (expressed in years).

THE IMPACT OF VOLATILITY AND TIME ON THE STANDARD DEVIATION

Volatility is the measure of the variation of a financial asset over a certain time period. An asset with high volatility displays sharp directional moves and large intraday moves; one can think of times when exchanges experience turbulent moments, when for instance geopolitical issues arise and investors seem to be panicking a bit. With low volatility one could think of the infamous summer lull; at some stage markets hardly move for days, volumes are very low and people are not investing during their summer holidays.

For T, the square root of time to maturity is represented in an annualised form, meaning that when maturity is in 3 months time, T will be ¼ (year), where its square root is ½.

So with a Future (F) trading at 50.00, volatility (σ) at 20% and maturity (T) 3 months (¼ year), the standard deviation will be: $\sigma \times \sqrt{T} \times F = 20\% \times \frac{1}{2} \times 50.00 = 5.00$. This implies that when 2 standard deviations are applied, the Future at maturity

Probability distribution different maturities and different volatility, Future at 50

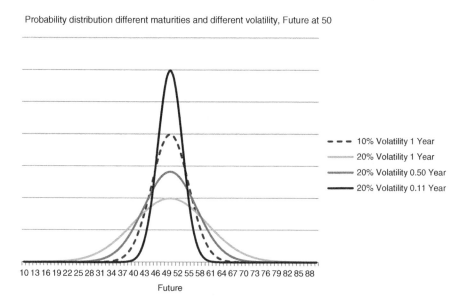

Legend:
- - - 10% Volatility 1 Year
——— 20% Volatility 1 Year
━━━ 20% Volatility 0.50 Year
━━━ 20% Volatility 0.11 Year

X-axis: 10 13 16 19 22 25 28 31 34 37 40 43 46 49 52 55 58 61 64 67 70 73 76 79 82 85 88

Future

CHART 2.2 Chart 2.2 shows the probability distributions for the Future, currently trading at 50, at two different volatility levels and three different times to maturity.

will be expected to be somewhere between 40.00 and 60.00 with 95% certainty (sometimes called the confidence level).

Obviously, when volatility and/or time to maturity increase the range gets larger (in essence an increase in the standard deviation); a decrease in volatility and/or time to maturity will result in a smaller range (a decrease in the standard deviation).

The dashed line in Chart 2.2 (10% volatility and 1 year to maturity) displays the distribution with a standard deviation of: $\sigma \times \sqrt{T} \times F$, being 10% times the square root of 1 times 50, which makes $5. When applying 3 standard deviations, the 35/65 range can be calculated (being $3 \times 5 = 15$ points lower and higher compared to the current Future level) where the 99.7% probability applies.

This is exactly the same as the distribution for the Future with a volatility of 20% and a maturity of 3 months (the earlier example). In the standard deviation formula ($\sigma \sqrt{T}$) the volatility has doubled from 10% to 20%. With regards to T, 3 months' maturity is one quarter of a year. By taking the square root of a quarter, it means that the T component has actually been halved. So by halving the standard deviation for the T component and multiplying it by 2 for the σ component, the outcome will be exactly the same probability distribution.

It is important to realise that the surface of the different distributions has the same size every time. The total chance has to be kept at 100% all the time. Maturity can be shorter, though the height of the chart will be higher then, in order to keep the surface at the same size. A higher volatility (with unchanged time to maturity) will result in a much broader/wider area in the Future; to compensate for that (keeping the total size of the charts at the same level) the height of the chart/distribution will be lower.

In conclusion: the effect on the standard deviations is linear with regards to volatility moves and has a square root function with regards to time changes. This feature will come back several times when discussing the Greeks. One just needs to recall how the charts will change (keeping size/surface constant) with changes in volatility and changes in time; it will help to explain other features in option theory as well.

CHAPTER 3

Volatility

Volatility is the measure of the variation (or the dispersion) of the returns (profits/losses) of a Future over a certain period of time.

One could say: the riskier the asset, the higher the volatility (think of market crashes). The lower an asset's risk, the lower its volatility (think of the summer lull). So, in highly volatile markets one could expect large moves of the Future where at low volatile markets there might be days where the Future hardly moves.

THE PROBABILITY DISTRIBUTION OF THE VALUE OF A FUTURE AFTER ONE YEAR OF TRADING

In option trading volatility is expressed on an annualised basis. It is a calculation of the daily returns based on a full year's expectation of the combined returns. The annualised volatility predicts the probability of the outcome of the value of a Future after one year of trading (usually 256 trading days).

The probability is based on the Gaussian distribution. With low volatility (for example, 10% as depicted in chart 3.1), one could expect the Future, which initially started at 50, to settle somewhere between 40 and 60 after one year of trading. (Here a 95% confidence level has been applied, being 95% of all probable occurrences, and hence 2 standard deviations of 10%.) If the volatility is twice as high (20%), the range for the Future to settle after one year of trading would (almost) double as well, now between 30 and 70.

When volatility is at 40%, the range (almost) doubles again.

NORMAL DISTRIBUTION VERSUS LOG-NORMAL DISTRIBUTION

Charts 3.1, 3.2 and 3.3 show that the distribution range for the Future to settle after one year of trading would double with double volatility, however the word "almost" has been added between brackets. This is the result of the convention in the financial markets to apply a log-normal distribution rather than a normal distribution.

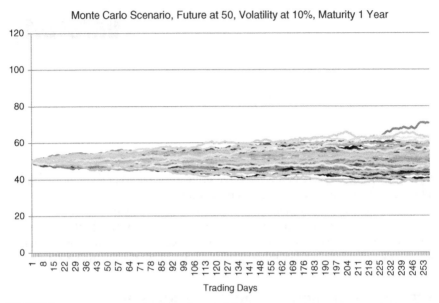

CHART 3.1   Probability distribution at 10% volatility

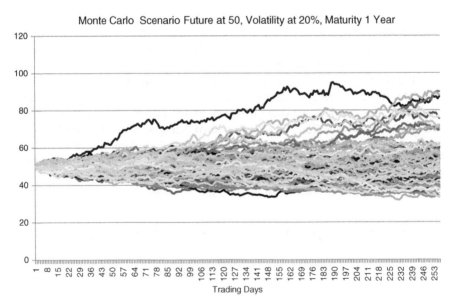

CHART 3.2   Probability distribution at 20% volatility

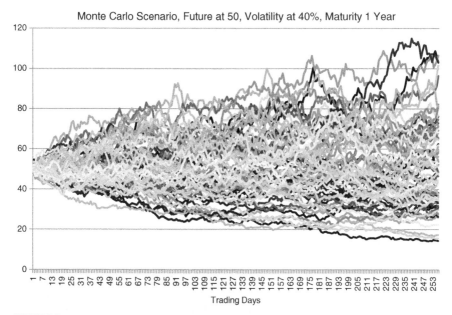

CHART 3.3 Probability distribution at 40% volatility

The application of a log-normal scale serves two purposes:

a. the Future cannot become negative;

b. the Future, not being able to go below zero, could in fact increase towards many times the initial value.

A Future, now trading at 50, can lose a maximum of $50 but could easily gain several hundreds of dollars. On a logarithmic scale the impact of an asset going up from 50 to 100 is equivalent to an asset going up from 100 to 200 – or, mathematically expressed in logarithmic returns: $\ln\left(\frac{50}{100}\right) = \ln\left(\frac{100}{200}\right)$. This is why the downside is somewhat limited $\ln\left(\frac{25}{50}\right) = \ln\left(\frac{50}{100}\right)$ (showing a 25 to 50 move being equivalent to a 50 to 100 move). In this way a $25 range on the downside is equivalent to a $50 range on the upside. Also a 10 to 50 range will be equivalent to a move from 50 to 250, a scenario where there is $40 on the downside versus $200 on the upside. When not applying the ln sign, the relationship will be clear as well: $\frac{25}{50} = \frac{50}{100}$ or $\frac{10}{50} = \frac{50}{250}$.

It is this relationship that tweaks the probability distribution for the Future somewhat. At 10% volatility and the Future trading at 50, the upper range (for a 95% confidence level, being two standard deviations) for the Future will be 2 times 10% times 50, resulting in a $10 move for the upside, being 60. The ratio $\left(\frac{60}{50}\right)$ is hence 1.2. When applying this ratio for determining the lower level of the range one will have to divide 50 by 1.2, making it $41\frac{2}{3}$. So at 10% volatility, the upper level for the range is $10 higher while the lower level of the range is only $8\frac{1}{3}$ lower. It will be quite easy to find the range levels now when applying different annualised volatility levels (applying two standard deviations for the upper level of the range).

TABLE 3.1

Volatility	Future level initially (F)	Upper level for the range	Ratio (R)	Lower level for the range (F/R)
10%	50	60	1.2	41.66
15%	50	65	1.3	38.46
20%	50	70	1.4	35.71
30%	50	80	1.6	31.25
40%	50	90	1.8	27.78

　　　The difference between a normal distribution and a log-normal distribution will have a clear impact on charts. When displaying a chart of a simple formula, being "sample value times 10" and using samples 1 to 100, the outcomes of the formula will lie between 10 and 1,000. The chart as displayed in Chart 3.4 using a normal axis will be a simple linear chart, while the chart with a logarithmic axis will look completely different, a feature one should be well aware of (e.g. think of technical analysis).

　　　In conclusion it could be said that, if volatility doubles the probability region for the Future to settle after one year of trading will (approximately) double as

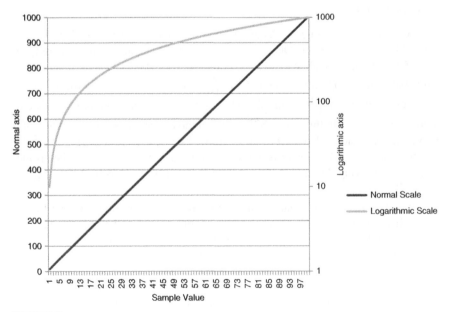

CHART 3.4　Normal scale versus logarithmic scale

well. This must then have an immense impact on the value of the options. And that is correct: when volatility doubles (with time to maturity and interest rate constant) the value of the at the money options will double as well. The impact of volatility is quite easy to measure, which in its turn facilitates valuing option prices.

CALCULATING THE ANNUALISED VOLATILITY TRADITIONALLY

When calculating the standard deviation of all daily (logarithmic) returns of the Future at close of day and then multiplying it with the square root of the amount of trading days in one year, the outcome is the annualised volatility.

This annualised volatility is called the historical volatility (or the realized volatility), as opposed to implied volatility, which is the measure of how the options are quoted by the market participants. As will be later shown in this chapter; quite often there is a (sometimes fairly large) discrepancy between the two. The annualised volatility will be called the historical volatility throughout the book.

In order to calculate the historical volatility, one first needs to calculate the variance of the daily returns of the Future.

In a formula, the Variance (σ^2) is as follows:

$$\sigma = \frac{1}{n-1} \sum_{i=1}^{n} (xi - \mu)^2$$

where:

- xi stands for the daily logarithmic return of each trading day

  xi = Logarithm (ln) of the Future value on day i divided by the Future value of the day prior to day $xi = \ln(\frac{Future\ Value\ on\ day\ i}{Future\ Value\ on\ day\ i-1})$;

- μ stands for the average of the computed daily logarithmic returns and n for the amount of trading days;

- $\sum$ is the symbol for Sum, just adding up all the values there are (in this case 1st to the nth value).

And the Standard Deviation (just being the square root of the variance) in formula:

$$\sigma = \sqrt{\frac{1}{n-1} \sum_{i=1}^{n} (xi - \mu)^2}.$$

As stated earlier, the historical volatility is calculated by multiplying the standard deviation of the daily returns with the square root of trading days: hence, $\sigma \times 16 (\sqrt{256})$. Bear in mind that in this chapter σ stands for standard deviation; however, further throughout the book, and also in the market, σ stands for annualised volatility.

The following table is an example of how to calculate the historical volatility of a set of 15 samples:

TABLE 3.2

Asset/Future 50	Daily Log Ret xi	$(xi\text{-}\mu)^2$		
49.66	−0.6765%	0.0111%	average (μ)	0.3788%
50.75	2.1637%	0.0319%	Variance	0.021%
51.20	0.8926%	0.0026%	Standard Deviation	1.44%
51.47	0.5260%	0.0002%	Trading Days	256
50.74	−1.4417%	0.0331%	Volatility	23.06%
50.61	−0.2516%	0.0040%		
50.03	−1.1472%	0.0233%		
51.17	2.2541%	0.0352%		
52.40	2.3646%	0.0394%		
52.84	0.8356%	0.0021%		
51.75	−2.0808%	0.0605%		
51.74	−0.0247%	0.0016%		
52.25	0.9924%	0.0038%		
51.84	−0.7891%	0.0136%		
52.92	2.0645%	0.0284%		

First the daily logarithmic returns (xi) will be calculated with $\ln(Fi / (Fi − 1))$, which generates the first value: ln (49.66/50). In total there are 16 values, although only 15 returns for the first value is the starting point of the Future. The outcomes are taken as a percentage: $\ln(\frac{49.66}{50}) = -0.006765$. Expressed as a percentage this is −0.6765%.

The next thing is to calculate μ by just averaging all daily log returns.

$(xi - \mu)^2$ speaks for itself, the square of a percentage is not the same as the square of the values and then the percentage sign added; for instance, $2\%^2$ is not 4% but 2% of 2%, which makes 0.04%.

The standard deviation is the square root of all $(xi - \mu)^2$ values together ($n = 15$) and divided by 14 $(n-1)$.

The calculation will end by multiplying the standard deviation with the square root of the amount of trading days in a year.

What, however, happens when the Future enters a trend and moves up exactly 2% every day compared to the day before? The value of xi (logarithmic) will be around 2%, while at the same time μ has exactly the same value as xi of around 2%. $(xi - \mu)^2$ will hence equate to 0.00% for every trading day. Thus, the result is a zero standard deviation which equates to a volatility of 0%, as shown in Table 3.3 on the following page.

So there is something wrong with this calculation and it is necessary to find a way to improve it. A Future which is moving will always have a volatility.

TABLE 3.3

Asset/Future 50	Daily Log Return xi	$(xi\text{-}\mu)^2$		
51	1.9803%	0.00%	average (μ)	1.9803%
52.02	1.9803%	0.00%	Variance	0.0000%
53.06	1.9803%	0.00%	Standard Deviation	0.000%
54.12	1.9803%	0.00%	Trading Days	256
55.20	1.9803%	0.00%	Volatility	0.00%
56.31	1.9803%	0.00%		
57.43	1.9803%	0.00%		
58.58	1.9803%	0.00%		
59.75	1.9803%	0.00%		
60.95	1.9803%	0.00%		
62.17	1.9803%	0.00%		
63.41	1.9803%	0.00%		
64.68	1.9803%	0.00%		
65.97	1.9803%	0.00%		
67.29	1.9803%	0.00%		

CALCULATING THE ANNUALISED VOLATILITY WITHOUT μ

Unfortunately, when looking for historical volatility calculation methods the fault mentioned in the former paragraph is very often found. One should be extremely careful with this traditional method for the calculation of the historical volatility of a Future which has moved considerably/ended in a trend in the observation period. With a sideways market, misinterpretation of historical volatility is less likely because μ will be close(r) to zero.

The formula needs a small adjustment, namely:

$$\sigma = \sqrt{\frac{1}{n-1}\sum_{i=1}^{n}(xi)^2} \; .$$

By simply deleting μ, market volatility is correctly calculated when the Future enters a trend.

Also, bear in mind that, when performing a calculation to determine the standard deviation, Excel will display the same issue; when computing the function "stdev" for logarithmic returns, the volatility of a trending Future will slide towards zero as well, it will have a dampening effect in all the cases.

This is an extremely important feature because a trader might err in selling options in the market since the options are trading at a much higher volatility (the implied volatility) than the (traditional) calculation of the historical volatility, which the trader had computed to be justifiable. The proper calculation (without using μ) might even entice him to buy the options instead of sell them.

When the formula is changed for the variance, and thus also for the standard deviation, the volatility calculation for trending Futures will result in a far more reasonable value. The computed volatility, when applying the same data as in the first shown traditional volatility calculation, is slightly higher.

TABLE 3.4

Asset/Future 50	Daily Log Ret x_i	$(x_i)^2$		
49.66	−0.6765%	0.0046%		
50.75	2.1637%	0.0468%	Variance	0.022%
51.20	0.8926%	0.0080%	Standard Deviation	1.49%
51.47	0.5260%	0.0028%	Trading Days	256
50.74	−1.4417%	0.0208%	Volatility	23.90%
50.61	−0.2516%	0.0006%		
50.03	−1.1472%	0.0132%		
51.17	2.2541%	0.0508%		
52.40	2.3646%	0.0559%		
52.84	0.8356%	0.0070%		
51.75	−2.0808%	0.0433%		
51.74	−0.0247%	0.0000%		
52.25	0.9924%	0.0098%		
51.84	−0.7891%	0.0062%		
52.92	2.0645%	0.0426%		

In Table 3.4 above, the same time series as in Table 3.2 has been computed. When using μ in the first example, the outcome was 23.06% annualised, now without using μ the outcome is 23.90% annualised – a small difference.

TABLE 3.5

Asset/Future 50	Daily Log Ret x_i	$(x_i)^2$		
51	1.9803%	0.0392%		
52.02	1.9803%	0.0392%	Variance	0.0420%
53.06	1.9803%	0.0392%	Standard Deviation	2.050%
54.12	1.9803%	0.0392%	Trading Days	256
55.20	1.9803%	0.0392%	Volatility	32.80%
56.31	1.9803%	0.0392%		
57.43	1.9803%	0.0392%		
58.58	1.9803%	0.0392%		
59.75	1.9803%	0.0392%		
60.95	1.9803%	0.0392%		

TABLE 3.5 *(Continued)*

Asset/Future 50	Daily Log Ret xi	$(xi)^2$
62.17	1.9803%	0.0392%
63.41	1.9803%	0.0392%
64.68	1.9803%	0.0392%
65.97	1.9803%	0.0392%
67.29	1.9803%	0.0392%

When calculating the volatility for a trending future using μ the outcome is 0%; leaving out μ would equate to a standard deviation of 2.050% multiplied by $16(\sqrt{256})$, resulting in a historical volatility of 32.80%, as shown above in Table 3.5. Now this is a huge and very striking difference. Next to that, when computing the Greeks (especially gamma and theta) in the Black & Scholes model, a volatility of around 32% is actually the right volatility.

CALCULATING THE ANNUALISED VOLATILITY APPLYING THE 16% RULE

Historical volatility is the result of the standard deviation of the Future over a certain time frame multiplied by the square root of the amount of trading days, in most cases 256 trading days, which results in a factor of 16. So quite simply said: if the standard deviation is 1%, the volatility should be 16%; if the standard deviation is 2%, the volatility would be 32%; and so on.

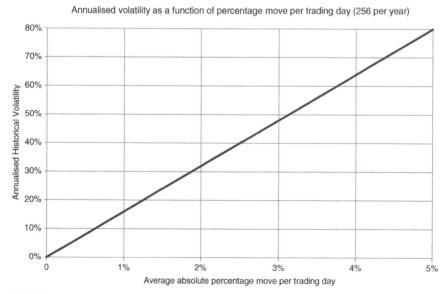

CHART 3.5 Volatility as a function of the daily percentage moves

Chart 3.5 shows that when the average is absolute (i.e. when the Future drops 1% in one day, the move is considered to be 1% positive) the daily percentage move is 1% and the volatility 16%. If there is a larger daily move, the historical volatility will be calculated by multiplying the average absolute percentage move per trading day times the square root of 256. The log return of a Future moving 1% will almost equal this 1% (0.995% versus 1%) or when moving 2% as well (1.9803% versus 2%). This is a very strong tool to estimate where the volatility is. When analysing historical volatility one sometimes just needs to look at the daily price changes to get a good feeling of where the volatility is at that moment, without actually computing it in a formula. The 16% rule is widely applied by traders in the business.

There is a caveat to this approach; when for instance a Future moves 1% for two days in a row its standard deviation will be 1%, just like the average absolute percentage, and a volatility of 16% will be justified. However if the Future moves 0.5% on day one and 1.5% on day two, the average absolute percentage move is 1% and the trader applying the 16% rule would come up with a volatility of 16%. The volatility calculation when leaving μ out, will, with these values, result in a standard deviation of 1.41 and a volatility of 22.6% – a large discrepancy. As a result, the 16% rule can only be applied when the Future shows stable daily returns; in other scenarios the 16% rule will underestimate the true historical volatility.

VARIATION IN TRADING DAYS

Although it is very unlikely, what if a certain future/asset class has less than 256 trading days in a year? As already mentioned, in order to calculate the historical volatility from the standard deviation, it just needs to be multiplied by the square root of the amount of trading days.

If an asset has a 2% standard deviation, but has only 100 trading days per annum, then the annualised volatility will be 2% multiplied by $10(\sqrt{100})$, making 20% volatility; with 256 trading days this would add up to 32% volatility.

Consider the charts at the beginning of the chapter: with only 100 trading days in a year, the charts should end somewhere in the middle. It is clear that the range where the Future could trade at maturity is much smaller than where it could trade after 256 trading days in a year. Next to that, the Black & Scholes model fully supports this approach.

APPROACH TOWARDS INTRADAY VOLATILITY

So far historical volatility has been calculated, based on close to close prices per trading day. A Future will however very often move in opposite directions during the day. When trading up, some traders might decide to take profit and start selling, pushing it lower again and vice versa. If, for instance, a Future moves up in the morning then down again, through profit taking, in the afternoon, closing unchanged at the end of the day, on a close to close basis it displays 0% volatility for that day, while actually it has displayed quite some volatility during the day.

This kind of volatility should be taken into account as well. Actually, if the level of the options volatility in the traded market (the implied volatility) is at the same level as the close to close historical volatility (with no other specific conditions ruling the market) then the options might be too cheap: there is always intraday volatility which actually should have been reflected in the calculation as well. A trader could take advantage of that. When the implied volatility is cheaper than the historical volatility there is a mismatch which could earn money when being long the cheaper options. The other way around works as well: being short at a higher implied volatility than the actual historical volatility would justify, makes money too.

So as a prudent trader one should be aware of the intraday volatility as well. Below are a few scenarios:

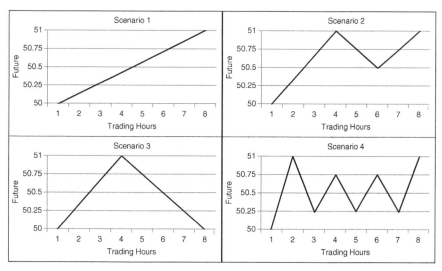

CHART 3.6 Four scenarios for intraday moves

In Scenario 1 the Future is moving from 50 to 51 in one trading day. To annualise its volatility on a close to close basis, a 2% move would be multiplied by $16(\sqrt{256})$ to end up at 32% volatility.

Scenario 2 would have the same volatility on close to close, but during the afternoon it dropped 1% and reversed again to finally end up 2% higher over the day. When the implied volatility was trading at around 32%, a trader could have benefitted (on this day) from the additional move the Future made in the afternoon.

Scenario 3 displays on close to close basis 0% volatility. However, the Future experienced some serious intraday moves, first trading up 2% to drop 2% in the afternoon again. In essence the Future showed a very large intraday volatility while the historical volatility on a close to close basis would actually be valued at 0%. A trader owning optionality would benefit from this move.

Scenario 4 depicts a very volatile Future: intraday the Future comes up and down several times. The trader being long optionality will seriously benefit from this intraday move.

So in these examples, except for Scenario 1, the historical volatility as calculated from close to close on a daily basis will actually be too low compared to the intraday moves. Scenario 2 and 4 display quite some discrepancy, but they still end up 2% higher on the day. Scenario 3, however, shows a 0% historical volatility, while at the same time the market went up 2% and in the afternoon dropped 2% again.

So something else needs to be added or changed with regards to the historical volatility calculation. One could of course compute volatility on an hourly basis – or even by the minute – but there are several volatility calculations available which take into account the high and low of the day and also those in combination with open and close levels. One of these calculations is the Parkinson calculation with the following formula:

$$\sqrt{\frac{\sum_{i=1}^{n} \frac{1}{4\ln 2} \times \left(xi^{HL}\right)^2}{n}}$$

Where $xi^{HL} = \ln \frac{FHi}{FLi}$, the logarithm of the high in the Future during the day is divided by the low of the Future during the day.

In some situations the Parkinson calculation can be a better estimator than the earlier mentioned volatility calculation (close to close). However, this valuation might also not be sufficient (it ignores gap openings, for instance).

Some other volatility measures are:

Garman–Klass;

Rogers–Satchel;

Yang–Zhang.

Scenario 4 shows, between the high and the low of the Future during the day, even more volatility, which should be taken into account. It should be clear that historical volatility is actually not easy to grasp. Volatility is also a result of unexpected events and therefore rigidly applying one of the volatility calculations could prove insufficient.

To determine the maximum volatility, each move can be broken into small parts (small time increments or directional moves) and added together again on a straight line. So, adding up all the absolute moves, something which may be called the stretch, as shown below in Chart 3.7:

It is quite interesting to see how 4 Scenarios of daily moves of a future, which in a sort of way resemble each other (the Future is everywhere trading in the same range), have such a huge difference in volatility realisation. Obviously, the "stretch" is the maximum for volatility calculation since the Future simply cannot move more.

Several ways of calculating volatility are shown, as well as what to take into account when trying to get a fair estimation. It is not recommendable to just compute the close to close volatility (and certainly not using the μ component), some additional volatility should be added. When trying to estimate the volatility one should really study the market and try to figure out how he would try to benefit from his optionality. Backtesting might give more information on how to implement/add

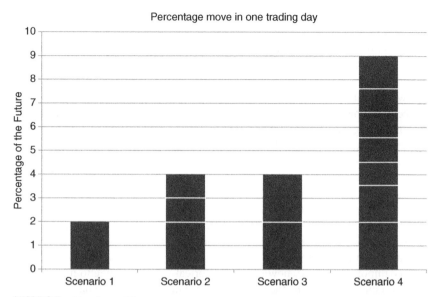

CHART 3.7 The "stretch"

additional intraday volatility in relation to trading the optionality and/or which estimator would be the most applicable. However, in the end it all depends on the way the trader exploits his optionality, a topic which will be discussed in the chapter about gamma and in the chapter about strategies: the wide versus the tight hedger. Someone being long an option, waiting for it to increase in value (or become in the money), will probably perform no intraday hedges, while another trader, exploiting the volatility of the market, will perform multiple hedges during the day. The first one will not be able to profit from these intraday moves and may have purchased his option at a too high price (since intraday volatility is also measured for determining the implied volatility).

HISTORICAL VERSUS IMPLIED VOLATILITY

Implied volatility has already had a few mentions; it is the volatility represented through option quotes. The market/implied volatility will be a reflection of supply and demand of the options and will quite often show a discrepancy with the (computed) historical volatility.

This discrepancy could be caused by future expectations: such as, the quarterly earnings figures of a company, important demand/supply data of a certain commodity, political decisions, geopolitical tensions, etc. Very often traders anticipate potential future market moves and will bid up the volatility in order to be able to buy enough optionality to profit from an event which results in a large move in the underlying. Many times (especially after the proverbial non-event) volatility will eventually come down to fair levels again – more in line with historical volatility. Sometimes this can happen very fast: perhaps within a day.

The implied volatility could be still high after a very volatile period where the historical volatility is already much lower, with the implied lagging behind. It could well be that there is some sort of pause and that historical volatility could come up again, which causes traders to be cautious with selling implied volatility. The same could be said if historical volatility is rising after a period of sustained low volatility in the underlying, but the implied is still at fairly low levels. Again the cautiousness of traders will cause the implied volatility to be lagging.

In a long lasting period of (fairly) stable historical volatility, either low or high, the implied volatility and historical volatility will converge more and more.

When entering into an option position, one should be aware of the discrepancies of the historical versus the implied volatility. A trader might also consider longer-term mid-level volatility in a specific asset, if this volatility reverts (how long is the mean reversion time?) to this mean. If the asset is part of a specific asset class, what is the implied (versus historical) volatility within this asset class? And very important as well, how did the historical volatility come to this specific number as computed? Maybe there has been an (unusual) big jump one day, which caused the volatility to be much higher compared to when filtering this one event out (valuation too high compared to normal). Or maybe in the computation there were no jumps, while actually one would have expected some jumps (valuation too low). When taking all possibilities into account, the trader should be able to come up with a fairly good assessment of where volatility should be. A fair volatility forecast means as well that there should be sufficient room for setting up a winning strategy (several volatility points). Trading to earn just one volatility point will in the end prove not to be a guaranteed winner: there should be at least some room for error/unexpected events, which could easily be that one volatility point.

Monitoring the market for wide spreads between historical volatility (computed in several ways) and implied volatility could be worthwhile. As stated before, one should be very cautious though and keep several scenarios in mind.

CHAPTER 4

Put Call Parity

Many people might look surprised when overhearing the phrase: "call is put and vice versa", but the truth is that calls and puts are directly related to each other and are "interchangeable". Discrepancies in this relationship can be easily arbitraged. The relationship also says something about the Greeks; when calls and puts are "interchangeable" and when arbitrage opportunities might arise when there are discrepancies, most of the Greeks (gamma, vega, theta) should be identical as well.

This chapter will describe how put call parity works and how, through so-called synthetics, calls can be converted into puts and vice versa. Firstly, a very obvious

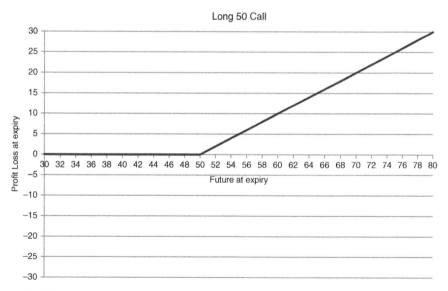

CHART 4.1   Long the 50 call

simple reflection of calls, puts and Futures is presented. Profit and loss charts of each one, long and short at 50, is shown.

A long 50 Call , as shown in Chart 4.1 on the previous page, at expiry obviously has no value when the Future is below 50. Anything above 50 is called intrinsic value and brings a straight profit (not taking the initial premium paid into account). The profit above 50 will be the Future level minus the strike level (F − K). So at 75 for instance, the profit of the option is $25 and so on.

A short 50 call will look as follows:

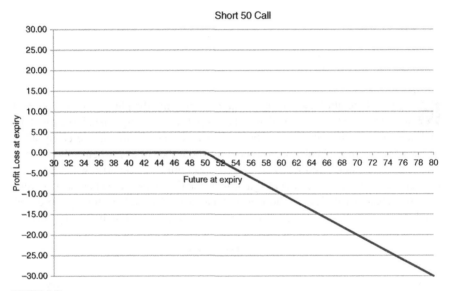

CHART 4.2   Short the 50 call

With a short 50 call, as shown above in Chart 4.2, at expiry, any level above 50 in the Future will create a loss in the option, equivalent to the strike minus the Future level (K − F). At 65 in the Future for instance, the short call will generate a loss of $15 (not taking initial premium received into account).

The owner of the 50 put, as shown in Chart 4.3 on the following page, will generate a profit when the Future is trading below 50 at expiry. At any level above 50 the put is worthless. At 40 in the Future, the put will generate a profit of $10 (not taking initial premium paid into account). The profit will be equivalent to K − F.

When the put is short, as shown in Chart 4.4 on the next page, the position will result in a loss when at expiry the Future is trading below 50. The loss is equivalent to F − K.

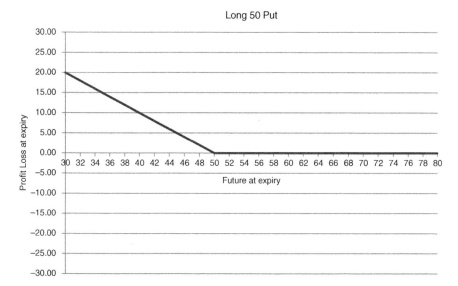

CHART 4.3 Long the 50 put

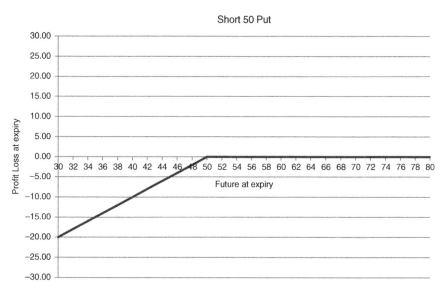

CHART 4.4 Short the 50 put

A long Future position, as shown below in Chart 4.5 entered at 50, will result in the following profit loss chart:

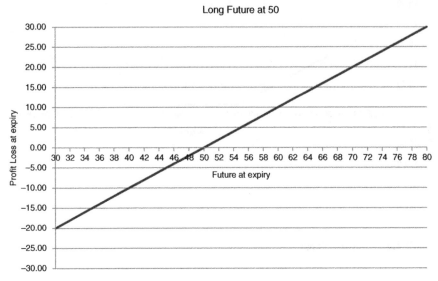

CHART 4.5   Long the Future at 50

Any level above 50 will result in a profit; below 50 the position will result in a loss.

A short Future at 50 will result in the following profit/loss chart, as shown below in Chart 4.6:

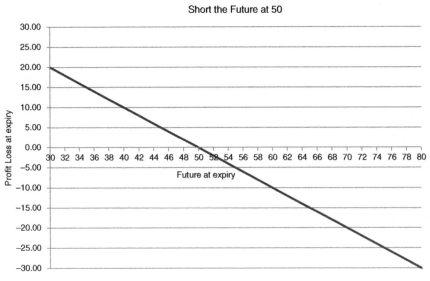

CHART 4.6   Short the Future at 50

SYNTHETICALLY CREATING A FUTURE LONG POSITION, THE REVERSAL

When combining a long call option (dark grey line), at the money strike (being 50) and a short put option (light grey line) of the same strike (maturity being the same) the outlook for the P&L at expiry will be as follows:

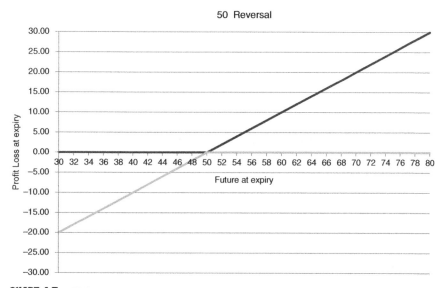

CHART 4.7 50 Reversal

Anything above 50 will yield a profit, one on one with the move of the Future; hence, $10 higher in the Future will imply a $10 profit in the option structure ($10 for the long call, zero for the short put). At the same time anything below 50 will yield a loss, one on one with the move of the Future. When the Future is, for instance, $15 lower at 35, the loss in the option combination will be $15 as well (zero for the long call, $15 for the short put). It actually has the same P&L distribution as a long Future, bought at 50.

When buying a call option and selling a put option of the same strike (both with the same expiry date) one synthetically creates a Future long position. Such a structure is called a reversal: Call – Put = Future or C – P = F. When setting up the reversal one is long the Future. Hedging the position to have a neutral P&L outlook can be done by selling a Future.

SYNTHETICALLY CREATING A FUTURE SHORT POSITION, THE CONVERSION

When setting up a long put and short call the profit loss distribution will appear as follows:

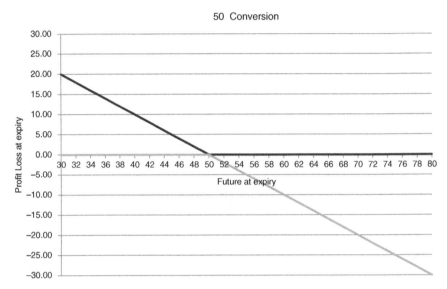

CHART 4.8   50 Conversion

This structure will yield exactly the same P&L as a short Future. By buying the put and selling the call one synthetically creates a Future short position. Such a structure is called a conversion: Put – Call = –Future or $P - C = -F$. Hedging the position in order to create a neutral P&L outlook can be done by buying a Future.

Reversals and conversions are set up by professional option traders to arbitrage small discrepancies in the market (firstly because of the bid ask spread in option quotes but also in relation to interest rate, dividend or small pricing errors). For the non-professional trader it makes no sense to enter into an option strategy when the only aim or result of the strategy is the (synthetic) creation of a long or short position in a Future. There is a simpler, cheaper and sometimes even more liquid way to do this: just enter into a position in the Futures market.

These two structures require the option Greeks for calls and puts to be identical. When the Greeks of a 50 put work differently from the Greeks of the 50 call, or have different values, the synthetic creation of Future long or short positions are not possible. The options would show different P&L distributions during their lifetime and/or at expiry and consequently arbitrage opportunities might arise.

Hence, "call is put and vice versa".

SYNTHETIC OPTIONS

When looking at the reversal $C - P = F$ and adding on both sides of the equation a put (which is allowed in accordance with algebra rules), the formula changes to:

$$C - P + P = F + P \text{ or } C = F + P.$$

So, a call would be equivalent to a long Future at 50 in combination with a long 50 put. In a chart it would look as follows:

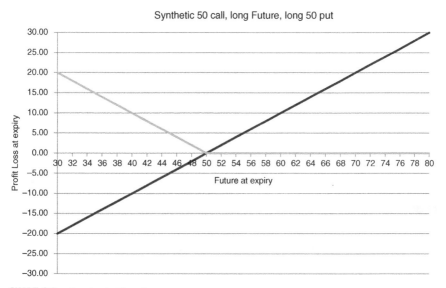

CHART 4.9 Synthetic 50 call

In Chart 4.9 the synthetic call is shown, created by a long Future position (dark grey line) in combination with a long 50 put position (light grey line). Below 50, the Future long position will generate a loss of one dollar for each dollar that the Future falls. However, this will be 100% offset by the long put option (generating a dollar profit for each dollar that the Future goes down). As a result, on the downside – below 50 – there will be no profit or loss generated. On the way up, anything above 50 will result in a profit; the owner of the strategy is long a Future, so for each dollar higher in the Future he will earn one dollar as profit. The put option will have no impact on the P&L above 50 (it will remain worthless). Actually these are the characteristics of a call option.

Taking the conversion $P - C = -F$ and adding on both sides of the equation a call, the formula would change into:

$$P - C + C = -F + C \text{ or } P = C - F.$$

(The same equation could be accomplished with the reversal, $C - P = F$, adding a put on both sides and at the same time subtracting a Future on both sides of the equation.)

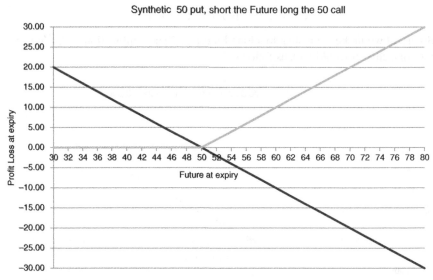

CHART 4.10 Synthetic 50 put

As shown above in Chart 4.10, the synthetic put is created by a long call option, represented by the light grey line and a short Future position represented by the dark grey line. Above 50 the short Future position will generate a loss, which is fully offset by the long call option. Below 50 the call option will not generate any P&L while the short Future position will yield a profit of one dollar for each dollar that the Future will trade lower. Actually these are the characteristics of a put option.

The reversal or conversion set up for the 50 strike, combined with the Future trading at 50, will yield no cashflow to make it P&L neutral compared to a Future long or short position. Any cashflow in one of the two combinations will immediately result in an arbitrage.

So far we have discussed at the money option positions, but what if the Future trades at 50 and a trader enters into a 45 reversal (buying calls, selling puts)? By entering into a reversal the trader will have to sell a Future to have a neutral position ($C - P = F$, so when having bought calls and sold puts one is actually long a Future, which can be offset by selling a Future. Sometimes this can be a bit confusing.).

The deals done by the trader are:

He buys the 45 call, sells the 45 put and sells the Future at 50, assuming this is done at no cost/no cashflow:

TABLE 4.1

Future at expiry	Profit Loss Future Position	45 call value	45 put value	Total Profit Loss
50	0	5	0	5
53	−3	8	0	5
70	−20	25	0	5
45	5	0	0	5
30	20	0	−15	5

In all the scenarios, as shown above in Table 4.1, the trader would make $5 profit from a structure without any cashflow (selling the puts at the same price as buying the calls). This is, however, impossible: any arbitrageur would have invested $4.90 for ending up with a small but certain profit.

The point is, when entering into the strategy, the call is already $5 in the money. So with the Future trading at 50, the 45 call should be worth $5 more than the 45 put. This $5 value is called the intrinsic value of the call.

With the Future at 50, a reversal or conversion set up for the 50 strike, has no cashflow. However, any other strike would imply that there should be a cashflow which equals the intrinsic value of the combination. For instance, in the 40 reversal the value would be $10, the call being $10 more worth than the put. The trader in this strategy will have to pay $10. For the 55 reversal, the 55 put will have intrinsic value (being $5). Hence, the trader entering into a 55 reversal (selling the put) should receive $5. When not receiving any cashflow, his strategy will always end with a $5 loss as shown below in Table 4.2:

TABLE 4.2

Future at expiry	Profit Loss Future Position	Cashflow	55 call value	55 put value	Total Profit Loss
50	0	0	0	−5	−5
55	−5	0	0	0	−5
70	−20	0	15	0	−5
45	5	0	0	−10	−5
30	20	0	0	−25	−5

When deducting the intrinsic value from the options (all the calls below 50 and all the puts above 50) when the Future is at 50, the extrinsic value will be left. Out of the money puts will have the same value as the extrinsic value of the calls of that specific strike. Out of the money calls will have the same value as the extrinsic value of the puts of that specific strike. With a Future trading at 50, volatility at 30% and maturity 1 year, prices will be as follows:

TABLE 4.3

Strike	Call	Intrinsic	Extrinsic	Put	Intrinsic	Extrinsic
35	15.72	15	0.72	0.72		0.72
40	11.77	10	1.77	1.77		1.77
45	8.51	5	3.51	3.51		3.51
50	5.96	0	5.96	5.96	0	5.96
55	4.07		4.07	9.07	5	4.07
60	2.72		2.72	12.72	10	2.72
65	1.79		1.79	16.79	15	1.79

In Table 4.3 any reversal or conversion has a value equal to the intrinsic value of the structure. The comparison of prices, or just the extrinsic values of calls and puts, might make the relationship between calls and puts already much more clear.

Earlier in this chapter it was mentioned that, because of the put call parity, the Greeks (gamma, vega and theta) will have to be identical for calls as well as for puts of the same strike (same maturity). This implies that, when referring to an in the money call, the gamma, vega and theta will be equivalent to those of the out of the money put of that same strike. For in the money puts it will be similar; those Greeks will be equivalent to the out of the money calls of that strike. Therefore, in several chapters on the Greeks there is only made a distinction between at the money options and out of the money options; in the money options will not be mentioned. The term "out of the money options" could thus apply to out of the money calls, which have the same characteristics as in the money puts and out of the money puts, which have the same characteristics as in the money calls. Next to that, most trading will take place in at the money and out of the money options. Trades in in the money options are very often the result of profit taking or stop loss trades.

COVERED CALL WRITING

The owner of assets/Futures, selling out of the money calls in order to create some additional profit (waiting for them to expire worthless and then repeating the strategy), which is called covered writing, is, in accordance with put call theory, actually selling in the money puts. An example is when the Future is trading at 50 and the owner of the Futures sells the 55 calls for the same volume as the amount of the Futures he owns. Assuming the 55 calls to be worth $1, according to put call theory the put should be worth $6 ($5 intrinsic and extrinsic value being the same as the call). His position is F (at 50) – C (55).

Above 50, his best performance would be at 55 or higher, making $5 profit with the Future at 55 and $1 for the calls he has sold, resulting in a $6 profit. At any higher level he would gain more with the Future; however, that is fully offset by being short the call.

Below 50, at 49, he has his break-even point. Having sold the 55 call for 1 he will break even after having lost $1 on his Future long position. For each lower dollar he will incur an additional loss of $1. As a result, the owner of this strategy has the same P&L distribution as the trader who is short the 55 put (receiving a cashflow of $6) without any further position in a Future.

SHORT NOTE ON INTEREST RATES

When setting up a reversal or conversion which is in the money, (a reversal with strike below 50 or a conversion with strike above 50 with the Future trading at 50) a cashflow will have to be paid. With a reversal above 50 (selling the in the money put) or a conversion below 50 (selling the in the money call) there is a cashflow to be received.

These cashflows will have to be adjusted for the interest rate. The trader paying for a strategy will have to borrow money, the trader receiving cash could deposit the money. As a result the cashflow will have to be discounted for the interest rate for the remaining time to maturity.

For a 40 reversal with the Future at 50, maturity 1 year and an interest rate of 5%, the resulting cashflow will not be $10 but $9.50. Or, to be more precise (with a continuous discount factor standardised in financial markets and the B&S model) $10 \times e^{-rt} = 9.51$, where e is the natural number, r the interest rate in percentage and t the time to maturity expressed in years.

The Future will not yield any cashflow (equities for instance would have yielded a cashflow); at expiry the difference between the level where the Future position was set up and where it actually expired will be financially settled.

Quite often there are margin requirements for Future positions; however, such a discussion falls beyond the scope of this book.

Delta Δ

Delta (the Greek letter ∂ or Δ for the capital letter) is the change of the option value compared to the change of the underlying value. It is the first derivative of the value of an option: $\frac{\partial V}{\partial F}$. The formula for calculating it is as follows: $\Delta call = \Phi(d1)$, $\Delta put = -\Phi(-d1)$ or $\Phi(d1) - 1$, where Φ is the standard normal cumulative distribution function where $d1$ stands for a specific formula.

With a long call option, one could expect an increase in value when the market increases. This change in the value of the option versus a one dollar change in the Future is called the delta. The delta of a call option has a positive value. Obviously a put option would lose value when the market rises, so put options have a negative delta: with a decreasing Future they increase in value.

Delta is a very important measure of a portfolio, it indicates how long or short one is. In this chapter the characteristics of the delta will be explained, how it changes and how it is distributed according to the Future level, volatility and time to maturity.

The delta is expressed in percentages (0 to 100% for calls and 0 to -100% for puts), but quite often also in basis points (for example, a 50 delta call or a 20 delta put, where one would need to realise that the put has a negative delta), and also just as a decimal (the option has a delta of 0.50). Throughout the book these different forms for expressing the value of the delta are all used.

Each strike will have a different delta. When a call option has a delta of 25%, it means that the value of the option would increase by 25¢ when the Future moves up one dollar; in fact, the call option represents 25% of one Future. When the call is very deep in the money, its value would increase by one dollar when the Future increases by one dollar; now the call represents one Future, being 100% delta. Obviously the delta cannot be more than 100% since by owning a call option one has the right to buy one Future (which is 100% of one Future). (Different markets have different specific volumes per option. This should be sorted out prior to trading.) The same works for a put option. With a delta of -40%, the option increases by 40¢ when the Future drops one dollar; in fact, the put option represents 40% of a short Future. When deep in the money, a put option represents a short position of one Future, being −100% delta.

For the options delta, the probability percentages, as applicable for the normal distribution, apply as well.

Simply put, there is a 50/50 chance of the market moving up or down. So, an at the money call or put has a 50% chance to move in the right direction (up for the call and down for the put) in order to generate a positive P&L for the trader. It is this percentage that will be applied to the delta of the at the money option. As shown in the chapter on volatility, the Future will have, when normally distributed, a 50% chance to be higher at maturity and 50% chance to be lower at maturity.

The at the money call option with the Future trading at 50 (hence the 50 strike) will have a delta of 0.50. It has a 50% percent chance to end up in the money and a 50% chance to expire worthless at maturity. As previously mentioned, in the Black Scholes model a logarithmic scale has been applied (the logarithmic returns of the Future are normally distributed). When the volatility is higher or the time to maturity increases, the distribution will be somewhat skewed. This is the reason why the at the money call will have a slightly higher delta, which will be discussed later in this chapter.

The Future has a delta of 100%, implying that a reversal will have a delta of 100% as well. So $C - P = 100\%$; when the call has a delta of 50%, the put should have a delta of −50% (resulting in 50% - -50% = 100%). Being short a Future would be equivalent to a delta of −100%, implying that a conversion will have a delta of −100% as well.

CHANGE OF OPTION VALUE THROUGH THE DELTA

The application of a 50% delta, as shown below in Table 5.1, for the at the money call, will mean that if the 50 call and the 50 put both have a value of $4.00, with the Future trading at 50 (volatility at 20%, maturity 1 year) and the market trades up 1 dollar (to 51), the value of the call would increase by $0.50 to $4.50 (being 50% of a 1 dollar move up), the value of the put would decrease to $3.50, a change of −$0.50, (being the result of −50% times a 1 dollar move up). On the other hand, a move towards 49 would cause the call to decrease by 50¢ towards $3.50. In this case the put will obviously increase in value.

TABLE 5.1

Underlying	50 Call	50 Put
50	4.00	4.00
51	4.50	3.50
49	3.50	4.50

Quite often the phrase "delta neutrality" is heard, which sometimes can be confusing. The buyer of a call option would like the Future to move up in order to generate a positive P&L. Hedging any delta on the way up would be a loss of opportunity; he would, therefore, never opt for delta neutrality. The delta neutral trader invests in other opportunities (this could be, for instance, a gamma or vega position), or is a market maker trying to earn a living from the bid ask spread he is quoting.

So, for instance, when the Future is at 50 and the trader sees fair value for the 50 call at $4.00, he might quote it at $3.90 at $4.10 when being asked for a market. When someone buys the call from him at $4.10, he ends up short half a Future per call option he has sold. He would, therefore, instantly hedge his position by buying 50% of the underlying at 50 (having sold 50% when he sold the put option). He is no longer exposed to the market, having hedged his short position resulting from the options with a long position in the underlying.

When the market stays at 50 and the market maker buys back the call option at $3.90, he is now long half a Future for each option he bought. He needs to sell the Future for 50% at 50 in order to make it a delta neutral trade again.

These are his trades:

TABLE 5.2

Sell 50 call	4.10	Buy F (50%) at 50	
Buy 50 call	3.90	Sell F (50%) at 50	
	P&L, 0.20	P&L, 0	Total result: 0.20

For a changing market:

When the market is at 50 the market maker would see fair value for the 50 call at $4.00. When being asked for a market, he will probably quote it $3.90 at $4.10. If someone sells the call to him at $3.90, he would instantly hedge his position by selling 50% of the Future at 50. His exposure to the market is no longer there; he has hedged his long position resulting from the options with a short position in the Future. Now the market moves to 51, where he sees fair value for the 50 call at $4.50. He sells the call at $4.60 now and hedges his delta exposure by buying 50% of the underlying at 51.

These are his trades:

TABLE 5.3

Buy 50 call	3.90	Sell F (50%) at 50	
Sell 50 call	4.60	Buy F (50%) at 51	
	P&L: 0.70	P&L: −0.50	Total result: 0.20

The loss on his Future hedge is 50 cents and not $1: each time he had to hedge 50% of the total volume of the option.

In the end, the bid ask spread the trader is applying has been honoured irrespective of where the market is; as long as he hedges his delta exposure to keep his book delta neutral he can focus on buying and selling with a positive margin – in traders' jargon this is called "scalping".

This is a simple representation of the risks of a trader earning a living on market making (actually, he has many more exposures). However, it shows how the delta neutral hedging works and why it is applied by market participants.

These examples refer to an option with a stable delta of 50%. However, a delta is dynamic, it changes all the time.

For expressing the delta in a portfolio, it may be preferable to use cents per dollar change in the underlying instead of percentages. Let's assume a portfolio with 10,000 calls long with a 0.50 (50%) delta, 8,000 calls long with a 0.40 (40%) delta, and 6,000 calls long with a 0.25 (25%) delta. Adding up in cents one could say I'm long 9.700 deltas, implying I would earn $9,700 when the market moves up a dollar. This is equivalent to a long position of 9,700 Futures. When adding up in percentages you could say I'm long 970.000%. It could be unclear to a bystander what the reference level is for the percentage; it is quite confusing (although correct). Mentioning a number in P&L per dollar with regards to a portfolio would make more sense and is easier to grasp for many people.

DYNAMIC DELTA

When owning a 50 call option which expires in a millisecond, at any level below 50 the option will be worthless. Regardless of whether the Future is at 40, 49, or even at 49.95, the value of the option remains 0.00 – its delta is zero. At any level above 50, the call will have intrinsic value, so if the market jumps from 50 to 51, the value of the call will increase towards 1 dollar. Any further move up in the Future will result in the same value increase for the option – so the delta will be 100%, as shown below in Chart 5.1.

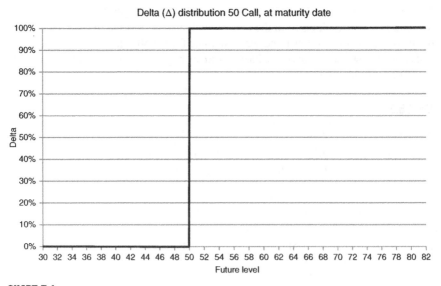

CHART 5.1   Delta distribution of the 50 call at expiry

DELTA AT DIFFERENT MATURITIES

If the time to expiry grows, the probability area where the future could be trading towards expiry will increase as well. A 50 call with expiry in a millisecond, and the Future trading at 40, will have no value and no delta (there is no chance that the call will end up in the money). However, when this call option has a long time to expiry, for instance ½ year, it will have some value. When looking at the probability distribution for the Future, there is some chance that it will expire above 50. This chance will result in a small value for the call: whenever there is a small probability of becoming in the money some people will be willing to invest in this option. The value of the option will increase when the market moves up and will decrease when the market moves in the opposite direction; hence, it must have a delta. When maturity is even longer, for instance 1 year, the probability area for the Future will be larger and as a result the value of the option and its delta is larger. It might already have some value with the Future trading at 35, as shown below in Chart 5.2.

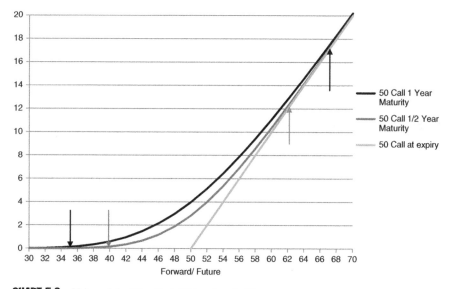

CHART 5.2 Value of the 50 call at different maturities

A 50 call with a maturity of ½ year will increase by one full dollar if the Future moves up one dollar at around 60–62 in the underlying. At that level the option has a 100% delta. With one year to maturity the delta of the option has grown towards 100%: somewhere around the 66–68 level in the underlying.

The fact that the delta of a call will grow on the way up, and hence its value increases gradually as depicted above, is sometimes called convexity.

At 20% volatility and 3 months to maturity, the convexity range for the 50 call will be somewhere between 38 and $66. The call will start to generate a delta around 38 in the Future; at 66 its delta will have grown to 100%, as shown in Chart 5.3.

At 20% volatility and 1 month to maturity, the range for the delta of the 50 call to grow from 0 to 100% will be somewhere between 42 and $60, as shown in Chart 5.4. Each time the maturity decreases, the probability range for the Future will decrease accordingly (square root function, see chapter on volatility).

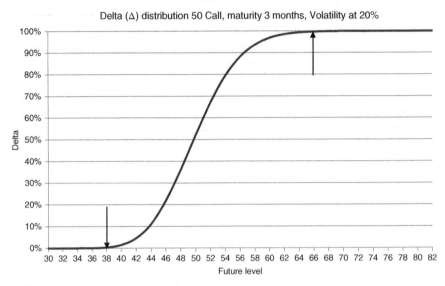

CHART 5.3   Delta distribution of the 50 call, volatility 20%, maturity 3 months

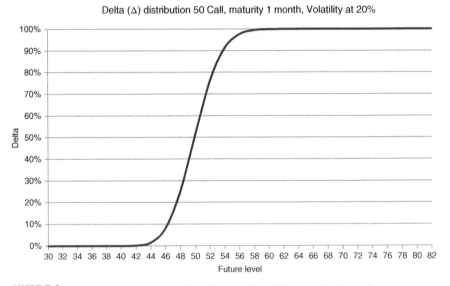

CHART 5.4   Delta distribution of the 50 call, volatility 20%, maturity 1 month

Delta (Δ) distribution 50 Call, maturity 1 month up to 12 months, Volatility at 20%

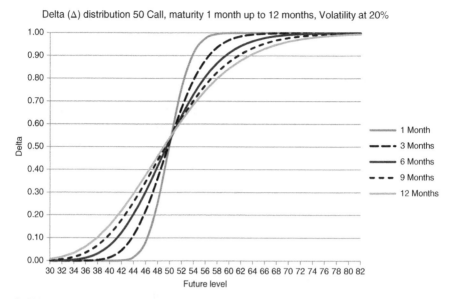

CHART 5.5   Delta distribution of the 50 call, volatility 20%, different maturities

Delta (Δ) distribution 50 Put, maturity 1 month up to 12 months, Vol 20%, i = 0%

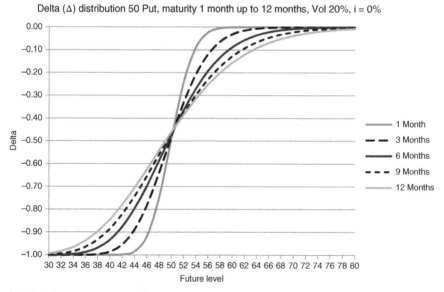

CHART 5.6   Delta distribution of the 50 put, volatility 20%, different maturities

The probability range will keep decreasing until the day of maturity itself – the expiration date – when the call option either has a delta of 0% or 100%.

Chart 5.5 shows that the longer the time to maturity is, the longer it takes for the delta of the 50 call to grow from 0 to 100%. At 20% volatility, and one month to expiry, the range will be around 43–58; with three months to expiry it will be 39–64; and with one year to expiry the range will be around 30–80.

The same applies to puts, as shown in Chart 5.6: with one year to maturity, the 50 put already has a small delta, with the Future trading at 80, while with one month to expiry it does not start to have a delta before the 58 level. On the way down, the put with a maturity of 1 month will have reached a delta of −100% around the 43 level in the Future versus a put with one year to maturity which will reach −100% delta not before the Future is trading around the 30 level.

DELTA AT DIFFERENT VOLATILITIES

The impact of volatility on the probability distribution for the Future is comparable to that of the time to maturity. In the chapter on normal probability distribution, the formula $\sigma \times \sqrt{T} \times F$ was introduced as a standard deviation. This formula shows, as discussed in the chapter on volatility, that any increase in volatility will result in higher standard deviation, which results in a larger probability area for the Future towards expiry. A higher volatility will thus result in a larger range where the delta of the call will grow from 0 to 100%, or the put will grow from 0 to −100%.

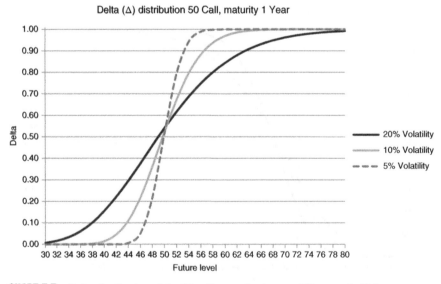

CHART 5.7   Delta distribution of the 50 call, maturity 1 year, different volatilities

Chart 5.7 displays the delta ranges at different volatility levels. When comparing chart 5.7 with chart 5.5, one could see that when volatility would halve from 20% to 10%, the range will go from 30 − 80 to 39 − 64. This feature will be exactly

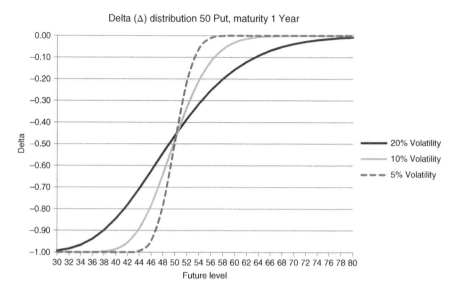

CHART 5.8 Delta distribution of the 50 put, maturity 1 year, different volatilities

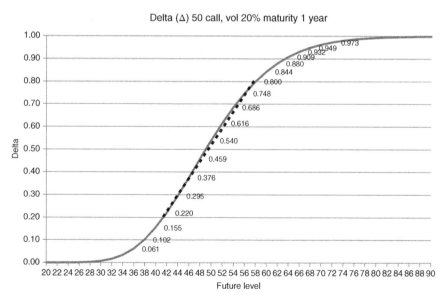

CHART 5.9 The 20–80% delta region

the same for when time to maturity goes from 1 year to 3 months. The impact of halve the σ on the standard deviation equals the impact of a quarter of the time to maturity.

20–80 DELTA REGION

The 20 to 80% delta region is almost linear, as shown in Chart 5.9. This linearity promotes working with a lot of rules of thumb and easy derivations for the Greeks. It is a strong tool for being able to come up with values for the Greeks without applying the option model. Strong also since it can, if volatility and time to maturity are large enough, represent a large area in terms of the Future level range. The range will be correlated with the formula for the standard deviation : $\sigma \times \sqrt{T} \times F$; the higher the volatility or the time to maturity, the larger the range for the Future level will be for the delta to be between 20% and 80%.

DELTA PER STRIKE

In the previous charts the 50 call has been depicted with Future values on the X-axis and delta on the Y-axis. In the following charts the X-axis will represent different call strikes and the Y-axis the delta again.

   When overseeing the lowest strikes, the deepest in the money calls on the left side of the X-axis, the delta will obviously have the highest value and the deltas of the out of the money calls, the lowest, will be shown on the right side of the chart. Obviously, a deep in the money call option has a delta growing towards 100%, the at the money 50% and the out of the money calls a delta decreasing towards 0%.

   Chart 5.10 displays the delta distribution of calls with a strike ranging from 30 to 80 with the Future trading at 50. The 30 call is so deep in the money that it has

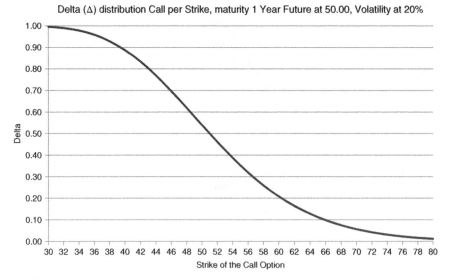

CHART 5.10   Delta distribution of the call, different strikes, volatility 20%, maturity 1 year

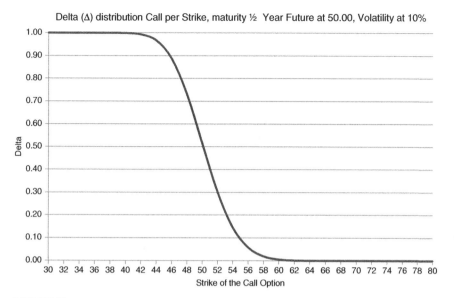

CHART 5.11   Delta distribution of the call, different strikes, volatility 10%, maturity 1/2 year

reached a delta of 100%, while the 80 call is so far out of the money that its delta is close to zero.

Chart 5.11 (10% volatility, 0.5 year maturity), has half the volatility and half the time to maturity of Chart 5.10. This will result in a standard deviation, which is half the value on the σ (volatility) component and $\sqrt{2}$ smaller on the T component. The outcome is a standard deviation which is ≈ 2.83 times smaller (2 times 1.414). Where in Chart 5.10 the 30 call has a delta which approaches 100%, in Chart 5.11 the 42 call already approaches 100%. For the out of the money calls, the 80 call in Chart 5.10 approaches a delta of 0 where in Chart 5.11 the 60 call already approaches a delta of 0. The delta decrease is much steeper in Chart 5.11, compared to Chart 5.10.

When comparing these two charts and studying the 80%–20% delta range:

Chart 5.12, on the following page, displays the delta decrease from 80% to 20%, from a distribution with a volatility of 20% and a maturity of one year, compared to a distribution with half the volatility, 10% and half the maturity, half a year. The first shows such a delta decrease in a range of $17, the latter a similar decrease in a range of $6. The ratio $\frac{17}{6}$ results in a value of 2.83.

DYNAMIC DELTA HEDGING

When discussing, at the beginning of the chapter, the delta hedging of a trader who trades in and out of the 50 call at different levels in the underlying (49 – 50 – 51), each time the same delta of 0.50 has been applied. The option model, however, is much more dynamic than these examples were implying. It should be clear that

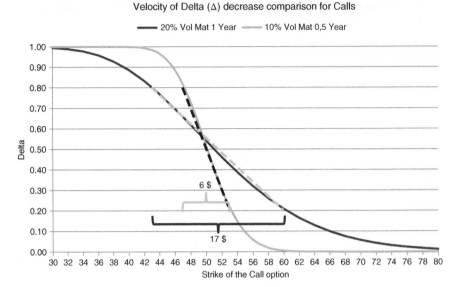

CHART 5.12   Velocity of the delta change

when the market is decreasing the delta of the 50 call will be decreasing as well (negative delta of the 50 put will become more negative) and vice versa.

In this paragraph the focus will be on the change of the delta and what it means to the trader, as shown in Chart 5.13 (this time the trader is not trading in and out, i.e. buying and selling the option). Let's assume a trader who is long the 50 call for 10,000 lots. The volatility is 20% and the maturity is 3 months. The trader wishes to keep his portfolio delta neutral at the end of each business day, so he is not aiming for a straight profit when the Future will reach higher levels (thanks to a delta long position when not having hedged anything); his strategy is based on the evolution of other Greeks in his portfolio. The Future is trading at 50 and (as mentioned earlier, there is a small discrepancy in the at the money delta) the delta of the 50 call is 0.52. In order to start with a delta neutral portfolio the trader has hedged his position and sold 5,200 Futures at 50.

The next trading day, the Future moves towards 54. Based on his option model, the delta of the 50 call is now 0.79; hence the calls represent 7,900 futures. Because he initially sold 5,200 Futures at 50 he now will need to sell another 2,700 Futures in order to neutralise his delta position.

The following day, the market retraces to end up at 50, the initial level where the trader entered into his position. Being long 10,000 calls and short 7,900 futures, his Future position against his option position in fact entails a net short position. With a 0.52 delta of the call at 50 he should buy back 2,700 futures at 50 to flatten/neutralise his delta position again.

The next two days the market goes down to 48: he needs to buy 1,600 futures because the delta of the calls is only 0.36 now and hence he has a net short position

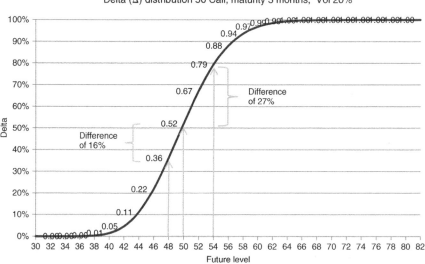

CHART 5.13   Delta distribution 50 call, volatility 20%, maturity 3 months

of 1,600. Later the Future trades up to 50 where the trader offloads these 1,600 futures (or deltas) again in order to neutralise his delta position.

In conclusion, the trader has done the following trades (scalps):

TABLE 5.4

	50	54	50	48	50	Total
Delta hedge	Sell 5,200	Sell 2,700	Buy 2,700	Buy 1,600	Sell 1,600	0
P&L at 50.00	0	$10,800	0	$3,200	0	$14,000

The trader made a large profit in a few days thanks to very large moves in the Future. The change in the delta enabled him to trade in a profitable way by selling at higher levels and buying back at lower levels (anyone could tell that's a good trading strategy). The way he has been profiting from these delta changes is called gamma trading. Gamma is the derivative of the delta, the change of the delta over a certain trajectory (what was called the velocity of the delta change in Chart 5.12). A few chapters later we will discuss gamma (γ) and its intricacies at more length.

One should have already figured out that, when referring to velocity, gamma is dependent on volatility and time to maturity. The velocity chart makes clear that when volatility is lower and time to maturity is lower as well, the delta change would be much more pronounced in a smaller range. Hence the trader will have more gamma to trade with.

It is a fantastic feature to be able to generate a profit based on the delta change of an option. However, there is a caveat: the trader is long the 50 strike. Since every day an option will get closer to maturity it will decrease in value (when being long the 50 call and the market stays at that level the option will expire worthless, while a 50 call, being at the money with a volatility of 20% and a maturity of 1 year will cost around $4.00). This decrease is called time decay or theta (Θ). His earnings in delta hedges, as a result of the gamma trading, should make up for the time decay of the options.

Against this trader might stand another trader, who is short the 50 calls. He might have decided to sell them to profit from the time decay. This counterparty will have to hedge his exposure for also having a delta neutral portfolio. However, he will have to trade the opposite: he will buy at higher levels and sell at lower levels. On the other hand he does "receive" the time decay of the options; when nothing happens he can buy back the options cheaper the next day.

This is an extreme example; as shown in the chapter on Volatility, a move from 50 to 54 is very unlikely when market volatility is at 20%. The trader being short the 50 call is the big loser in this strategy, the only upside for him will be when the market becomes quiet with small changes in the Future and as a consequence minimal negative delta hedges where he can fully benefit from the daily time decay. A trader will only set up a gamma short strategy when he has the view that the market will be rangebound in the near future or when he sees the time decay being larger than the cost of his negative scalps on the back of his strategy.

THE AT THE MONEY DELTA

The delta formula in the model is: $\Delta call = \Phi(d1)$, being the normal cumulative distribution function of $d1$.

$$d1 = \frac{\ln\dfrac{F}{K} + (r + \frac{1}{2}\sigma^2) \times T}{\sigma \times \sqrt{T}}$$

where F stands for Future, K for Strike, σ for volatility in % and T for time to maturity, expressed in years (days to maturity divided by 365 days). Throughout the book the interest rate r will be set at 0% and as a result d1 will be:

$$d1 = \frac{\ln\dfrac{F}{K} + \frac{1}{2}\sigma^2 \times T}{\sigma \times \sqrt{T}}$$

Chart 5.14 displays the delta of a call option compared to the value of d1. d1 should be seen as the standard deviation. For instance, when trying to find the probability for a one standard deviation move (or less) it should be between d1=−1 and d1=1, when normally distributed, 68.2% should be expected. When d1 has a value

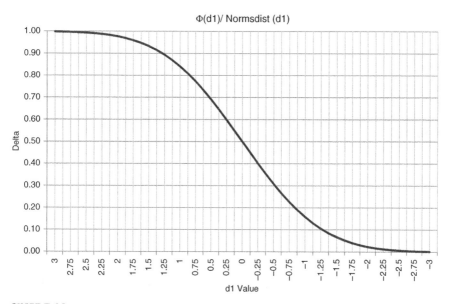

CHART 5.14   Delta distribution versus d1

of 1, the value on the Y-axis is 84.1% and with d1 being -1, the value on the Y-axis is 15.9, the difference of the two is 68.2. The difference between d1 = 2 and d1 = −2 will obviously be 95.4%.

D1 is normally distributed, however one component of d1 is logarithmic, being $\ln \frac{F}{K}$. This is why it is said that the logarithmic returns of the asset are normally distributed in the Black and Scholes model.

So far the at the money delta has been treated as a 50% delta. This is, however, never the case (be it sometimes accidentally due to discounting, for the interest rate, of the delta with e^{-rT}). Due to the d1 formula the delta for the at the money call will always be higher than 50%. In principle the discrepancy is small, but the longer the time to maturity and the higher the volatility, the bigger it will get, sometimes even to proportions where one could consider to abandon the Black and Scholes model (for instance, when volatility is at 100% and maturity 1 year, d1 for the at the money 50 call will be 0.5, which equals to an at the money delta of 69%). For the at the money call to have a delta of exactly 50%, d1 should have a zero value.

When having a look at the delta formula $\Delta call = \Phi(d1)$ and d1 being:

$d1 = \dfrac{\ln \frac{F}{K} + \frac{1}{2}\sigma^2 \times T}{\sigma \times \sqrt{T}}$ it can be concluded that $\ln \frac{F}{K}$ will be zero when the Future will have the same value as the strike ($\ln(1) = 0$, $e^0 = 1$). So the delta formula for an at the money call will thus be:

$$\Phi(d1) \text{ and d1 being: } d1 = \frac{\frac{1}{2}\sigma^2 \times T}{\sigma \times \sqrt{T}} = \Phi(\tfrac{1}{2}\sigma\sqrt{T}).$$

So in order for d1 to have a 0 value, either way σ or $\sqrt{T}$ will have to be zero. When there is zero volatility or no time to maturity there is simply no optionality, hence this is not possible. Only at expiry will d1 be zero when being exactly at the money, and thus the call will have a delta of 50%. At any other time d1 will have a value, in all circumstances a positive number, and thus the at the money call will have a delta which is bigger than 50%, as shown in Table 5.5.

TABLE 5.5

d1	0.5	0.4	0.3	0.2	0.1	0
Delta call	69.1%	65.5%	61.8%	57.9%	54%	50%

For a better understanding, one can take a deep in the money call where the Future trades at a much higher level than the strike. If a low volatility or a short time to expiry is then applied one can see easily that the delta of the call will be soon at the 100% level, the value of d1 is at least higher than 3. The lower the volatility or the shorter the time to maturity, the larger the value for d1 for an in the money option: if one divides something by a small fraction the outcome will be a large number (d1 is the outcome of a value being divided by $\sigma\sqrt{T}$; if any of the two is close to zero, the value of d1 will be very high as a result).

A few examples for the calls, applying $\Delta call = \Phi(d1)$:

When F = 50, K = 20, $\ln\frac{F}{K} = 0.916$ and when volatility will be 10% and T 1 Year,

$$d1 = \frac{0.916 + \frac{1}{2}(0.1)^2 \times 1}{0.1\sqrt{1}} \approx 9.21$$ in Chart 5.14 the delta of the call is already 100% with a d1 value of 3, hence the delta of the 20 call is definitely at 100%.

For a more at the money call option the following will apply:

When F = 50, K = 45, $\ln\frac{F}{K} = 0.105$ and when volatility will be 10% and T 1 Year,

$$d1 = \frac{0.105 + \frac{1}{2}(0.1)^2 \times 1}{0.1\sqrt{1}} \approx 1.10$$ which corresponds, as shown in Chart 5.14, with a delta of around 87%.

For a far out of the money call $\ln\frac{F}{K}$ will have a negative number. Dividing that by a small σ or short time to maturity quite easily a large negative number could be the outcome, and already at -3 for the d1 value the call will hardly have any delta anymore.

When F = 50, K = 80, $\ln\frac{F}{K} = -0.47$ and when volatility will be 10% and T 1 Year,

$$d1 = \frac{-0.47 + 0.005}{0.1} \approx -4.65$$ in the matrix the call delta is already 0% with a d1 value of -3, hence the delta of the 80 call is 0%.

For a more at the money call option the following could apply:

When F = 50, K = 55, $\ln\frac{F}{K} = -0.095$ and when volatility will be 10% and T 1 Year,

$$d1 = \frac{-0.095 + 0.005}{0.1} \approx -0.90$$ which corresponds with a delta of around 18%.

A few examples for the puts, applying $\Delta put = \Phi(d1) - 1$:

When F = 50, K = 20, $\ln\frac{F}{K} = 0.916$ and when volatility will be 10% and T1 Year,

$$d1 = \frac{0.916 + \frac{1}{2}(0.1)^2 \times 1}{0.1\sqrt{1}} \approx 9.21$$ in Chart 5.14 the call delta is 100%, resulting in a put delta of 100% − 100% = 0% for the 20 put.

For a more at the money put option the following will apply:

When F = 50, K = 45, $\ln\frac{F}{K} = 0.105$ and when volatility will be 10% and T1 Year,

$$d1 = \frac{0.105 + \frac{1}{2}(0.1)^2 \times 1}{0.1\sqrt{1}} \approx 1.10$$ which corresponds with a delta of around 87% for

the call, resulting in a put delta of 87% − 100% = −13% for the 45 put.

A few examples for the puts, applying $\Delta put = -\Phi(-d1)$:

When F = 50, K = 80, $\ln\frac{F}{K} = -0.47$ and when volatility will be 10% and T1 Year,

$$d1 = \frac{-0.47 + 0.005}{0.1} \approx -4.65, -d1 = 4.65, \Phi(4.65) = 100\%, -\Phi(4.65) = -100\%,$$

the 80 put will thus have a delta of −100%.

For a more at the money put option the following could apply:

When F = 50, K = 55, $\ln\frac{F}{K} = -0.095$ and when volatility will be 10% and T 1 Year,

$$d1 = \frac{-0.095 + 0.005}{0.1} \approx -0.90, -d1 = 0.90, \Phi(0.90) = 82\%, -\Phi(0.90) = -82\%,$$

the 55 put will thus have a delta of −82%.

For the at the money, the $\ln\frac{F}{K}$ component will have a zero value and hence the formula for $d1 = \frac{1}{2}\sigma\sqrt{T}$. When looking at the left side of the d1/Delta chart, one could see that if volatility were 100% and time to maturity 1 year (the resulting value for d1 is $\frac{1}{2} \times 1$ (or 100%) $\times \sqrt{1}$ which makes 0.5) the corresponding delta of the at the money call option is 69.1%, a very high delta for an at the money call option. If volatility or maturity approaches the zero level, d1 will gradually decrease towards 0.00 and the call will have a corresponding delta of 50%. In the two examples mentioned above, the delta of the at the money put, $\Phi(d1) - 1$, will be −30.9% and gradually decreasing towards −50%.

These values (with volatility at 100% and maturity 1 year) explain why at the beginning of the paragraph, the remark has been made, that the delta of the at the money call sometimes increases to proportions where one could consider to abandon the Black and Scholes model, because it really looks like it doesn't make sense. On the other hand, in time (or when volatility drops) the delta will decrease gradually towards the 50% level, as long as one would adhere to the model, all will look more reasonable in the end.

DELTA CHANGES IN TIME

As shown in the paragraph before, deltas will change in time and in relation to volatility for at the moneys as well. Delta changes in time are sometimes called "Charm" or DdeltaDtime, mathematically $\frac{\delta\Delta}{\delta T}$.

With the Future trading at 49 and maturity a week from now; the 50 call is around the at the money and has a delta of around 40%. However, on the last day its delta has completely disappeared: it is an out of the money call now.

So the definition for in, out and around the at the money might shift somewhat. An option with a 50 strike with the Future trading at 49 and maturity one year is definitely an around the at the money option, while the same option with one day to maturity is definitely an out of the money option for calls, and an in the money option for puts. There is not a hard line of distinction in time, it's more the probability which determines the definition.

The trader who is used to always hedging his deltas, and is long 10.000 of the 50 calls, will have against his option portfolio a Future portfolio consisting of 4.000 Futures short. These Futures he will have to buy back in the coming week towards expiry in order to have a flat delta position, because in time the deltas from his option portfolio will disappear (which is quite logical). The trader has to be aware of that and trade accordingly. Many traders have had the experience of coming into the office one day to discover that they have an unanticipated (unwanted) delta position due to the change of the delta of the option in relation to time, the so-called DdeltaDtime, which went against them.

In the money calls, when maturity is long enough and volatility high enough, have a delta smaller than 100% (unless they are very deep in the money of course). When maturity is getting shorter and/or volatility is decreasing their delta will slowly grow towards 100%. A trader who has hedged his long delta position – caused by his long (in the money) call option position by selling Futures, will find himself net long when time matures and/or volatility drops (one should be aware that a drop in volatility has the same effect as a decrease in time towards maturity). In essence, he didn't sell enough futures to hedge the calls, as shown below in Table 5.6.

TABLE 5.6

Time to maturity	Strike	Future	Delta	Hedge	Net position
1 year	45	50	74%	−74%	0%
3 months	45	50	86%	−74%	12%
1 day	45	50	100%	−74%	26%

Out of the money puts, when maturity is long enough and volatility high enough, have a delta between 0 and (smaller than) -50%. When maturity is getting shorter and/or volatility is decreasing their delta will slowly decrease towards 0%. A trader who has hedged his short delta position, caused by his long out of the money put option position, by buying Futures will find himself net long when time matures and/or volatility drops (one should be aware that a drop in volatility has the same effect as a decrease in time towards maturity). In essence he bought too may futures to hedge the puts.

So the trader with a position which consists of long in the money call options or long out of the money put options (where both calls and puts have a strike which is lower than the prevailing underlying Future price), and who delta hedged his position, will encounter an increase of his delta position stemming from the options when time gets closer to maturity and/or volatility decreases, and hence will end up with a net long position.

The other way around, with out of the money calls and in the money puts, options with a strike price which is higher than the prevailing underlying Future price, the trader will find a position which will get net shorter when time matures and/or volatility decreases.

CHAPTER 6

Pricing

In this chapter we will briefly discuss the pricing of the model. There is a very simple rule of thumb to price at the money options. At the money straddles (calls and puts of the same strike) will be valued first; later, the value of this straddle will be used as a sort of standard deviation in the pricing of other options in order to compute the value and Greeks of option combinations and spreads.

As shown before, the standard deviation of a Future is $\sigma\sqrt{T}$. This implies that with a volatility of 10% (annualised) and the future at 50, in a year's time the Future will trade somewhere between 45 and 55 with a 68% probability and between 40 and 60 with a 95% probability. If the time would double, the standard deviation will become $10\% \times \sqrt{2} \times 50$, being around $7 as a standard deviation with a 68% probability for the Future to trade somewhere between 43 and 57 and a 95% probability for the Future to trade somewhere between 36 and 64. With volatility at 15%, time to maturity 1 year and the Future at 50, the standard deviation will be 7.50 and so on.

With regards to option theory, the value of the at the money straddle can be applied as a sort of standard deviation which will be of great help in computing the value of options prices and their Greeks. As shown in the former chapter, the 20% to 80% delta region is a fairly linear area; the 20% to 80% delta region is in the range from approximately 1 straddle in the money (a strike which is one straddle value below the at the money strike) to 1 straddle out of the money (a strike which is one straddle value above the at the money strike). This linearity can be worked with and one can consequently come up with good valuations for a large variety of options, options combinations and their Greeks without applying the model and therefore knowing the value of this straddle will facilitate as well in understanding the delta distribution.

TABLE 8.1

d1	d2	φ(d1) Normsd (d1)	φ(d1) Normsd (d2)
0,5	−0,5	0,691	0,309
0,45	−0,45	0,674	0,326
0,4	−0,4	0,655	0,345
0,35	−0,35	0,637	0,363
0,3	−0,3	0,618	0,382
0,25	−0,25	0,599	0,401
0,2	−0,2	0,579	0,421
0,15	−0,15	0,560	0,440
0,1	−0,1	0,540	0,460
0,05	−0,5	0,520	0,480
0	0	0,500	0,500
−0,05	0,05	0,480	0,520
−0,1	0,1	0,460	0,540
−0,15	0,15	0,440	0,560
−0,2	0,2	0,421	0,579
−0,25	0,25	0,401	0,599
−0,3	0,3	0,382	0,618
−0,35	0,35	0,363	0,637
−0,4	0,4	0,345	0,655
−0,45	0,45	0,329	0,674
−0,5	0,5	0,309	0,691

Vol	T (years)	d1	d2	Normsdist d1	Normsdist d2	Call	Put	Straddle
5%	1	0,025	−0,025	0,510	0,490	0,997	0,997	1,995
10%	1	0,050	−0,050	0,520	0,480	1,994	1,994	3,988
15%	1	0,075	−0,075	0,530	0,470	2,989	2,989	5,979
20%	1	0,100	−0,100	0,540	0,460	3,983	3,983	7,966
25%	1	0,125	−0,125	0,550	0,450	4,974	4,974	9,948
30%	1	0,150	−0,150	0,560	0,440	5,962	5,962	11,924
35%	1	0,175	−0,175	0,569	0,431	6,946	6,946	13,892
40%	1	0,200	−0,200	0,579	0,421	7,926	7,926	15,852

Vol	T (years)	d1	d2	Normsdist d1	Normsdist d2	Call	Put	Straddle
20%	0,25	0,050	−0,050	0,520	0,480	1,994	1,994	3,988
20%	0,5	0,071	−0,071	0,528	0,472	2,819	2,819	5,637
20%	0,75	0,087	−0,087	0,535	0,465	3,451	3,451	6,901
20%	1	0,100	−0,100	0,540	0,460	3,983	3,983	7,966
20%	1,25	0,112	−0,112	0,545	0,455	4,451	4,451	8,902
20%	1,5	0,122	−0,122	0,549	0,451	4,874	4,874	9,748
20%	1,75	0,132	−0,132	0,553	0,447	5,262	5,262	10,524
20%	2	0,141	−0,141	0,556	0,444	5,623	5,623	11,246

CALCULATING THE AT THE MONEY STRADDLE USING BLACK AND SCHOLES FORMULA

The calculation for the at the money straddle is depicted on the former page, nr 56: on the left the computation of d1, d2 and $\Phi(d1)$ and $\Phi(d2)$; on the upper right side is a calculation with different volatilities, keeping the time to maturity constant; and on the lower right side with different maturities, keeping the volatility constant. It might look a bit complicated, but it is actually fairly simple and can be easily performed in Excel. According to put call parity, the at the money calls will have the same value as the at the money puts.

The value of a call option $= \Phi(d1)F - \Phi(d2)K$ or $Normsdist(d1)F - Normsdist(d2)K$ (normsdist is the normal standard distribution as used in Excel) when applying an interest rate level of 0%.

$$d1 \text{ being: } d1 = \frac{\ln \frac{F}{K} + \frac{1}{2}\sigma^2 \times T}{\sigma \times \sqrt{T}}$$

and

$$d2 \text{ being: } d2 = d1 - \sigma\sqrt{T}.$$

Before calculating the at the money straddle, one should be aware that the Future level is the same as the strike level, hence $F = K$ resulting in $\frac{F}{K}$ is 1. The logarithm of 1 is zero ($\ln(1) = 0$ *because*: $e^0 = 1$), so for an at the money option $\ln\frac{F}{K}$ can be deleted from the equation.

$$\text{Hence } d1 = \frac{\frac{1}{2}\sigma^2 \times T}{\sigma \times \sqrt{T}} = \frac{1}{2}\sigma\sqrt{T}$$

and

$$d2 = d1 - \sigma\sqrt{T} = \frac{1}{2}\sigma\sqrt{T} - \sigma\sqrt{T} = -\frac{1}{2}\sigma\sqrt{T}.$$

It is now a simple calculation to derive, for instance, the value of the at the money 50 call, with a volatility of 20% and a maturity of 1 year.

$$d1 = \frac{1}{2} \times 0.20 \times \sqrt{1} = 0.1, Normsdist(0.1) = 0.54.$$
$$d2 = -\frac{1}{2} \times 0.20 \times \sqrt{1} = -0.1, Normsdist(-0.1) = 0.46.$$

Calculating the value of the call: $Normsdist(d1)F - Normsdist(d2)K$ will result, with a Future at 50, in $0.54 \times 50 - 0.46 \times 50$ being $4 (see values in the diagram as shown in Table 6.1). Due to rounding errors, the outcome is $4, the Black and

Scholes model comes with a value of $3.99. Throughout the book the rounded value will be used, it is a nice round number and it only represents a small error in comparison with the Black and Scholes model.

Since, in accordance with put call parity, put is call or $C = P$, the put can also be valued at $4. Hence the 50 straddle, being at the money, with a volatility of 20% and maturity of 1 year is valued at $8. In the next chart, the value of the at the money call is computed for several different volatilities:

Chart 6.1 shows the linear relationship of the at the money call value compared to the volatility level σ($\sigma\sqrt{T}$ application); with a volatility of 10% the atm call represents a value of $2, when volatility would double to 20% its value will be $4, at 40% volatility the value would increase to 8$ (almost, due to the rounding error).

Chart 6.2 shows that, for the at the money strike, the value for the straddle will be twice the value of the call option. According to put call parity, $C = P$, hence the call value can be simply doubled in order to get to the straddle value.

When applying different times to maturity, the following values can be seen for the straddle:

Chart 6.3 displays the relation of the at the money straddle compared to the time to maturity ($\sigma\sqrt{T}$ application). It is a function of the square root of time; the value of the straddle with for instance 1.8 year to maturity, being $10.67, is three times as expensive as the straddle with 0.2 year to maturity, being $3.57 ($\sqrt{9}$ relationship). The straddle with 0.5 year maturity, being worth $5.64, is half the value of the straddle with 2 year maturity, being worth $11.25 ($\sqrt{4}$ relationship), there are some small deviations due to rounding errors.

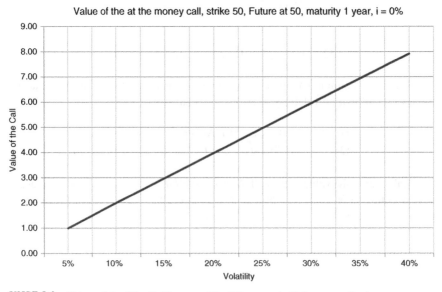

Value of the at the money call, strike 50, Future at 50, maturity 1 year, i = 0%

CHART 6.1   Value of the 50 call, Future at 50, different volatilities, maturity 1 year

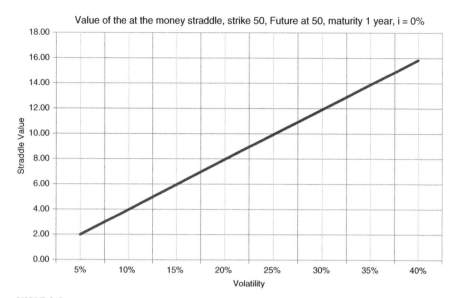

CHART 6.2   Value of the 50 straddle, twice the value of the call

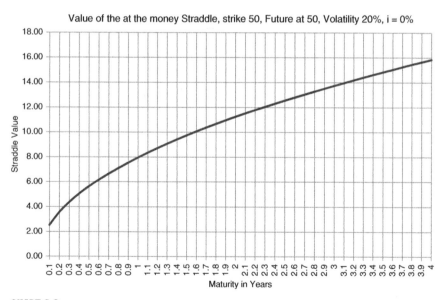

CHART 6.3   Value of the 50 straddle, Future at 50, volatility 20%, different maturities

DETERMINING THE VALUE OF AN AT THE MONEY STRADDLE

Chart 6.2 displays a linear graph for the straddle. Its value is $0.8 \times \sigma \times \sqrt{T} \times F$ (or K, since for an at the money option F = K). Applying this formula, with maturity at 1 year and volatility at 5% and the Future trading at 50, the straddle will be valued at $0.8 \times 5\% \times \sqrt{1} \times 50 = \$2$, at 30% volatility: $0.8 \times 30\% \times \sqrt{1} \times 50 = \$12$. With volatility at 20%, maturity at ¼ year and the Future trading at 50, the straddle will be valued at: $0.8 \times 20\% \times \sqrt{¼} \times 50 = \$4$. With volatility at 25%, maturity at ¼ year and the Future trading at 100, the straddle will be valued at: $0.8 \times 25\% \times \sqrt{¼} \times 100 = \$10$, and so on.

Another approach is applying the following formulas for calls and puts:

$$C = 0.4 \times \sigma \times \sqrt{T} \times F \text{ (or K, since for an at the money option F = K).}$$
$$P = 0.4 \times \sigma \times \sqrt{T} \times F \text{ (or K, since for an at the money option F = K)}$$

Half of the value of the straddle is the value for the call and the other half of the straddle is the value for the put.

At very high volatilities or very long times to maturity, the Black and Scholes values tend to be slightly lower than the outcome of the formula. However, application of this rule of thumb proves to be very valuable. Below are some tables showing how the $0.8 \times \sigma \times \sqrt{T} \times F$ formula relates to the outcome of the Black and Scholes model at different Future levels, volatility levels and time to maturity.

TABLE 6.2

Future	Volatility	Maturity	$0.8\sigma\sqrt{T}F$	Black Scholes	Error
50	10%	1 year	$4	$3.99	0.25%
50	15%	1 year	$6	$5.98	0.33%
50	25%	1 year	$10	$9.95	0.5%
50	50%	1 year	$20	$19.74	1.3%

TABLE 6.3

Future	Volatility	Maturity	$0.8\sigma\sqrt{T}F$	Black Scholes	Error
100	10%	1 year	$8	$7.98	0.25%
75	15%	1 year	$9	$8.97	0.33%
50	25%	1 year	$10	$9.95	0.5%
25	50%	1 year	$10	$9.87	1.3%

TABLE 6.4

Future	Volatility	Maturity	$0.8\sigma\sqrt{T}F$	Black Scholes	Error
50	10%	¼ year	$2	$2.00	0%
50	15%	½ year	$4.24	$4.23	0.25%
50	25%	2 year	$14.14	$14.03	0.8%
50	20%	4 year	$16	$15.85	1%

CHAPTER 7

Delta II

The previous chapter showed how to calculate the straddle value at a certain Future level, volatility and maturity. In principle one should be able now to value this for a very large variety of at the money options.

In the first chapter on delta, all the charts made clear that at specific levels the delta of an option is 0 or 100% for calls, 0 or −100% for puts. The longer the time to maturity, or the larger the volatility, the later this would happen. Just a millisecond before expiry the delta of the option would grow from 0 or 100% in a tiny range: from just slightly below 50 to just slightly above 50. At 40% volatility and 1 year to maturity, this range would be from around 27.50 to 90.

The main importance is to understand that when having a 0% delta an option is void. When a call or put, the value of a 0% delta option is zero. It has no chance (statistically) to end up in the money within the time left to maturity. The call value (out of the money call, already worth 0) will not change when the Future drops, the put value (out of the money put) will not change when the Future goes up. Hence, both call and put keep a 0% delta: there is no change in delta, so the option has no gamma either. The same will apply to an option which has a delta of 100% or −100%: these two will have the same characteristics as an option with 0% delta (Think of put call parity: the characteristics of a call with a delta of 100% will be equivalent to the put of the same strike which has a 0% delta. The same applies to a put with −100% delta which will have the same characteristics as the call of the same strike which has a delta of 0%).

DETERMINING THE BOUNDARIES OF THE DELTA

These options (at 0%, 100% or −100% delta) are at the boundaries of the statistical distribution. Anything beyond has no convexity any more – no gamma, no other Greeks; they are out of scope.

The options either way behave as if they are worthless, not subject to any Greeks. Or, in the case of deep in the money calls: will be the same as a Future long (delta 100%); or, in the case of deep in the money puts: will be the same as a Future short position (delta −100%).

Before further discussing the Greeks, it is important to determine the boundaries for the statistical distribution of the options. This will be done by applying the value of the straddle as a standard deviation.

For the normal distribution, when applying 3 standard deviations from the mean, it is known that 99.7% of all the samples will fall within this specific range; when applying 4 standard deviations this percentage will increase towards 99.999%. So, with a standard deviation of $\sigma\sqrt{T}$, as discussed in the first part, one could say that within $4 \times \sigma\sqrt{T} \times F$ (being 4 times the standard deviation) all the samples of a group of outcomes will fall within the distribution.

In the chapter on Pricing, the standard deviation/at the money straddle for the options was computed at $0.8 \times \sigma\sqrt{T} \times F$. In order to get to $4 \times \sigma\sqrt{T} \times F$, the standard deviation or straddle for the options will need to be multiplied by 5. So, by applying 5 times the value of the straddle the upper boundary of the distribution will be found; beyond this level no Greek has any value/meaning anymore.

Since the model has a lognormal distribution, this will be the boundary for the higher level strikes. The boundary for lower level strikes will be calculated by applying the ratio laid out in the chapter on volatility (the difference is that in that chapter a two standard deviation was applied). With a Future at 50, volatility at 20% and a maturity of 1 year, all optionality is assumed to have disappeared beyond: $50 + (5 \times 0.8 \times 20\% \times \sqrt{1} \times 50) = \$90$. At 10% vol, 3 months to maturity and the same level in the Future, the boundary will be situated at: $50 + (5 \times 0.8 \times 10\% \times \sqrt{1/4} \times 50) = \$60$.

Applying this in combination with the Future trading at 50, volatility at 20% and maturity at 1 year, with an upper boundary of $90 (which is actually a ratio of 1.8 versus 50), the lower boundary can be determined by dividing 50 by 1.8, making it: $27\frac{7}{9}$. From $27\frac{7}{9}$ to 50 is equivalent to from 50 to 90: both are 1.8 times the base value.

So, in this example, the puts with a strike below 27.77 and the calls with a strike of above 90 have no value and no delta any more, and hence are not subject to any form of optionality.

For the other example (volatility 10%, maturity ¼ year), with an upper boundary of 60, the lower boundary can be determined at 50 divided by 1.2, making $41\frac{2}{3}$.

With the Future trading at 50, maturity at 1 year and volatility at 20% the boundaries are at $27\frac{7}{9}$ and 90, and with maturity at ¼ year and volatility at 10% the boundaries are at $41\frac{2}{3}$ and 60. Above the 60 strike (10% volatility and maturity at ¼ year) and the 90 strike (20% volatility and maturity at 1 year), the delta of the call option has reached 0%, which is obviously the minimum delta for a call option (the delta of a call option cannot turn negative, changing from a right to buy a Future into the right to sell a Future), hence there is also no gamma anymore. When the call option has a delta of 0%, applying put call parity, the put will thus have a delta of −100%.

At any strike below $41\frac{2}{3}$ (10% volatility and maturity at ¼ year) and $27\frac{7}{9}$ (20% volatility and maturity at 1 year), the delta of the put option has reached 0%, which is the minimum for a put option – any strike lower will yield a 0% delta, and no gamma anymore. Any call option with a strike below $41\frac{2}{3}$ and $27\frac{7}{9}$ respectively will have a delta of 100%.

To conclude, at the boundaries of the distribution the delta cannot change anymore, calls are at a maximum delta with a strike at the lower boundary (deep in the money calls, a call cannot get a higher delta than 100%) and puts are at their maximum negative delta with a strike at the higher boundary (deep in the money puts, a put cannot get a delta larger than -100%). This feature no longer allows any gamma for the options: the delta doesn't change anymore and hence there shouldn't be any gamma.

Gamma for 2 different Maturities with different Vols, Future at 50

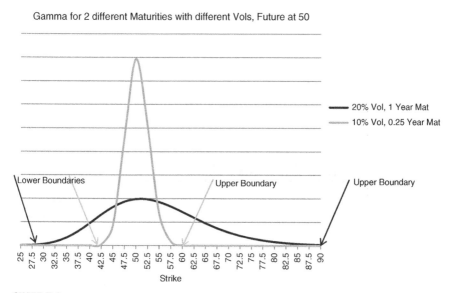

CHART 7.1   The gamma boundaries for 2 different maturities with different volatilities

Chart 7.1 shows the boundary levels for the delta by displaying the gamma boundaries, for two different maturity and volatility levels; the Future is trading at 50. Lower boundaries are at $27\frac{7}{9}$ and $41\frac{2}{3}$, upper boundaries are at 60 and 90. At any level where there is no gamma any more, the delta of the options have reached either 0% or 100% / -100%.

Chart 7.2 displays the gamma distribution for calls (or puts, since their gamma is the same) in combination with the deltas of the calls. The Future is trading at 50, volatility at 20% and maturity is at 1 year. At any strike below $27\frac{7}{9}$ there will be no gamma anymore and at the same time the delta of the call option will be 100%. Around the 90 strike, there is also no remaining gamma and the delta has reached the minimum value, being 0%. Beyond these levels there will be no changes anymore in either gamma or delta. (One could see some tiny value for the gamma around 90; this has to do with the fact that 4 standard deviations is also slightly less than 100% of the distribution. This value is, however, so small that it can be disregarded.)

Delta for call options versus gamma, Future at 50,00, Volatility at 20% Maturity 1 Year

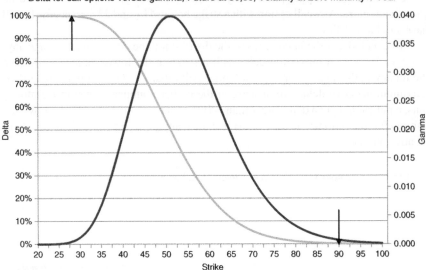

CHART 7.2   The delta and gamma boundaries for calls, Future at 50, volatility 20%, maturity 1 year

VALUATION OF THE AT THE MONEY DELTA

In the chapter on Pricing we discussed the delta for an at the money call, being $\Phi(d1)$ and d1 – for an at the money call, $\frac{1}{2}\sigma\sqrt{T}$. When σ and T are known, the at the money delta can be easily derived. When assuming maximum volatility at 100% and maximum time to maturity at 1 year, the maximum value for d1 will be $0.5(\frac{1}{2} \times 100\% \times \sqrt{1})$. In the range d1 between 0 and 0.5, $\Phi(d1)$ has an almost linear shape.

$\Phi(d1)$ with d1 at 0, results in a 50% delta (at the money delta at expiry), and $\Phi(d1)$ with d1 at 0.5 (100% volatility, maturity 1 year) results in approximately 70% delta – hence a difference of 20% delta. So each step of 0.1 for d1 will result in an additional 4% delta, as shown in Chart 7.3 on the following page. So, for instance, with volatility at 20% and time to maturity at 1 year, d1 can be valued at $\frac{1}{2} \times 20\% \times \sqrt{1} = 0.1$. The delta of the at the money call will thus be 50% +4%, being 54% (−46% for the at the money put). In the table below some examples are displayed:

TABLE 7.1

Volatility	Maturity	d1	$\Phi(d1)$ approximation	$\Phi(d1)$ Delta
10%	¼ year	0.025	51%	51%
25%	1 year	0.125	55%	55%
20%	1 year	0.1	54%	54%
30%	½ year	0.106	54.2%	54.2%
60%	1 year	0.3	62%	61.8%

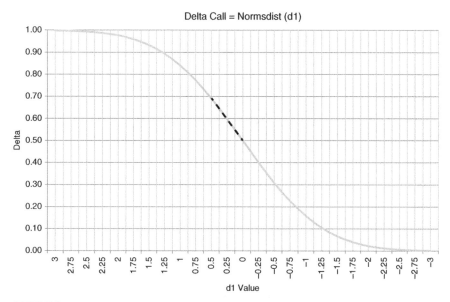

CHART 7.3 The lineair shape of the delta with d1 between 0 and 0.5

DELTA DISTRIBUTION IN RELATION TO THE AT THE MONEY STRADDLE

As being mentioned before in the chapter Delta I, sensible things can be said about options based on the linearity of the delta chart between roughly 20% and 80% for the calls (and hence −20% and −80% for the puts). Compared to the at the money delta of (around) 50% for the call and (around) −50% for the put, there is an area comprising 30% in deltas either direction of the at the money level where the delta chart is more or less linear.

Chart 7.4 shows the 50 call with a delta of 54%, the 42 call with a delta of around 83%, and the 58 call a delta of around 26%. When applying the straddle formula $0.8 \times \sigma\sqrt{T} \times F$ its value (with the Future trading at 50, volatility at 20% and maturity at 1 year) will be $8. At the same time, the call which is one straddle in the money (the 42 call) will have a delta of 83%, which is approximately 30% higher in delta. The call which is one straddle out of the money (58 call) will have a delta of 26% –approximately 30% lower in delta compared to the at the money strike.

TABLE 7.2

Strike	Call delta	Put delta	Reversal (as a check)
42	83%	−17%	100%
50	54%	−46%	100%
58	26%	−74%	100%

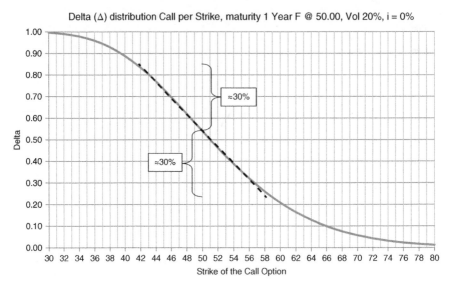

CHART 7.4   The 30% rule for one straddle in or out of the money

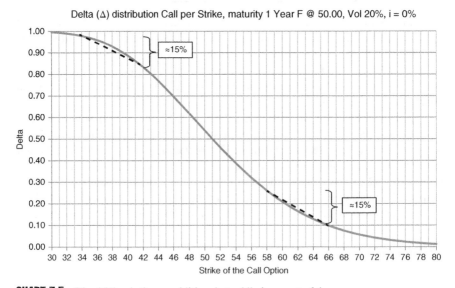

CHART 7.5   The 15% rule for an additional straddle in or out of the money

When taking the delta of a reversal (i.e. 100% when applying an interest rate of 0%) into account, the 50 put will thus have a delta of −46%, the 42 put, being one straddle out of the money, will have a delta which is approximately 30% less negative (−17%) and the 58 put, being one straddle in the money and thus having a delta which is approximately 30% more negative, is −74%.

This so-called 30% rule can be applied to all kinds of volatilities and maturities. There are some small discrepancies compared to the Black and Scholes model, but the rule of thumb holds very well in general.

When referring to a strike which is two straddles in the money or out of the money there will be an additional 15% change in delta.

When comparing the 34 call with the 42 call, chart 7.5 shows that, when two straddles in the money, the delta of the call is approximately 15% higher compared to the strike, which is one straddle in the money (the 42 call). The 66 call (being two straddles out of the money) will have a delta which is approximately 15% lower compared to the 58 call (being one straddle out of the money). Obviously the deltas for the puts will change in the same way when one straddle deeper in the money or further out of the money.

TABLE 7.3

Future at 50, volatility 10%, maturity 1 year, $0.8 \times \sigma \sqrt{T} \times F = \$4$			**Black and Scholes Model**
Calls	**Strike**	**Delta**	**Delta**
2 straddles in the money	42	97%	96%
1 straddle in the money	46	82%	81%
At the money	50	52%	52%
1 straddle out of the money	54	22%	24%
2 straddles out of the money	58	7%	8%

TABLE 7.4

Future at 50, volatility 20%, maturity 1 year, $0.8 \times \sigma \sqrt{T} \times F = \$8$			**Black Scholes Model**
Calls	**Strike**	**Delta**	**Delta**
2 straddles in the money	34	99%	98%
1 straddle in the money	42	84%	83%
At the money	50	54%	54%
1 straddle out of the money	58	24%	26%
2 straddles out of the money	66	9%	10%

TABLE 7.5

Future at 50, volatility 10%, maturity ¼ year, $0.8 \times \sigma\sqrt{T} \times F = \$2$			Black Scholes Model
Calls	Strike	Delta	Delta
2 straddles in the money	46	96%	95%
1 straddle in the money	48	81%	80%
At the money	50	51%	51%
1 straddle out of the money	52	21%	23%
2 straddles out of the money	54	6%	7%

Tables 7.3, 7.4 and 7.5 above show that, for different volatilities as well as for different maturities, the 30% and 15% delta rule of thumb works very well. These two percentages are rough percentages and could be fine-tuned: 29% for one straddle in the money calls and 15% additional for two straddles in the money calls (and thus 29% for one straddle out of the money puts and 15% for the additional straddle out of the money puts) and 28% and 16% for one straddle out of the money calls and two straddles out of the money calls, respectively. However, the 30%/15% delta rule of thumb will suffice – it is easy to remember and will not result in a very large deviation.

APPLICATION OF THE DELTA APPROACH, DETERMINING THE DELTA OF A CALL SPREAD

Applying this simple 30% delta rule can very much assist in determining the delta of an option with a certain strike, but also in valuing option combinations: like spreads and, for instance, specific structures like butterflies.

When entering in a (long) call spread, one buys one strike and sells a higher strike. For the (long) put spread it's the other way around, buying the higher strike and selling the lower strike. The initial investment is obviously lower than just buying the call option at the first strike; the investment of the lower strike call will be partly offset by receiving the premium of the higher strike call being sold.

When the Future is trading at 50, a trader, being bullish on the market, could for instance buy the 50–54 call spread, buying the 50 call, selling the 54 call. His P&L at expiry would look as follows:

Chart 7.6 displays the profit & loss distribution of the 50–54 call spread. At any level below 50 it has no value; above 50 it will gradually grow to a maximum value of $4 when having reached 54. At any point higher than 54 the additional profit generated by the 50 call will be offset by the short position in the 54 call and thus the P&L will stay at $4. The initial investment has not been taken into account, so it will have to be deducted from the P&L distribution. Obviously the chart displays the P&L distribution at expiry. Below 50 the structure will have a 0% delta; above 50, the delta will be 100%, above 54, yielding a delta of 0% again.

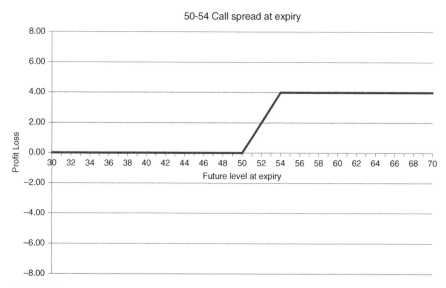

CHART 7.6 50-54 call spread at expiry

During its lifetime, the spread will have a certain delta. The 30% rule can be easily applied here. When, for instance, the Future is trading at 50, the volatility is at 20% and maturity at 1 year; the value of the at the money straddle is $8 and the 54 call is thus half a straddle out of the money – resulting in a delta which is 15% (half of 30%) lower than the delta of the 50 call. Hence the call spread, at that specific time, has a delta of 15%.

If the volatility was 10% with a maturity at 1 year, or 20% volatility with a maturity at ¼ year, the value of the at the money straddle would have been $4, resulting in a 30% delta (or more precisely 28%) for the call spread.

If the Future traded at 46 instead of 50 and a volatility of 20% and time to maturity ¼ year (straddle being around $4), the 50 call would be around one straddle out of the money and the 54 around two straddles out of the money, resulting in a delta of 15% for the call spread. (One should keep in mind that the straddle value for the 46 strike is slightly smaller than the 50 strike; but it's all an approximation.)

CHAPTER 8

Gamma

Gamma is the change of the delta of an option in relation to the change in the underlying Future.

Gamma (γ or Γ for the capital letter) is the first derivative of delta, or the second derivative of the value of the option (as delta is the first derivative of the value of an option), mathematically: $\frac{\partial \Delta}{\partial F}$ or $\frac{\partial^2 V}{\partial F^2}$ ($\Delta = \frac{\partial V}{\partial F}$), which actually doesn't say more than – it's the change of the delta relative to the change of the Future (or to make it more accurate: the change of the change of the value of the option relative to the change of the Future). Throughout this book the Greek letter γ or simply gamma is used for denoting the gamma. The formula for calculating it is as follows: $\gamma = \frac{\varphi(d1)}{F\sigma\sqrt{T}}$ where φ is the probability density function (for d1 see chapter on delta).

As shown in the chapter on delta, and depicted in chart 8.1, the change in the delta of a 50 call option could bring a large profit by each time hedging the delta position. When the market moves up (e.g. from 50 to 54), the owner of the 50 calls can sell Futures (27% of total volume of the option position) in order to flatten/neutralise his delta position; if the market moves down, he can achieve this by buying Futures. So, he is locking in his profit by selling at higher levels in the underlying and buying it at lower levels. The continuous delta hedging on the back of a changing delta position of a portfolio of options is called gamma hedging/trading. Obviously the trader being short the 50 calls, will have to perform the opposite hedging transactions, i.e. buying Futures when the market is going up to hedge his short delta position and selling Futures when the market is going down.

Gamma expresses the change of the delta of an option compared to a \$1 change of the Future. Since delta is often expressed in different ways – in percentages, pips/basis points behind the comma, or just by leaving out the comma altogether (as explained in the Delta chapter) – sometimes it can be a bit confusing. This is the case for gamma, the derivative, as well. In this book gamma will be

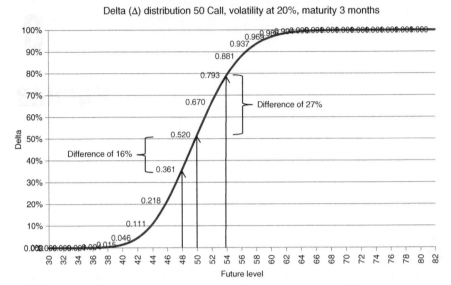

CHART 8.1   Displaying the change in delta from a 50 call, relative to a change in the Future from 50 towards 48 and 54.

expressed as a percentage or as basis points (so for instance 20% gamma will be the same as a gamma of 0.20). Axes on charts reflecting the gamma will be treated the same way.

Where the delta has a distinction between a positive value and a negative value for, respectively, the call and the put, the gamma will be positive for owning the options (irrespective of calls or puts) and negative for being short on them. Put call parity dictates gamma to have the same value for the calls as well as for the puts, when having the same strike and same time to maturity. Whenever discrepancies exist, they can easily be arbitraged by entering into a conversion (when owning a put this is more attractive – i.e. generates more gamma – than owning the call) or reversal (the other way around).

The fact that the delta of a put option is negative sometimes results in the belief/misunderstanding in the market that the gamma of a put option should be negative as well, as opposed to a positive gamma for the call option.

The put option, which has a negative delta by nature, will find its delta becoming more negative as the Future moves down (up to a max of -100%): it gets deeper in the money as the market drops. So if the Future retreats by a dollar – i.e. the market $= -\$1$ – the gamma must be positive in order for the delta to become more negative ($\gamma \times -\$1$ results in a negative number only when gamma is positive, as it should be, while $\gamma \times -\$1$ results in a positive number when gamma is negative, which it shouldn't be.).

The gamma will have different values for different strikes, as well as different values for different maturities and volatilities.

THE AGGREGATE GAMMA FOR A PORTFOLIO OF OPTIONS

For a portfolio (Portfolio I, Table 8.1), the gamma will be expressed in total (aggregate) delta change per dollar. So, if a portfolio consists of 10,000 calls with 20% gamma/$, the gamma of this portfolio will be expressed for the full delta change in total volume per dollar, being: $10,000 \times 20\% = 2,000$. This portfolio will generate a short position of 2,000 deltas (or Futures, since delta is in fact a Future) when the Future would drop $1; it will generate a long position of 2,000 deltas when the Future would move up by $1. The resulting position could be hedged by selling 2,000 Futures with the market trading $1 higher or by buying 2,000 Futures with the market trading $1 lower.

TABLE 8.1

Portfolio I, starting point flat Δ position, Future 50, Vol 15%, maturity 1 month

Strike	Volume	γ per option	Gamma/$	Δ position, Fut $1 lower	Δ position, Fut $1 higher
50 Call	10,000	20%	2,000	$-2,000$	2,000
Total			2,000	$-2,000$	2,000

TABLE 8.2

Portfolio II, starting point flat Δ position, Future 50, Vol 15%, maturity 1 month

Strike	Volume	γ per option	Gamma/$	Δ position, Fut $1 lower	Δ position, Fut $1 higher
50 Call	10,000	20%	2,000	$-2,000$	2,000
52.50 Call	20,000	10%	2,000	$-2,000$	2,000
Total			4,000	$-4,000$	4,000

TABLE 8.3

Portfolio III, starting point flat Δ position, Future 50, Vol 15%, maturity 1 month

Strike	Volume	γ per option	Gamma/$	Δ position, Fut $1 lower	Δ position, Fut $1 higher
47.50 Put	$-15,000$	9%	$-1,350$	1,350	$-1,350$
50 Call	10,000	20%	2,000	$-2,000$	2,000
52.50 Call	20,000	10%	2,000	$-2,000$	2,000
Total			2,650	$-2,650$	2,650

TABLE 8.4

Portfolio IV, starting point flat Δ position, Future 50, Vol 15%, maturity 1 month

Strike	Volume	γ per option	Gamma/$	Δ position, Fut $1 lower	Δ position, Fut $1 higher
47.50 Put	20,000	9%	1,800	−1,800	1,800
50 Call	−10,000	20%	−2,000	2,000	−2,000
52.50 Call	20,000	10%	2,000	−2,000	2,000
Total			1,800	−1,800	1,800

Portfolio II, as shown in Table 8.2, consists of two option strikes, the former 50 calls plus an additional 20,000 52.50 calls with a gamma of 10% per option (thus a different gamma value). With an initial flat delta position, the 50 calls, just as in Portfolio I, generate a delta change of 2,000 per $ change in the underlying. The 52.50 calls, being long 20,000, also generate a gamma of 2,000 deltas per $ change in the market. Each strike generates a 2,000 delta short position when the market drops by $1, an aggregated 4,000 deltas short for the whole portfolio. Furthermore, each strike generates a 2,000 delta long position when the market would moves up by $1, totalling a length of 4,000 deltas. The gamma of the two strikes can be added up to value the gamma of the total position/portfolio. When having the total gamma value of the portfolio one doesn't need to monitor the separate options to have the total delta change of the portfolio when the market would move up or down.

Portfolio III, as shown in Table 8.3, is a combination of portfolio II and a short position of 15,000 47.50 puts. The short position generates a negative gamma (owning options creates a gamma long position, being short creates a gamma short position). The gamma of the puts is 1,350 short; so, when the market drops $1 it generates a 1,350 long delta position (−$1 times −1,350 delta), and with the market $1 higher it will generate a short position of 1,350 deltas ($1 times −1,350 delta). Adding up all the gammas generates the same delta changes per $ move of the market as monitoring each option separately.

Portfolio IV, as shown in Table 8.4, is long the 47.50 puts, and therefore they generate a positive gamma. However, now the portfolio is short the 50 calls – they now generate a negative gamma. Monitoring the delta of the aggregate position will result in the same delta changes with a market move as monitoring each strike separately.

When a portfolio consists of 4,000 gamma, the delta increases by 2,000 when the market moves only 50¢ up; when moving up $2, the delta generated by the gamma position would be 8,000; a fall of $3 generates a short position of 12,000 deltas. And so on. When gamma is negative it results in a delta long position when the market goes down and a delta short position when the market moves up.

THE DELTA CHANGE OF AN OPTION

Table 8.5 shows how the delta of a 50 put option, starting at 50 in the Future, changes according to its gamma of 10%. Each time the market goes down the delta of the put option becomes more negative. The deeper in the money a put is, the more negative its delta is. When going up, the delta of the option gets smaller (i.e. less negative), which is consistent with how the delta of a put should evolve in relation to changes in the Future.

TABLE 8.5

The impact on the delta as a result of Future changes for a 50 Put with a gamma of 10%, Future 50, Vol 10%, maturity 3 months

Future	Change F	Delta Before	γ	Delta Change (Change F × γ)	New Delta
50			10% or 0.10		−50%
48	−2	−50%	10%	−20%	−70%
49	1	−70%	10%	10%	−60%
51	2	−60%	10%	20%	−40%
47	−4	−40%	10%	−40%	−80%

TABLE 8.6

The impact on the delta as a result of Future changes for a 50 Call with a gamma of 10%, Future 50, Vol 10%, maturity 3 months

Future	Change F	Delta Before	γ	Delta Change (Change F × γ)	New Delta
50			10% or 10		50%
48	−2	50%	10%	−20%	30%
49	1	30%	10%	10%	40%
51	2	40%	10%	20%	60%
47	−4	60%	10%	−40%	20%

The call option, as shown in Table 8.6, has the same positive gamma value; each time when the Future rises the delta of the call increases, and vice versa. This is all consistent with how the delta of a call should evolve in relation to changes in the Future.

When combining the two tables, setting up a conversion/reversal will result in a −100%/100% delta position respectively (when the interest rate is at zero). If at any time the gamma were different for the call or the put, it would immediately have been visible when looking at these two strategies as its delta would deviate from these two values.

When a trader reports that he is short gamma, this means that he has a portfolio with a negative gamma, which implies that he is short options in general. He will be long gamma when long in options in general (here we refer to an option position in one or a few strikes; in a portfolio with positions in multiple strikes and/or multiple maturities it could happen that a trader is net long options, while being short gamma. This is a result of either horizontal spreads, time spreads or a combination of the two).

THE GAMMA IS NOT A CONSTANT

In Tables 8.5 and 8.6 of the previous paragraph, a stable 10% gamma was applied to demonstrate the fact that the gamma of an option has a positive value. In the real world this gamma changes over the distribution.

As was presented in the Delta chapter, the delta change is steepest around the at the money area. When the delta is approaching 100%/−100% or decreasing towards 0% (what were called the boundaries in the delta chapter) the delta changes will be much slower. Gamma, reflecting the change of the delta of an option, is thus the highest when the option strike is at the money and lowest when deep in the money or far out of the money.

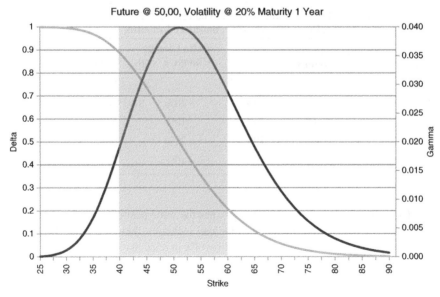

CHART 8.2   The delta and gamma distribution over a range of different option strikes

LONG TERM GAMMA EXAMPLE

Chart 8.2 shows that the delta (light grey line), when being deep in the money, slowly decreases, just 12 deltas, from 100 at the 25 strike towards 88 at the 40 strike, when around at the money (grey area) 68 deltas between the 40 and 60 strike, and when out of the money 20 deltas between the 60 and 90 strike. So in a range of $65, the delta has decreased from 100% to 0% (100% move, as shown in Table 8.7). The dark grey line represents the gamma, it already indicates that when deep in the money or (far) out of the money the delta change compared to the change of the Future will be the least, the derivative $\frac{\partial \Delta}{\partial F}$ (the gamma) will go towards zero, or in this specific example when comparing strikes: $\frac{\partial \Delta}{\partial K}$. The gamma is highest when precisely at the money, at 50.

TABLE 8.7

Strike Range	Delta difference	Strike difference	$\frac{\partial \Delta}{\partial F}$	γ (average of the range)
25–40	12%	15	12%/$15	0.8%/$
40–60	68%	20	68%/$20	3.4%/$
60–90	20%	30	20%/$30	0.66%/$

SHORT TERM GAMMA EXAMPLE

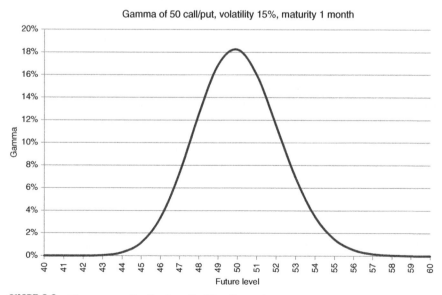

CHART 8.3 The gamma distribution of a 50 strike option

In Chart 8.3 the distribution of the gamma of a 50 call/put at 15% volatility and one month to maturity is depicted. Call and put both have the same positive gamma (put call parity, otherwise arbitrage opportunities might arise).

At 50 the gamma is around 18%, meaning a long position of 10,000 50 calls or puts would generate a delta change of 1,800 per dollar. The gamma changes quite rapidly (due to fairly low volatility and a short time to expiry). At 53 the gamma is only 7% and around 58 there's no gamma anymore in the 50 strike. On the way down all gamma has vanished around 43.

Since gamma is changing all the time, the delta change will be according to the average gamma in a certain range (the range shouldn't be too large since the change in the gamma distribution is not a linear one).

VERY SHORT TERM GAMMA EXAMPLE

When there is a long position in a 50 call, the Future is trading slightly below 50 and the expiry is in one millisecond; the delta, zero, will not change up to the 49.999 level. Just above 50, at 50.001, the delta will be 100%. So in a move of two thousandths of a dollar, the delta of the option grew from zero to 100% (100% move), as shown below in Table 8.8.

TABLE 8.8

Strike Range	Delta difference	Strike difference	$\frac{\partial \Delta}{\partial F}$	γ (average of the range)
25–49.999	0%	24.999	0%/$25	0%/$
49.999–50.001	100%	0.002	100%/$0.002	50.000%/$
50.001–90	0%	39.999	0%/$40	0%/$

Applying the gamma formula $\frac{\partial \Delta}{\partial F}$ equals $\frac{100\%}{0.002}$, being 50.000%. When further narrowing the levels in between where the delta moves from 0 to 100% (e.g. from 49.99999 to 50.00001), gamma actually could become infinite, be it within a very small range (provided time to expiry is ultra short).

Because gamma is in fact the delta change per $1 change in the Future, the maximum gamma per $ for one option should be 100%, as shown in Table 8.9.

TABLE 8.9

Strike Range	Delta difference	Strike difference	$\frac{\partial \Delta}{\partial F}$	γ (average of the range)
25–49.50	0%	24.50	0%/$25	0%/$
49.50–50.50	100%	1.00	100%/$1	100%/$
50.50–90	0%	39.50	0%/$40	0%/$

The Black and Scholes model, however, values gamma as is shown in Table 8.8. Gamma is computed at exactly the input level for the Future and not for a specific range. Thus when exactly at the money, gamma could be extremely high; when slightly in the money, or out of the money within a small range, gamma could already have been heavily reduced.

That's why, from a risk management perspective, so often it doesn't make sense to have gamma limits for a trader. A scenario analysis over a certain range would be more sensible: while the explosive gamma position is only there in a very small area, other option positions might mitigate the risk.

Gamma, as a derivative of delta, should be considered as dynamic as delta. It changes over the range of a series of option strikes, in relation to volatility, the level of the at the money strike (or the Future), and also in relation to maturity, where it even could go towards infinity when the time to maturity is extremely small.

DETERMINING THE BOUNDARIES OF GAMMA

The 0–100% delta range of the example in the prior paragraph, with its expiry in one millisecond, was based on a very small price increment of the Future. However, Chart 8.2 reflected a longer term example: the call option with a 100% delta when very deep in the money, the 25 strike with the Future trading at 50 and a 0% delta when very far out of the money, the 90 strike with the Future trading at 50. These are two "extreme" scenarios in which the delta changes 100%. While it might seem a bit arbitrary, the model is quite consistent in the ranges in which the delta makes a 100% move.

The delta chapter discussed boundaries: the level where the out of the money calls have a delta of 0% and the in the money puts have a delta of -100%; and, on the other side, the level where the in the money calls have a delta of 100% and the out of the money puts have a delta of 0%. These levels are: on the upside, 5 times the straddle value and, on the downside, the Future level divided by the ratio of the first one (due to lognormal distribution).

Setting the boundaries for options with a Future at 50, volatility at 10% and maturity 1 year, with a straddle value of 4 (as shown in the Pricing chapter) the outcome will be 70 (50 plus 5 times the straddle value, being 20) for the upside boundary (any call option with a strike above 70 will have a zero delta). The lower boundary will be 50 divided by the ratio of the former, $\frac{70}{50} = 1.4$, resulting in $\frac{50}{1.4} \approx 35$ (any put option with a strike below 35 will have a zero delta).

Since a call option is the right to buy one Future (being 100%), the delta can never be higher than 100% and will never drop below 0% and since the put option is the right to sell one Future (being -100%), the delta could never get more negative than -100% when in the money, or above 0% when out of the money. This implies that, whenever a delta of 100%, -100% or 0% has been reached, the delta cannot go beyond these levels: i.e. will not change anymore. With γ being $\frac{\partial \Delta}{\partial F}$ and $\partial \Delta$ being zero, γ has to be zero as well. In conclusion: the gamma will have the same boundaries as the delta. Beyond these levels the gamma doesn't exist anymore (provided all the other parameters stay the same), as shown in Chart 8.4.

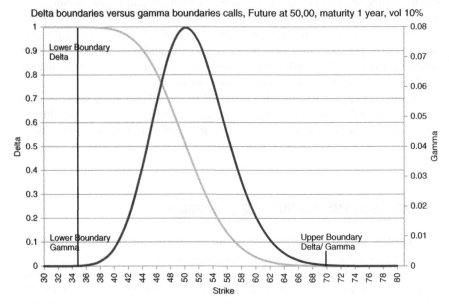

CHART 8.4   The boundaries for the delta in comparison with the boundaries for the gamma

For the delta (light grey line), there is a lower boundary of 35 where any strike below or at 35 will have a 100% delta for the calls and 0% delta for the puts; for the gamma, 35 is the lower boundary as well – any option with a strike of 35 or lower will have 0 gamma. The upper boundary at 70 determines the level where any strike above will have a 0% delta for the calls and −100% delta for the puts. Any strike above 70 will have 0 gamma.

The gamma has a Log Normal distribution, simply because the delta has a Log Normal distribution and the gamma is its derivative.

DETERMINING THE GAMMA VALUE OF AN AT THE MONEY STRADDLE

In the pricing chapter the values of the at the money straddle were shown in relation to the volatility and underlying, which is a linear function, and in relation to the time to maturity, which is a square root function.

The basis for the at the money straddle value is: 10% volatility with a maturity of 1 year results in a straddle which is worth 8% of the underlying or strike ($F = K$)

with interest rate at 0%. With the Future at 50 the straddle is worth \$4.00. When applying \$4 as a basis one could multiply it with the ratio of the Future (actual Future compared to 50), the ratio of the volatility (actual volatility compared to 10%) and the ratio of the maturity (actual maturity compared to 1 year maturity). As already shown in the chapter on pricing, below, in Table 8.10, 8.11 and 8.12, some more examples are depicted in order to show the accuracy and the simplicity of it at the same time:

It is also known that when the market moves up or down one straddle value, this will be equal to one standard deviation in the options.

Where in a normal distribution the probability for being within one standard deviation is 68%, for gamma a 64% delta range in one straddle move will be applied – a small adjustment, the "64 gamma rule". So if the straddle is worth \$8, the gamma will be: $\frac{\partial \Delta}{\partial F} = \frac{64\%}{\$8} = 8\%/\$$ (4% for the call and 4% for the put).

TABLE 8.10

Future	Volatility	Maturity	F ratio × Vol ratio × Mat ratio ($\sqrt{}$)	Straddle value
50	10%	1 Year	1	4.00
50	15%	1 Year	1.5	6.00
50	20%	1 Year	2	8.00
50	25%	1 Year	2.5	10.00

TABLE 8.11

Future	Volatility	Maturity	F ratio × Vol ratio × Mat ratio ($\sqrt{}$)	Straddle value
50	10%	1 Year	1	4.00
50	10%	½ Year	$\sqrt{½}$	2.82
50	10%	¼ Year	$\sqrt{¼} = ½$	2.00
50	10%	4 Year	$\sqrt{4} = 2$	8.00

TABLE 8.12

Future	Volatility	Maturity	F ratio × Vol ratio × Mat ratio ($\sqrt{}$)	Straddle value
50	10%	1 Year	1	4.00
100	20%	½ Year	$2 \times 2\sqrt{½} \approx 2.83$	11.31
25	12.5%	2 Year	$½ \times 1¼\sqrt{2} \approx 0.88$	3.54
25	10%	¼ Year	$½\sqrt{¼} = ¼$	1.00

TABLE 8.13

Future	Volatility	Maturity	Straddle value	γ Straddle (64%/Straddle)	γ Call or γ Put	B.S. Model
50	10%	1 Year	4.00	16%	8%	7.97%
50	15%	1 Year	6.00	10.66%	5.33%	5.30%
50	10%	¼ Year	2.00	32%	16%	15.95%
125	16%	1 Year	16.00	4%	2%	1.99%

The gamma values in Table 8.13 are all approximations, but they are very very close to the Black and Scholes outcome. At least they are useful for a sanity check. Or, if a trader has to quickly decide whether to do a trade or not, he could easily know what volume of gamma he would be trading.

In the chapter on delta we showed that a one straddle in the money call will have a delta which is 30% higher than the at the money delta. The put of that strike will have a delta which is 30% more positive (−20% instead of −50%). As a result, the strike which is one straddle in the money will have a delta which is around 60% higher than the at the money, instead of the applied 64%. Due to the fact that gamma is not linear, the 64% approach works better.

GAMMA IN RELATION TO TIME TO MATURITY, VOLATILITY AND THE UNDERLYING LEVEL

Being the first derivative of the delta, gamma is 100% related to the outlook of the delta. The shorter the time to expiry is, the narrower the 0–100% delta range for calls and 0 to −100% for puts will be. So, gamma must be very high and will cease to exist quite early (boundaries are very near when time to maturity is short). If time to maturity gets longer, the delta change will be less pronounced and the 0–100% delta range will be much larger. This indicates that gamma for the at the money options will be smaller, but overall gamma will be there in a large array for the options (more strikes will have gamma, while with short term options the gamma is only concentrated on a few strikes around the at the money). As a result, out of the money strikes will have an increasing gamma and at the same time strikes which had no gamma before will then commence to generate gamma.

The lower the volatility, the earlier the boundaries are reached. The delta will very rapidly travel along the 0–100% path and the gamma is concentrated in a few around the at money strikes. In a high volatility environment, the delta change will be less pronounced/lower and the gamma is distributed over many more strikes.

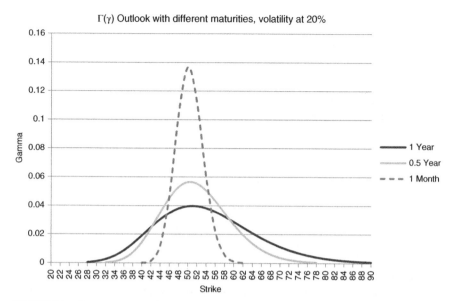

CHART 8.5 The gamma distribution with a stable volatility and alternating maturities

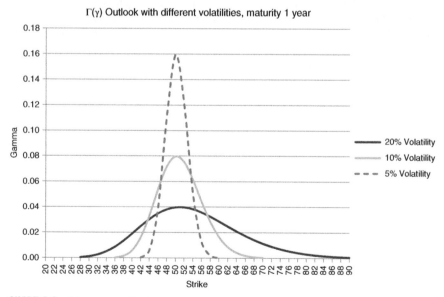

CHART 8.6 The gamma distribution with a stable maturity and alternating volatilities

In Chart 8.5, at stable volatility the time to maturity determines the gamma. It is just like, when time to maturity increases one has to grab the short term gamma graph and "stretch" it out in order to cover a larger range in the underlying Future which is eligible for gamma. This is actually a fair approach, because the surface area of the distribution always has an aggregate value of 100% or 1. When time to maturity increases, the gamma of at the money options decreases, the gamma of out of the money options increases.

In Chart 8.6 something similar has been depicted. However, this time it refers to a stable maturity with varying volatilities. The volatility is increasing, and as a result the gamma for the at the money strikes decreases, while at the same time the gamma for the out of the moneys will increase. In essence, the boundaries for the delta have widened due to higher volatility; gamma, as a derivative of the delta, will hence have increasing boundaries as well. So there will be some strikes which had hardly any, or even zero, gamma that suddenly acquire a more pronounced gamma.

So far there have been many examples showing the Future (and the at the money level for the options) trading at 50, but what happens to the gamma when the Future (and hence the at the money level as well) trades at a different level?

If the Future was trading at 100 instead of 50, and applying the same volatility and the same time to maturity, the range of one standard deviation up and down would be twice as large as with the Future at 50. Applying that to $\frac{\partial \Delta}{\partial F}$ where $\partial \Delta$ remains the same but ∂F is double, the result is an at the money gamma which is half the value. Using this method to determine what the gamma of a 25 call or put should be when the Future is trading at 25: $\partial \Delta$ is the same but ∂F will be half the initial value; accordingly, the gamma of the at the money option will double.

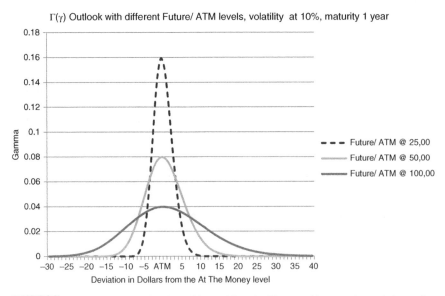

$\Gamma(\gamma)$ Outlook with different Future/ ATM levels, volatility at 10%, maturity 1 year

CHART 8.7   The gamma distribution with a stable volatility, a stable maturity and alternating Future levels (which are at the money).

The out of the money strikes/options will increase in gamma when the Future level increases, and vice versa, as shown in Chart 8.7.

Using the stretching features laid out in the charts, an option trader can always understand/consider the implications for gamma on the back of higher/lower volatility, decreasing time to maturity and changing underlying levels for the at the money options.

The gamma formula $\frac{\varphi(d1)}{F\sigma\sqrt{T}}$ indicates for the at the money options that the gamma has an inverted linear relationship with volatility. So, when volatility doubles the gamma will halve – an inverted linear relationship with regards to the Future/at the money level; when the at the money Future level halves, the gamma will double and the other way around. For time to maturity this relationship is an inverted square root function: when the time to maturity doubles the gamma will be $\sqrt{2}$ times as small. $\varphi(d1)$ will not change for different Future levels, $(d1)$ will be determined by $\ln \frac{F}{K}$, which remains unchanged for the at the moneys: 0. For volatility and time to maturity changes $\varphi(d1)$ will change slightly: it is fractional and can be neglected in the approximations for gamma.

PRACTICAL EXAMPLE

In the chapter on delta, Chart 8.8 below, was shown, depicting the delta and the velocity of the delta decrease (i.e. gamma) when the market moves up.

At 20% volatility, maturity 1 year and the Future at 50, the delta of the 43 call, being 80%, decreases towards a delta of 20% for the 60 Calls. In a range of $17 the delta decreases by 60%, being 3.5% on average per $($\frac{\partial \Delta}{\partial F} = \frac{60\%}{\$17\$} = 3.5\% / \$)$.

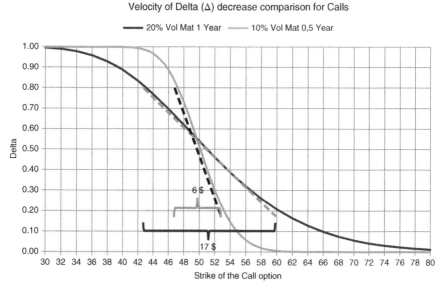

Velocity of Delta (Δ) decrease comparison for Calls

CHART 8.8 The velocity of delta change for a range of call option strikes.

Also shown:

At 10% volatility, maturity ½ year and the Future at 50, the delta of the 47 call, being 80% decreasing towards a delta of 20% for the 53 calls. In a range of $6 the delta decreased by 60%, being 10% on average per $($\frac{\partial \Delta}{\partial F} = \frac{60\%}{\$6\$} = 10\%/\$$). These values are estimations; for reasons of simplicity the range values were given a round number.

Please note that, bearing in mind the gamma formula $\frac{\varphi(d1)}{F\sigma\sqrt{T}}$, when the gamma at 20% vol and 1 year to maturity is 3.5% (on average), the gamma at 10% vol and ½ year to maturity should double on the back of the volatility decrease, and increase by a factor $\sqrt{2}$ on the back of the maturity. Thus, it should be 2 times 1.414, being 2.83 times as high, resulting in 9.98%/$ (where the Black and Scholes model has a ratio of 2.84 due to a small discrepancy in $\varphi(d1)$).

The following is an initial simple valuation for the gamma for the above example. The percentage is per option. So, if someone owns 10,000 of one of these options and hedges his position to a delta neutral portfolio he knows that, in the first case, he has a positive gamma of 350 per $ (3.5% of 10,000), meaning that, if the Future moves up $1 he will be long 350 deltas or 350 Futures; when going up another $ it will be 700 deltas. In the second case, the gamma is larger (due to lower volatility and shorter time to maturity), namely 1,000 per $. Two $ higher the owner would be long 2,000 deltas, as shown in Table 8.14.

Comparing these two portfolios, the gamma is assumed to be constant.

TABLE 8.14

	Gamma	Δ position at start	Δ position $2 higher	Average Δ position long	Profit & Loss
First Case	350	0	700	350	700
Second Case	1,000	0	2,000	1,000	2,000

This works on the way down as well:

TABLE 8.15

	Gamma	Δ position at start	Δ position $2 lower	Average Δ position short	Profit & Loss
First Case	350	0	−700	−350	700
Second Case	1,000	0	−2,000	−1,000	2,000

Obviously, the trader would choose the scenario in which he owns the most gamma, for it creates the most P&L. So, when a market becomes volatile, one wants to be as long as possible in gamma for reaping profits from trading the gamma.

HEDGING THE GAMMA

A combination of a long gamma position and a volatile Future market can contribute immensely to the creation of P&L for the trader. As much gamma as possible is the adage, though gamma comes at a cost.

It is important to understand that every day an option is worth less than the day before (time decay or theta). With 30% volatility, Future at 50 and maturity 1 year, a 50 straddle will cost $12. If absolutely nothing further happened the buyer of the straddle would lose this amount. The theta can be computed on a daily basis.

The trader buying gamma actually expects/hopes that the daily moves of the Future will be larger than the implied volatility justifies or he bets on an increase of volatility in the near term. When the implied volatility is the same as the historical volatility, and remains that way during the option's lifetime, statistically the trader will end up with a zero P&L.

A trader who does not expect a sharp move in volatility should not, therefore, enter into a position when implied volatility is at the expected level compared to historical volatility. When expecting lower volatility he could sell gamma and wait for the daily time decay value, which he "receives" to become bigger than the impact of his negative delta hedges on his gamma short position (buying high, selling low). When expecting higher volatility he expects the returns of his positive delta hedges on the back of his gamma long position to outperform the cost of maintaining his position and paying for the theta. Such a trade should not be initiated for just one volatility point; the risk for it to go against you is too big compared with the reward when having put on the right trade. There should be a substantial discrepancy between implied and historical volatility before entering into such a position.

In the next examples a stable gamma will be assumed for a long option position. When just owning options in 1 strike, the gamma will be very dynamic; however, when there are more strikes in the portfolio one should be able to create a kind of stable gamma along a fairly wide range.

The following table displays the position of a trader long 2,500 gamma with the Future trading at 50.

TABLE 8.16

Week	Future Level	γ position	Δ position	P&L
Start	50	2,500	0	0
1	51	2,500	2,500	1,250
2	52	2,500	5,000	5,000
3	53	2,500	7,500	11,250
4	54	2,500	10,000	20,000

Over four weeks, the Future rose from 50 to 54.

In the first week the trader was initially flat delta but ended up 2,500 delta long. On average he was long 1,250 deltas over a dollar move, making a profit of $1,250. The trader made no hedges on the way up.

In week 2 the trader was already long 2,500 deltas and gained another 2,500 deltas on the way up towards 52. From 50 to 51 he made 1,250 profit and from 51 to 52, where he was 2,500 long at 51 which grew to 5,000 long at 52, he made an average of 3,750 over 1 dollar increase, creating a P&L of $3,750. When added to the first 1,250 he made, the result totals $5,000.

To simplify the calculation somewhat, one should have a look from the start to week 2 directly. The trader is 5,000 delta long at 52; he will be long 2,500 on average from 50 to 52, resulting in a P&L of $5,000.

From 50 to 54, he will end up being 10,000 deltas long, so on average he's long 5,000 deltas/Futures over a path of $4, resulting in a profit of $20,000.

Because of the stable gamma, the mathematics in this example is quite simple – it's linear. Thanks to the gamma his P&L looks more like an exponential function. This is typically the case for gamma; it could look like a modest gamma initially, however if a trader lets it run when the market is moving (i.e. not hedging his deltas) his P&L could grow exponentially. If the market had gone to 60, the trader would have been long 25,000 deltas at that level, being 12,500 deltas on average over a $10 trajectory – which makes a fantastic $125,000 profit.

Certainly this is a highly unlikely scenario. The trader has performed no hedges on the way up, and at the high at 60 he sells all his deltas/Futures. But, what if the market had gone only to 59 (the trader is waiting for the 60 level to sell 25,000 Futures) and then straight back to 50. He wouldn't have made any money, while he experienced a massive move in the underlying (in just 4 weeks an $18 move: 9 up and 9 down). His manager wouldn't have believed him if he told him that he made no money after such a move; in fact, he lost money because of time decay. So, either way the trader must be an enormous bull and dare to let it go, and even risk his job perhaps, or he simply needs to hedge some exposure.

The trader should at least hedge a part of his position, just in case it moves up and will later retrace. Maybe something like this:

Table 8.17 illustrates the prudent trader who sells his deltas on the way up, just to make sure that he makes money as well if the market retraces. For instance,

TABLE 8.17

Week	Future Level	γ position	Δ position	P&L without hedging	Δ Hedge	P&L of Hedges	P&L Total
Start	50	2,500	0	0			0
1	51	2,500	2,500	1,250	−2,500	0	1,250
2	52	2,500	2,500	5,000	−2,500	−2,500	2,500
3	53	2,500	2,500	11,250	−2,500	−7,500	3,750
4	54	2,500	2,500	20,000	−2,500	−15,000	5,000

if the market went to 51 and the week after retraced to 50, the trader could show a profit of 2,500 deltas sold at 51 and 2,500 deltas bought back at 50, making $2,500.

In these two examples, two extremes have been depicted: firstly, the trader who doesn't hedge at all and makes $20,000 when the market goes to 54; and secondly, the prudent trader who only makes $5,000 when the market goes to 54, but does make some money as well when the market retraces after a modest move up. The trader who hasn't hedged anything has the greatest opportunity when the market continues to go up, but will make nothing when the market settles. The trader hedging his deltas with each dollar higher (or even in smaller increments) is called a tight hedger; the trader who waits a few dollars before (partly) hedging his position is a wide hedger. The feature of tight/wide hedging strategies will be lengthily discussed in the chapter on strategies.

When being opportunistic, a trader likes to perform no hedges on the way up when a market is trending (applying the wide hedging strategy) and he prefers to hedge/sell aggressively when the market goes up, buying it back aggressively when the market retraces (the tight hedging strategy). All this to create the best possible P&L. Unfortunately things are not that easy, in order to maximise his P&L the trader will have to forecast market behaviour. This often makes it very hard for traders to find the best way to hedge their gamma.

The trader must hope that he is right in the hedging strategy he pursues in accordance with his market assessment. The prudent trader should hedge some of his deltas, but not all. Hedging all gives away almost all opportunity if the market ends up in a trend. Hedging part of his deltas enables the trader to generate some profit when the market trades sideways, but will also create opportunities when a trend develops. In the end, the trader will have to decide how to set up the hedging strategy. Quite often it is experience and personal preferences that determine the strategy.

In the chapter on Strategies, at the end of the book, several gamma hedging strategies are discussed at more length.

DETERMINING THE GAMMA OF OUT OF THE MONEY OPTIONS

Here we will briefly discuss how to come up with gamma values of other strikes. This becomes less reliable because a linear function will be applied for the gamma determination while it has a log normal distribution. Still it will give some idea of gamma levels.

When taking an at the money straddle with the Future at 50.00, volatility at 15% and maturity 1 year, the value of the straddle is $6.00 and the gamma 10.66% for the straddle ($\frac{\partial \Delta}{\partial F} = \frac{64\%}{\$6\$}$), making the gamma for either way call or put 5.33%. The boundaries for the gamma distribution are for the upside: $50 + (5 \times 6) = 80$ and for the downside $50/(80/50) = 31.25$.

For the gamma distribution for a range of strikes, the assumption will be that the boundaries are at 3½ times the straddle for the upside and 2½ times the straddle for the downside; hence, with $6 in the straddle, they will be at $50 + 21 = 71$ and at $50 - 15 = 35$. When drawing a straight line from the top to the 71 level and another one towards the 35 level, as shown in Chart 8.9, those lines will be assumed to be the gamma distribution. Now it's simple to come up with the values for the gamma, as shown in Table 8.18 below:

TABLE 8.18

Parameters:	Strike	Computed γ	Black and Scholes γ
	35	0	0.3%
Future @ 50,00	38	1.1%	0.9%
Volatility @ 15%	41	2.1%	2.0%
Maturity: 1 Year	44	3.2%	3.5%
50 Straddle: $6.00	47	4.3%	4.7%
	50	5.3%	5.3%
	53	4.6%	5.1%
	56	3.8%	4.2%
	59	3.1%	3.1%
	62	2.3%	2.1%
	65	1.5%	1.3%
	68	0.8%	0.8%
	71	0%	0.4%

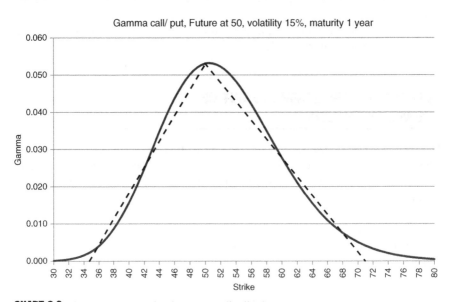

CHART 8.9 Linear approach for the gamma distribution

Chart 8.9 shows that there are quite some discrepancies, but at the same time it gives some idea of where the gamma is distributed over the curve.

DERIVATIVES OF THE GAMMA

This chapter has shown that changes of the gamma are subject to changes in volatility, time to maturity and the underlying level.

So, one should be able to compute the derivatives $\frac{\partial \Gamma}{\partial \sigma}, \frac{\partial \Gamma}{\partial T}$ and $\frac{\partial \Gamma}{\partial F}$ (which are actually fairly simple formulas, although not further specified here).

The change of the gamma in relation to the changes of volatility $\frac{\partial \Gamma}{\partial \sigma}$ or $\frac{\partial^3 V}{\partial F^2 \partial \sigma}$ is called zomma or DgammaDvol.

The change of the gamma in relation to the change of time $\frac{\partial \Gamma}{\partial T}$ or $\frac{\partial^3 V}{\partial F^2 \partial T}$ is called colour, gammableed or DgammaDtime.

The change of the gamma in relation to the change of the underlying $\frac{\partial \Gamma}{\partial F}$ or $\frac{\partial^3 V}{\partial F^3}$ is called speed or DgammaDspot.

These are all third-order Greeks, at the same time first order Greeks of the gamma (being a second order Greek).

In principle, knowing the stretching features (stretching out the chart of the gamma distribution when volatility, time to maturity or underlying levels increase) will suffice for understanding and considering how it works. However, sometimes it is very useful for a trader with a large portfolio of options with different strikes and maturities to quantify this as well. When not quantifying, playing with the parameters of the portfolio, changing maturity, volatility and underlying levels (even into extremes) in the model could also give much/sufficient information about the gamma distribution and the impact of changing parameters for the whole portfolio.

Vega

Vega (ν, sometimes kappa is used: κ) is the change of the value of an option in relation to the change of the (implied) volatility.

It is the derivative of the value of an option in relation to the volatility of the underlying, mathematically: $\frac{\partial V}{\partial \sigma}$. Throughout the book the Greek letter ν will be used for denoting the vega. The formula for calculating it is as follows: $\nu = \frac{F\varphi(d1)\sqrt{T}}{100}$, where φ is the probability density function. The vega has a log normal distribution.

As earlier mentioned; put call parity dictates vega to be the same for calls and puts, otherwise arbitrage opportunities may arise. Vega will be positive for owning the options (irrespective of calls or puts) and negative for being short them.

The vega is expressed in dollars per option. So if an option would have a vega of $0.20, like the 50 strike as shown in Chart 9.1, a 1% increase in volatility would make the option (call or put) 20¢ more expensive. A 1% decrease in volatility would result in a 20¢ lower value for the option. For the 60 strike, having a vega of $0.04 a change in volatility would result in an increase of the option value of $0.04 when volatility would go up 1% and a decrease of $0.04 when volatility would drop 1%.

When a trader reports that he is short vega, it means that he has a portfolio with a negative vega, implying that he is short options in general. He will be long vega when being long options in general (There is an exception; in a portfolio with positions in multiple strikes and/or multiple maturities it could happen that a trader is net long options, however short vega. This is a result of either horizontal spreads, time spreads or a combination of the two).

When the vega position/portfolio is stable along a range in the underlying, computing the resulting P&L from a change in volatility is fairly simple. The result will be the change in the market volatility times the vega position, being impacted by that change, as shown in Table 9.2.

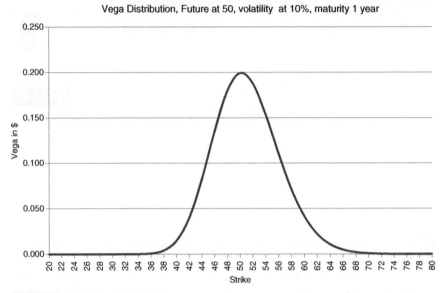

CHART 9.1   Vega distribution

TABLE 9.1   The vega distribution in values from the 36 to 72 strike, Future at 50.00, Volatility 10% and Maturity 1 year

	Calls	Strike	Puts	Vega
	14,001	36	0,001	0,001
	12,004	38	0,004	0,004
	10,020	40	0,020	0,015
	8,075	42	0,075	0,040
	6,223	44	0,223	0,083
	4,543	46	0,543	0,135
	3,114	48	1,114	0,180
ATM	1,994	50	1,994	0,199
	1,188	52	3,188	0,188
	0,658	54	4,658	0,154
	0,340	56	6,340	0,111
	0,163	58	8,163	0,071
	0,074	60	10,074	0,041
	0,031	62	12,031	0,022
	0,012	64	14,012	0,011
	0,005	66	16,005	0,005
	0,002	68	18,002	0,002
	0,001	70	20,001	0,001
	0,000	72	22,000	0,000

TABLE 9.2

Vega position	Market volatility	New volatility	Change in vol% × Vega position	P&L
10,000	20%	22%	2 × 10,000	20,000
8,000	23%	20%	−3 × 8,000	−24,000
−12,000	14%	18%	4 × −12,000	−48,000

DIFFERENT MATURITIES WILL DISPLAY DIFFERENT VOLATILITY REGIME CHANGES

For a portfolio of options one could aggregate all vega and compute the total exposure for when volatility would change. The P&L for the vega of all the options together is the same as the aggregated P&L's computed for all the strikes separately, as shown in Tables 9.3 and 9.4.

A trader should, however, be careful while at changing volatility regimes: the implied volatility changes for the options could differ with respect to different maturities, as already mentioned in the chapter on Volatility. For instance, when market volatility explodes, the impact is much bigger on short term options than on longer dated options. The daily time decay should be justified by the daily moves, while at the same time a large jump in volatility will quite often retrace/mean revert. So paying up for longer-term options implies that there should be the expectation that the higher volatility regime will be long-lasting, which is obviously very often not the case. But also, the other way around, when volatility is dropping, quite often one could see the short-dated options affected the first; the potential retracement/mean reversion in volatility regime will cause the volatility of longer dated options to lag behind.

TABLE 9.3

Strike	Volume	Vega Strike	Total vega	Initial Vol	New Vol	P&L
46	5000	0.135	675	10%	12%	1,350
48	10,000	0.18	1,800	10%	12%	3,600
50	10,000	0.199	1,990	10%	12%	3,980
Total			4,465	10%	12%	8,930

TABLE 9.4

Strike	Volume	Vega Strike	Total vega	Initial Vol	New Vol	P&L
46	10,000	0.135	1,350	10%	12%	2,700
48	−5,000	0.18	−900	10%	12%	−1,800
50	5,000	0.199	995	10%	12%	1,990
Total			1,445	10%	12%	2,890

TABLE 9.5

Maturity	Initial Volatility	Vega Position (total 8,000)	New volatility	Change in vol × Vega position	P&L
Up to 3 months	23%	−$5,000	20%	−3 × −$5,000	$15,000
3–6 months	23%	$3,000	21%	−2 × $3,000	−$6,000
6–12 months	23%	$1,000	22%	−1 × $1,000	−$1,000
Over 12 months	23%	$9,000	23%	0 × $9,000	$0
Total		$8,000			$8,000

In Table 9.5 above there will be a closer examination of an example of lagging volatility. When considering different maturity periods (bucketing) and differing impacts from dropping volatilities, the following could be a potential scenario.

So a fairly simple evaluation of a vega portfolio could become much more complex when different maturities behave in different ways compared to changes in volatility. With an overall 3 points drop in volatility for all maturities, the trader, with a total long vega position of 8,000, would have lost $24,000. However, now with the different behaviour of different maturities, the trader actually made $8,000 with a volatility drop of 3 percentage points (in the front maturities). Obviously (in this particular situation) he had the right position, being short the front vega and being long the back end vega.

So, when trying to quantify a vega position, one should be very careful when having the aggregate vega position spread over different maturities. An assessment should be made on the potential impact of different volatility scenarios per maturity period/bucket.

DETERMINING THE VEGA VALUE OF AT THE MONEY OPTIONS

In the chapter on pricing it was shown that, for the value of an at the money straddle, a simple linear formula could be used: $0.8\sigma\sqrt{T}F$. This would be for the at the money call or put, half of it being: $0.4\times\sigma\times\sqrt{T}\times F$. As shown in Chart 9.2, the at the money call (K = 50, maturity 1 year) has a value of $2 at 10% volatility and $4 at 20% volatility. When drawing the chart more to the left, it shows that at 5% volatility the price of the call option is $1 and obviously at 0% its value is zero. So for each set of 5 percentage volatility steps, the value of the option increases by $1, being 0.20 per percentage point. So per 1% change in volatility the call (and thus also the put option) will change by $0.20.

An at the money option at volatility X is built up by X identical little increments of $0.4\%\times\sqrt{T}\times F$ (which is actually the pricing formula for an at the money call or put when applying 1% for the volatility).

Chart 9.2 shows that the vega of the at the money option can be computed by setting σ at 1% and applying the $0.4\times\sigma\times\sqrt{T}\times F$ formula, which then results in $\frac{0.4\times\sqrt{T}\times F}{100}$ (because 1% $\sigma = 0.01/\frac{1}{100}$).

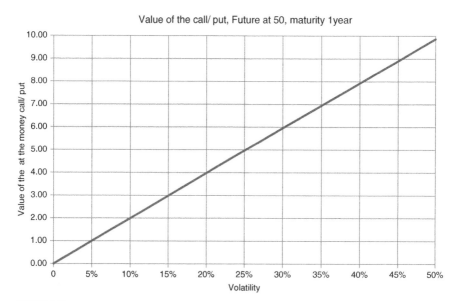

CHART 9.2   The linearity of the price of an option compared to the volatility level

When comparing this approximation with the actual vega formula ($\frac{F\varphi(d1)\sqrt{T}}{100}$), the following could be said: when d1 has a (near) zero value (when being at the money, low volatility and short term to maturity) $\varphi(d1)$ will have a value of 0.3989. In that perspective, the simple formula for pricing a straddle ($\frac{0.4\sqrt{T}F}{100}$) to determine the value of the vega (for the at the money option), very much resembles the vega formula ($\varphi(d1)$ has a value of 0.3989, so being very close to 0.4). It will start however to deviate a bit with volatilities at levels higher than 30% (at 30% volatility $\varphi(d1)$ has a value of 0.395; at a volatility of 50% $\varphi(d1)$ is even further reduced to 0.387). In conclusion: $\frac{0.4\sqrt{T}F}{100} \approx \frac{0.3989\sqrt{T}F}{100}$, which actually means that this rule of thumb can be applied without causing large deviations in value.

VEGA OF AT THE MONEY OPTIONS COMPARED TO VOLATILITY

In the formula for computing vega, $\nu = \frac{F\varphi(d1)\sqrt{T}}{100}$, the only component impacted by volatility is in the $\varphi(d1)$ part of this formula. And as shown before: for at the money options, with a volatility below let's say 40%, $\frac{0.4\sqrt{T}F}{100}$ as a formula could be used to compute the vega.

With some negligible differences, the next table shows that the at the money vega levels are quite easy to estimate without using the Black Scholes model (they are actually very accurate).

The table above has also shown that vega (for the at the money options) is independent from the volatility level (which is a curiosity not many people and traders are aware of). Further, as shown before, when volatility rises the probability distribution for the range in which a Future will be at maturity will widen. This implies

TABLE 9.6

Volatility	Time to Maturity	F level (= K)	$\frac{0.4\sqrt{T}F}{100}$ computation	$\frac{F\varphi(d1)\sqrt{T}}{100}$ (Black and Scholes) computation
25%	1 year	50	0.20	0.20
10%	¼ year	50	0.10	0.10
15%	½ year	100	0.28	0.28
30%	2 year	25	0.14	0.14
20%	1 year	25	0.10	0.10

that the vega of out of the money options should increase when volatility rises and decrease when volatility drops.

In Chart 9.3 the vega distribution is displayed at different volatilities, while at the same time keeping the time to maturity stable at 1 year and the Future at 50. The at the money vega will remain stable while the vega of out of the money options will change according to a changing volatility regime. Just as with gamma, the vega of out of the money options will increase when volatility goes up and will decrease when volatility drops. The difference with γ is that the at the money vega will remain unchanged at different volatilities (and therefore the surface area of the vega distribution will alter, where the surface area of the gamma will be 1/100% at any volatility level, as shown in Chart 9.4, the so-called stretching feature as mentioned in the chapter on gamma).

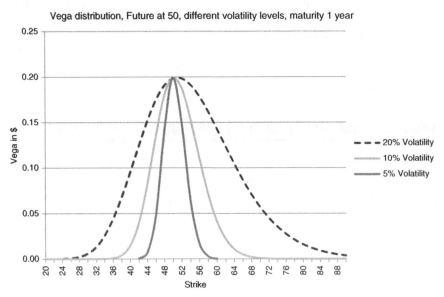

CHART 9.3 Vega distribution resembling gamma distribution. However, at the money vega is stable with regards to volatility

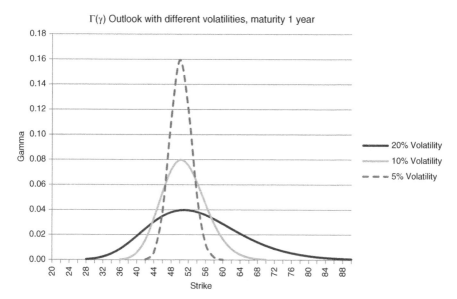

Γ(γ) Outlook with different volatilities, maturity 1 year

— 20% Volatility
— 10% Volatility
– – 5% Volatility

CHART 9.4   Distribution of gamma, Future at 50, maturity 1 year

VEGA OF AT THE MONEY OPTIONS COMPARED TO TIME TO MATURITY

In the vega formula $\nu = \frac{F\varphi(d1)\sqrt{T}}{100}$, the time component is a simple square root function. So, when time to maturity quadruples, the vega for the at the money options will be $\sqrt{4}$ times as big, being twice as much. For out of the money options the $\varphi(d1)$ component will kick in and hence they are more difficult to estimate. In a later paragraph a simple estimation, similar to what has been performed with the gamma, will be discussed.

In Chart 9.5, the vega distribution with different times to maturity is displayed, while keeping the Future level and the volatility stable. The square root function of time is easy to detect, when comparing the vega of the at the money option (50 strike) for a maturity of ¼ year ($0.10) with the vega for a maturity of 1 year ($0.20); when time to maturity quadruples, the vega will double. The vega of out of the money options will go up when time to maturity increases and will decrease when time to maturity will be shorter. So the vega of an at the money option 1 year to maturity should be $\sqrt{12}$ times as big as the at the money option with a maturity of 1 month. With vegas of 0.1992 and 0.0576 respectively for the two options this approach is correct (the ratio of the two is 3.46 which is equivalent to $\sqrt{12}$).

VEGA OF AT THE MONEY OPTIONS COMPARED TO THE UNDERLYING LEVEL

The last component of the vega formula is the level where the Future is trading. It's a linear function which makes it very easy to value at the money vega at different

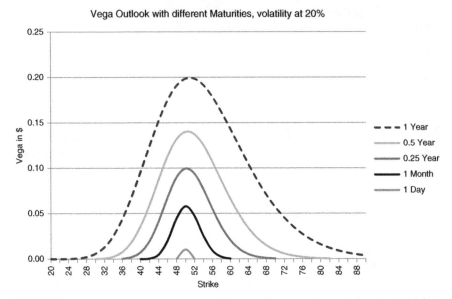

CHART 9.5 Vega distribution with changing time to maturity, Future at 50, volatility at 20%

Future levels. So if F doubles, the at the money vega, being $\nu = \dfrac{F\varphi(d1)\sqrt{T}}{100}$, should double as well, as shown in Chart 9.6.

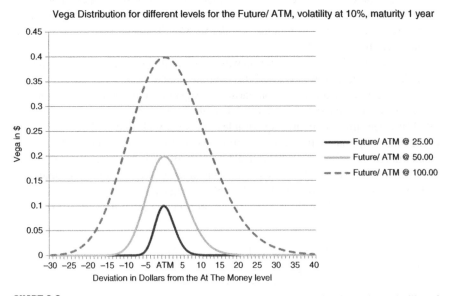

CHART 9.6 Vega distribution at different Future/at the money levels with stable volatility of 10% and maturity of 1 year.

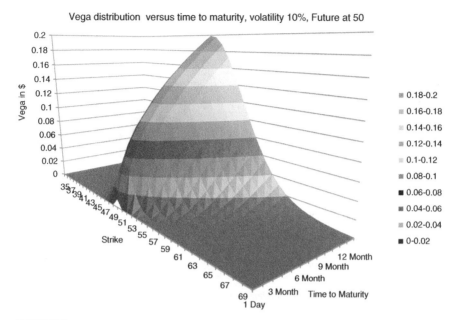

Vega distribution versus time to maturity, volatility 10%, Future at 50

CHART 9.7 Vega distribution over time with stable volatility of 10% and Future at 50

VEGA ON A 3-DIMENSIONAL SCALE, VEGA VS MATURITY AND VEGA VS VOLATILITY

Chart 9.7 displays the vega evolution over time with a stable volatility of 10% and Future level at 50. The shorter the time to maturity the less pronounced the vega will be. The out of the money options have their vega when time to expiry will be long enough. However, in time their vega will fairly quickly vanish. The 50 call/put will see its vega decrease the most from $0.20 to $0.01 from 12 months to maturity to 1 day before maturity. The ratio of these two values will be the square root of 365 days being around 19.

Chart 9.8 displays the vega distribution with different volatilities with a time to maturity of 1 year and Future at 50. The feature of stable vega for the at the money options in relation to changing volatilities is clearly detectable. At higher volatility levels the out of the money options get a higher vega value, the increase in volatility will increase the distribution as there is a higher probability for the Future to end in a much larger range when at maturity.

Chart 9.9 shows what would happen when the maturity is a quarter of a year instead of 1 year. The at the money vega has been halved ($\sqrt{1/4}$ for T) and now has a value of $0.10. Since time to maturity decreased the probability distribution for the Future has become much smaller and hence the out of the money strikes will have a less pronounced vega as well.

Vega distribution versus volatility level, Future at 50, maturity 1 year

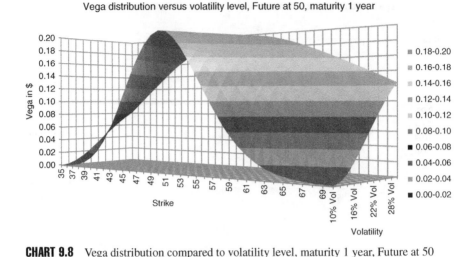

CHART 9.8   Vega distribution compared to volatility level, maturity 1 year, Future at 50

Vega distribution versus volatility level, Future at 50, maturity ¼ year

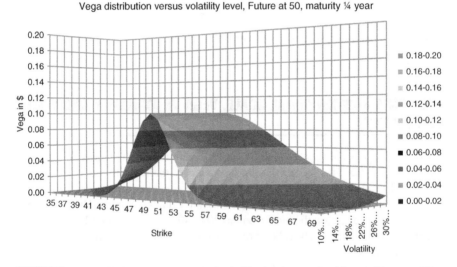

CHART 9.9   Vega distribution compared to volatility level, maturity ¼ year, Future at 50

DETERMINING THE BOUNDARIES OF VEGA

There is a simple way to consider where the boundaries of vega should be, when assuming a deep in the money call which has a delta of 100%. With an interest rate level at 0% this call option will have intrinsic value only, at 10% volatility with 1 year to maturity and Future at 50, the 36 call would be such a 100% delta option as shown in the table below. The put has no value, so put call parity dictates the call being worth $14, hence only intrinsic value. When the 36 call (or put) still has a vega, the call should trade below $14 when the volatility drops, which is impossible, since minimum value is intrinsic, or the put would trade at a negative value, which is also not possible. So, whenever a call option reaches 100% delta or the put option reaches 0% delta, the vega will have reached a zero value.

The same could be argued for deep in the money puts with a delta of −100% (or far out of the money calls with 0% delta). With the same parameters, the 70 put would have only intrinsic value, the 70 call would have no value anymore. When having (positive) vega the value should be decreasing when volatility drops, resulting in a put value below intrinsic value or a negative value for the call, something which is clearly wrong!

In conclusion: any option with a delta of 100%/−100% or 0% has no vega anymore, as shown below in Table 9.7.

The Black and Scholes print below gives the values for the vega for different strikes with a volatility of 10%, maturity at 1 year and the Future at 50.00. Those values are used for Chart 9.10 to show that the boundaries for the vega are at the same levels as the boundaries for the delta. As discussed in the Delta chapter, these boundaries are situated at 5 times the straddle value for the upside, being 70 and for the downside $50/\frac{70}{50}$ (applying the ratio) being around 36.

TABLE 9.7 Vega values, Black Scholes model, maturity 1 year, volatility 10% Future at 50

	Calls	**Strike**	**Puts**	**Delta Call**	**Delta Put**	**Vega**
	14,001	36	0,001	1,000	0,000	0,001
	12,004	38	0,004	0,997	−0,003	0,004
	10,020	40	0,020	0,989	−0,011	0,015
	8,075	42	0,075	0,964	−0,036	0,040
	6,223	44	0,223	0,908	−0,092	0,083
	4,543	46	0,543	0,812	−0,188	0,135
	3,114	48	1,114	0,677	−0,323	0,180
ATM	1,994	50	1,994	0,520	−0,480	0,199
	1,188	52	3,188	0,366	−0,634	0,188
	0,658	54	4,658	0,236	−0,764	0,154
	0,340	56	6,340	0,139	−0,861	0,111
	0,163	58	8,163	0,076	−0,924	0,071
	0,074	60	10,074	0,038	−0,962	0,041
	0,031	62	12,031	0,018	−0,982	0,022
	0,012	64	14,012	0,008	−0,992	0,011
	0,005	66	16,005	0,003	−0,997	0,005
	0,002	68	18,002	0,001	−0,999	0,002
	0,001	70	20,001	0,000	−1,000	0,001
	0,000	72	22,000	0,000	−1,000	0,000

Delta boundaries calls versus vega boundaries, Future at 50.00, maturity 1 year, vol 10%

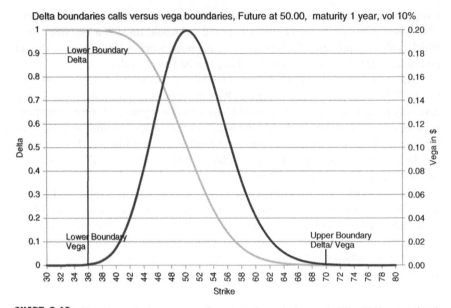

CHART 9.10   Vega boundaries compared to delta boundaries, volatility 10%, maturity 1 year, Future/at the money level at 50.00

COMPARING THE BOUNDARIES OF VEGA WITH THE BOUNDARIES OF GAMMA

Chart 9.10 bears a remarkable resemblance to the chart which was depicted in the chapter on gamma, showing that the gamma boundaries are at the same level as the delta boundaries, as shown in Chart 9.11 on the following page. It shows a high at the 50 level and has the same log normal distribution. The only difference is its value, vega being 0.20 at the high and gamma at 0.08.

Where gamma is expressed in percentages or pips and at the same time vega is expressed in dollars, however, in the whole distribution the ratio vega/gamma will remain at 2.5 (0.20 divided by 0.08).

When comparing the formula of vega with the formula of gamma a fixed rule will appear:

$$\nu = \frac{F\varphi(d1)\sqrt{T}}{100} \quad \text{and} \quad \gamma = \frac{\varphi(d1)}{F\sigma\sqrt{T}}$$

$$\frac{\nu}{\gamma} = \frac{\dfrac{F\varphi(d1)\sqrt{T}}{100}}{\dfrac{\varphi(d1)}{F\sigma\sqrt{T}}} = \frac{F\varphi(d1)\sqrt{T}}{100} \times \frac{F\sigma\sqrt{T}}{\varphi(d1)} = \frac{F^2\sigma T}{100}$$

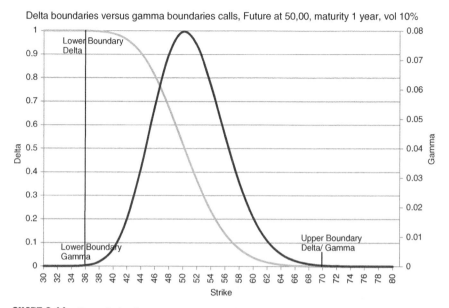

Delta boundaries versus gamma boundaries calls, Future at 50,00, maturity 1 year, vol 10%

CHART 9.11   Boundaries for gamma, compared to boundaries for delta

In this particular case $(F = 50, \sigma = 10\%, T = 1)$ the ratio $\frac{v}{\gamma}$ computes to $\frac{2500 \times 0.1 \times 1}{100} = 2.5$.

Hence, in the chapter on put call parity the close relationship between calls and puts was discussed; now another close relationship has been shown: the gamma–vega relationship, which in any distribution of options of different strikes has a fixed ratio.

When knowing the boundaries for gamma and applying a ratio, one should realise that the boundaries, where gamma has zero value, should be exactly the same for vega. When applying a fixed ratio (for certain parameters) it should be evident as well that the shape of the distribution of vega should be the same as the shape of the gamma, as shown in Charts 9.12 and 9.13. The last column in the Table 9.8 shows the ratios (all the same) when dividing the vega by the gamma.

DETERMINING VEGA VALUES OF OUT OF THE MONEY OPTIONS

Just like determining gamma for out of the money options, the same assumptions will be applied for the vega; 3½ straddles for the way up, 2½ straddles for the way down. So with an at the money 50 straddle of $4 (10% volatility, 1 year maturity), the boundaries for vega will be (artificially) set at 64 for the upside and 40 for the downside. (In the gamma example the parameters used were, volatility 15%, maturity 1 year, Future at 50.00; hence wider boundaries there.)

TABLE 9.8 Print from Black Scholes model, Future/at the money at 50, volatility at 10%, maturity 1 year

	Calls	Strike	Puts	Gamma	Vega	Ratio v/γ
	14.001	36	0.001	0.000	0.001	2.500
	12.004	38	0.004	0.002	0.004	2.500
	10.020	40	0.020	0.006	0.015	2.500
	8.075	42	0.075	0.016	0.040	2.500
	6.223	44	0.223	0.033	0.083	2.500
	4.543	46	0.543	0.054	0.135	2.500
	3.114	48	1.114	0.072	0.180	2.500
ATM	1.994	50	1.994	0.080	0.199	2.500
	1.188	52	3.188	0.075	0.188	2.500
	0.658	54	4.658	0.062	0.154	2.500
	0.340	56	6.340	0.044	0.111	2.500
	0.163	58	8.163	0.029	0.071	2.500
	0.074	60	10.074	0.017	0.041	2.500
	0.031	62	12.031	0.009	0.022	2.500
	0.012	64	14.012	0.004	0.011	2.500
	0.005	66	16.005	0.002	0.005	2.500
	0.002	68	18.002	0.001	0.002	2.500
	0.001	70	20.001	0.000	0.001	2.500
	0.000	72	22.000	0.000	0.000	2.500

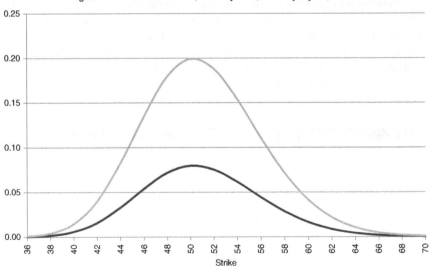

Vega and Gamma distribution, volatility 10%, maturity 1 year, Future at 50

CHART 9.12 Comparing vega distribution with gamma distribution

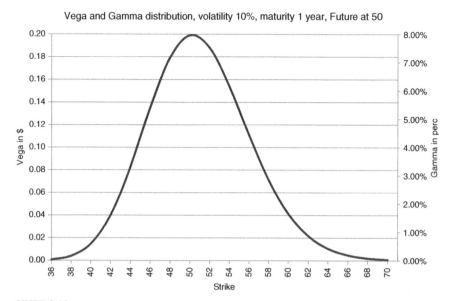

CHART 9.13 Vega is Gamma, when multiplying gamma by 2.5 the values will be identical

When drawing a straight line from the top to 64 for the upside and drawing a line from the top to 40 for the downside, it will be easy to compute the vega. The vega for the 50 strike is known and thus it is simple to derive vega levels for a linear relation for the downside: a $10 range for $0.20 making $\frac{0.20}{10} = \$0.02$ decrease in vega per dollar change in the strike.

For the upside: a $14 range for $0.20, making $\frac{0.20}{14} = \$0.0143$ decrease in vega per dollar change in the strike, as shown in Table 9.9 below.

TABLE 9.9

Parameters:	Strike	Computed Vega call or put	Black Scholes Vega
	38	0	0
Future @50,00	42	0.04	0.04
Volatility @ 10%	46	0.12	0.13
Maturity: 1 Year	50	0.20	0.20
50 Straddle: $4.00	54	0.14	0.15
	58	0.09	0.07
	62	0.03	0.02
	66	0	0.01

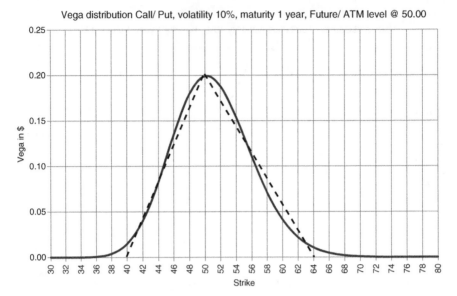

CHART 9.14   Linearisation of the vega distribution

Chart 9.14 depicts the linearisation of the vega distribution. This linearisation is performed in order to get a sense of how the vega is distributed along the curve. It is not a very accurate approximation, however it gives a fairly good idea about the distribution.

DERIVATIVES OF THE VEGA

The vega, as being dependent on time to maturity, Future and volatility, has its derivatives $\frac{\partial v}{\partial T}$.

The change of the vega in relation to changes of the volatility $\frac{\partial v}{\partial \sigma}$ is called vomma or DvegaDvol.

The change of the vega in relation to the change of time, $\frac{\partial v}{\partial T}$ is called veta or DvegaDtime.

The change of the vega in relation to the change of the underlying, $\frac{\partial v}{\partial F}$ is called vanna or DvegaDspot.

VOMMA

Vomma is also called vega convexity, convexity because it has resembling features with a gamma position. When being long vomma one could profit from increasing and decreasing volatility, just like scalping the Futures with a gamma long position. In the following position, maturity 1 year, volatility 10%, Future at 50 a trader has a vega neutral position, the volatility will move to 12.5%:

TABLE 9.10

Strike	Call position	Future level	Vega @ 10% Vol	Aggr Vega	New Future level	Vega @ New Vol 12.5%	Aggr Vega
50	−5,000	50	0.20	−1,000	50	0.20	−1,000
60	24,000	50	0.042	1,000	50	0.075	1,800
Total				0			800

The position, as shown above in Table 9.10, changed from a flat vega position into a position of 800 vega long at 2.5 volatility points higher, still at the same Future level of 50 and hence will generate a profit (of 2.5% times $400/% on average being $1,000, when applying linearity). If the market also moved to the upside, the 50 strike would lose vega value (getting more out of the money) and the 60 strike would gain vega (getting more at the money) and hence the full position would gain additional vega. With a Future level of 55 the position would look as shown in Table 9.11:

Now the position will be long $3,500 of vega and the profit is also much higher (2.5% times $1,750/% on average being $4,375, when applying linearity). In reality volatility increases usually take place when there is a big change in the underlying or news is expected to be reported soon either way (geo)politically or in relation to the specific asset. In a stable Future environment, volatility has a tendency to come off somewhat. Therefore, the second scenario is the more realistic one with increasing volatility. If the market is stable the volatility most likely would come off (for instance to 7.5%), resulting in the following position as shown in Table 9.12:

At the stable scenario, the vega position will go negative on the back of dropping volatility.

TABLE 9.11

Strike	Call position	Future level	Vega @ 10% Vol	Aggr Vega	New Future level	Vega @ New Vol 12.5%	Aggr Vega
50	−5,000	50	0.20	−1,000	55	0.16	−800
60	24,000	50	0.042	1,000	55	0.18	4,300
Total				0			3,500

TABLE 9.12

Strike	Call position	Future level	Vega @ 10% Vol	Aggr Vega	New Future level	Vega @ New Vol 7.5%	Aggr Vega
50	−5,000	50	0.20	−1,000	50	0.20	−1,000
60	24,000	50	0.042	1,000	50	0.012	275
Total				0			−725

So in both cases, increasing market with increasing volatility and stable market with decreasing volatility, the trader is able to earn money: he can flatten his position by selling vega in the first scenario and buying vega in the second scenario and maybe play the game once more. (In the first scenario he will have to rebalance his strikes as well.)

This vega convexity works on the upside as well as on the downside, selling at the money options and buying (in ratio) out of the money puts will generate similar results. It has to be in a ratio when the preference is to have a flat vega position initially.

Setting up vega convexity strategies will be further discussed in the chapter on strategies under Vega convexity/Vomma.

CHAPTER 10

Theta

Theta (θ or for the capital letter Θ) is the change of the value of an option in relation to the change in time, also called time-decay.

It is the derivative of the value in relation to time, mathematically: $\frac{\partial V}{\partial T}$. Throughout the book the Greek letter Θ will be used for denoting the theta, sometimes time decay will be used. The formula for calculating it is as follows: $\Theta = -\frac{F\varphi(d1)\sigma}{2\sqrt{T}} \times \frac{1}{365}$ (interest rate and dividend yield at 0%), where φ is the probability density function. Theta has a log normal distribution.

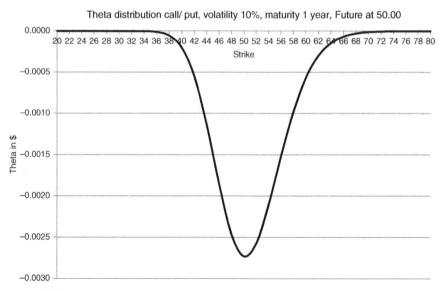

Theta distribution call/ put, volatility 10%, maturity 1 year, Future at 50.00

CHART 10.1 Theta distribution call/put, Future at 50, volatility at 10%, maturity 1 year

The theta, as shown in Chart 10.1, is expressed in dollars (or rather cents) per day. The theta value indicates the amount with which the value of an option will decrease overnight. An option will get cheaper every day towards maturity. At expiration date the option (when not in the money) has lost all of its value, each time decreasing in value at a daily time decay rate.

When the interest rate and the dividend yield are both at 0%, theta for calls will be the same as theta for puts. Theta is highly related to gamma; a gamma position will directly result in a theta position.

When a trader reports that he has a portfolio with a negative theta, it means that he is long options in general, he will lose money due to theta/value decrease of his option portfolio. When short options the theta will be positive, the time decay will have a positive effect on the P&L of the trader being short options: he could buy them back cheaper the next day, locking in a profit (there is an exception. In a portfolio with positions in multiple strikes and/or multiple maturities it could happen that a trader is net short options, however having a negative theta, hence paying for time decay. This is a result of horizontal spreads, time spreads, or a combination of the two.

When entering into a long gamma position, a trader will instantly incur the cost of theta. The opportunity he will get by being able to delta hedge (scalping the Futures) his gamma position in his portfolio in a profitable way will be offset by the cost of theta. When the implied volatility is equivalent to the historical volatility, the trader being long gamma and paying for time decay, as well as the trader being short gamma and receiving theta, will statistically both end up with a zero P&L.

One of the reasons for a trader to enter into a gamma long position could be the view that the market volatility will outperform the time decay/theta of the options. Intra day moves will add to the P&L by scalping Futures on the back of the gamma. Or he bets on a trending underlying which he will hedge according to the wide hedging strategy, as discussed in the chapter on gamma.

A PRACTICAL EXAMPLE

In the next two tables a stable gamma has been used at a volatility of 16% and a maturity of 3 months. With these parameters the theta of such a gamma position is $175/day. Two weeks are computed; on day 6 and day 7 (the weekend) there will be no trading obviously, however the owner of the position will still incur a daily time decay of $175 on these days. 16% volatility (256 trading day rule) implies a daily return of 1% of the underlying. Starting at 50.00 for the Future, each trading day the market will move by 50¢. The P&L for the Δ is computed by comparing the Δ hedges with the closing price of the last trading day of week 2.

TABLE 10.1

Week 1	γ	New Delta	Δ Hedge	Δ Hedge level	Δ after hedging	Θ	P&L Δ Hedge
50.50	2,000	1,000	−1,000	50.50	0	−175	500
51.00	2,000	1,000	−1,000	51.00	0	−175	1,000
51.50	2,000	1,000	−1,000	51.50	0	−175	1,500
51.00	2,000	−1,000	1,000	51.00	0	−175	−1,000
50.50	2,000	−1,000	1,000	50.50	0	−175	−500
50.50	2,000	0	0		0	−175	0
50.50	2,000	0	0		0	−175	0
Total						−1225	1500

TABLE 10.2

Week 2	γ	New Delta	Δ Hedge	Δ Hedge level	Δ after hedging	Θ	P&L Δ Hedge
50.00	2,000	−1,000	1,000	50.00	0	−175	0
49.50	2,000	−1,000	1,000	49.50	0	−175	500
49.00	2,000	−1,000	1,000	49.00	0	−175	1,000
49.50	2,000	1,000	−1,000	49.50	0	−175	−500
50.00	2,000	1,000	−1,000	50.00	0	−175	0
50.00	2,000	0	0		0	−175	0
50.00	2,000	0	0		0	−175	0
Total						−1225	1000

After two weeks the P&L of the position consists out of 2 components, being the P&L of the Δ hedges minus the theta over 14 days, which makes $2,500 − $2,450 = 50. This example shows that the opportunity created by a gamma long position will be offset by theta. The position will only generate a positive P&L when the market volatility and/or intraday volatility is higher than the implied volatility of the options; the profit from the delta hedging of the gamma in portfolio will then outweigh the cost of theta. When the market volatility is lower it means that the cost of theta outweighs the potential creation of P&L by hedging the deltas on the back of the gamma position. Hence, theta has a very strong relation with gamma. The ratio gamma/theta (sometimes called alpha, α) is an important measure to see if a gamma long portfolio has a fair chance of generating a decent P&L.

In the examples in Tables 10.1 and 10.2, the assumption of valuing volatility of a Future, when moving 1% per day, has been applied at 16%. So in 2 trading days the Future, starting at 50.00, will move 50¢ up and then 50¢ down again, and the next 2 trading days it will trade at 49.50 and then retrace to 50.00. In this example, a trader who is long 2,000 gamma, could earn $1,000 by selling 1,000 Futures at 50.50 and buying them back at 50.00 and buying 1,000 Futures at 49.50 and selling them again at 50.00. So, on average, each trading day he would earn $250, 5 trading days a week, generating $1,250 per week.

For theta to offset this weekly profit, $1,250 has to be divided by 7 (daily theta, also during the weekend) resulting in slightly less than $180 per day. Hence, in this particular environment, with the Future at 50.00 and volatility at 16%, a 1,000 gamma position would cost approximately $90 per day.

THETA IN RELATION TO VOLATILITY

In the theta formula $\Theta = -\dfrac{F\varphi(d1)\sigma}{2\sqrt{T}} \times \dfrac{1}{365}$ the σ or volatility component for the options is a linear one, as shown in Chart 10.2, meaning that when volatility doubles the theta should double as well for the at the money options ($\varphi(d1)$ will remain fairly stable). For out of the money options the $\varphi(d1)$ component will be subject to changes (which will not be further discussed) and hence all will work differently.

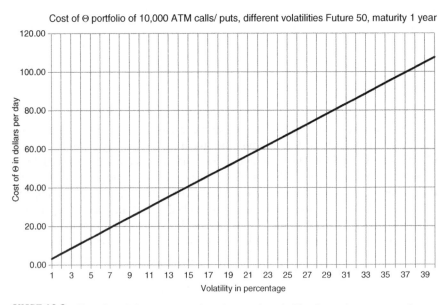

Cost of Θ portfolio of 10,000 ATM calls/ puts, different volatilities Future 50, maturity 1 year

CHART 10.2　linearity of theta compared to changes in volatility for at the money options

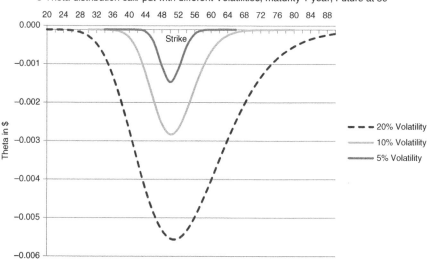

CHART 10.3 Distribution of theta different volatilities, maturity 1 year, Future at 50

A very logical way to consider the cost of theta when, for instance, volatility would double is to look at the ATM straddle value: $0.8\sigma\sqrt{T}F$. When volatility doubles, the straddle will be worth twice as much, so theta should be twice as much as well, which it is, as shown in Chart 10.3.

In Chart 10.3, the linearity, with regards to volatility, for the 50 (ATM) strike is evident. When volatility doubles theta will double as well. The theta of the 50 call/put at 10% volatility is 0.00273 (¼ of a cent) where the theta at 20% volatility is 0.00544 (half a cent).

THETA IN RELATION TO TIME TO MATURITY

When looking at a maturity of 3 months, instead of 1 year, the cost of theta for the at the moneys should have doubled: T now being a quarter of the initial 1 year to maturity. With $\Theta = -\frac{F\varphi(d1)\sigma}{2\sqrt{T}} \times \frac{1}{365}$, −the new theta is initial theta divided by the square root of T. When T is ¼ the new theta will be: $\frac{initial\,\Theta}{\frac{1}{2}} = \frac{2 \times initial\,\Theta}{1} = 2 \times initial\,\Theta$. At the same time gamma has doubled as well (dividing by a fraction is the same as multiplying by the reciprocal).

When comparing the values of Chart 10.2, maturity 1 year, and Chart 10.4, maturity 3 months, we find that theta has doubled. At 1 year maturity theta will add up to $55 where at 3 months maturity theta has doubled to 110, when applying a volatility of 20%.

The distribution, for different strikes and different maturities, will look as shown in Chart 10.5:

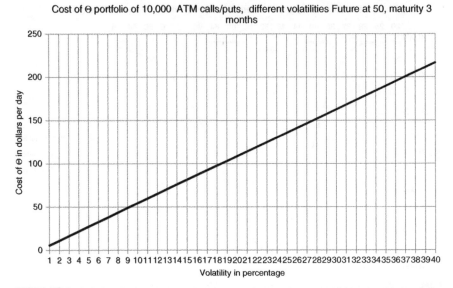

CHART 10.4   Cost of theta of a portfolio of 10,000 ATM options, Future at 50, maturity
3 months

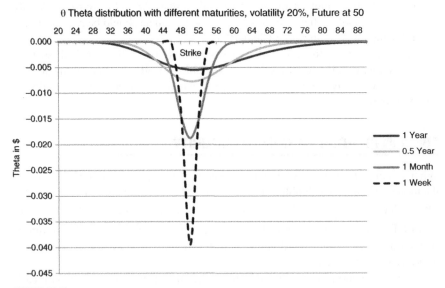

CHART 10.5   Theta distribution, Future at 50, volatility 20%, different maturities

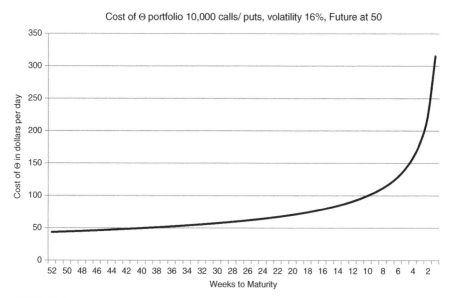

Cost of Θ portfolio 10,000 calls/ puts, volatility 16%, Future at 50

CHART 10.6 The evolution of theta in time for a portfolio of 10,000 calls/puts, volatility 16%, Future at 50

THETA OF AT THE MONEY OPTIONS IN RELATION TO THE UNDERLYING LEVEL

This should also be a linear relationship according to the formula. Chart 10.7 below will show theta values for a portfolio consisting of 10,000 calls/puts with volatility at 25% and maturity 1 year Chart 10.8 on the following page shows the full distribution..

Future/ATM level	Θ in Dollars
25	34
50	68
100	136
200	271

Chart 10.7 Linear relationship between theta and the Future/ATM level for a portfolio of 10,000 calls/puts at 25% vol and 1 year maturity.

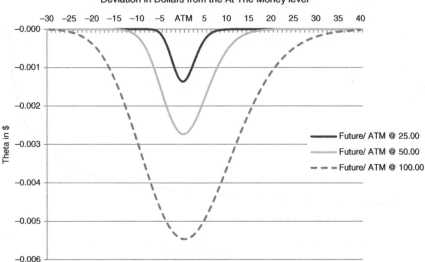

CHART 10.8   Theta distribution at different at the money levels

DETERMINING THE BOUNDARIES OF THETA

There is a simple way of considering where the boundaries of theta should be: when assuming a deep in the money call which has a delta of 100%. With an interest rate level at 0% this call option will have intrinsic value only, at 10% volatility with 1 year to maturity and Future/ATM level at 50, the 36 call would be such a 100% delta option. The put has no value, so put call parity dictates the call being worth $14. When the 36 call (or put) still would have a theta value, the call should trade below $14 the next day, which is not possible since minimum value is intrinsic or the put should trade at a negative value, which is also not possible. So whenever a call option reaches 100% delta or the put option reaches 0% delta, the theta will have reached a zero value.

The same could be argued for deep in the money puts with a delta of -100% (or far out of the money calls with 0% delta). With the same parameters, the 70 put would have only intrinsic value – the 70 call would have no value anymore. When having (negative) theta the value should decrease as time passes, resulting in a put value below intrinsic value or a negative value for the call – which is clearly wrong!

In conclusion: any option with a delta of 100%/-100% or 0% has no theta anymore.

Hence, just like gamma and vega theta will have its boundaries at the level where the delta boundaries are situated: 36 for the lower boundary and around 70 for the upper boundary , as shown in Table 10.3 and Chart 10.9.

TABLE 10.3 Theta values (for calls), Black Scholes model, maturity 1 year, volatility 10%, Future/ATM level @ 50.00

	Calls	Strike	Puts	Delta Call	Delta Put	Theta Call
	14.001	36	0.001	1.000	0.000	−0.00001
	12.004	38	0.004	0.997	−0.003	−0.00006
	10.020	40	0.020	0.989	−0.011	−0.00020
	8.075	42	0.075	0.964	−0.036	−0.00055
	6.223	44	0.223	0.908	−0.092	−0.00113
	4.543	46	0.543	0.812	−0.188	−0.00185
	3.114	48	1.114	0.677	−0.323	−0.00246
ATM	1.994	50	1.994	0.520	−0.480	−0.00273
	1.188	52	3.188	0.366	−0.634	−0.00258
	0.658	54	4.658	0.236	−0.764	−0.00211
	0.340	56	6.340	0.139	−0.861	−0.00152
	0.163	58	8.163	0.076	−0.924	−0.00098
	0.074	60	10.074	0.038	−0.962	−0.00057
	0.031	62	12.031	0.018	−0.982	−0.00030
	0.012	64	14.012	0.008	−0.992	−0.00015
	0.005	66	16.005	0.003	−0.997	−0.00007
	0.002	68	18.002	0.001	−0.999	−0.00003
	0.001	70	20.001	0.000	−1.000	−0.00001
	0.000	72	22.000	0.000	−1.000	−0.00000

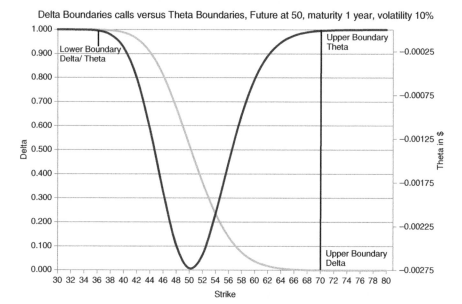

Delta Boundaries calls versus Theta Boundaries, Future at 50, maturity 1 year, volatility 10%

CHART 10.9. Theta has the same boundary levels as delta, gamma and vega

THE GAMMA THETA RELATIONSHIP α

In the last few pages the relationships between theta and volatility, time to maturity and Future/ATM level have been discussed. There is a very strong relationship with gamma, as explained in the tables for the two weeks of trading at 16% volatility. The Future moves 1% per day in relation to the daily gamma of 2,000 and costs $180 per day; a 1,000 gamma position would cost $90 per day.

So what would happen if the volatility doubled?

When taking a look again at the gamma distributions it is clear that when volatility doubles the gamma would halve for the at the moneys. The formula for $\gamma : \frac{\varphi(d1)}{F\sigma\sqrt{T}}$ also clarifies this feature. It is also known that the theta would double: the straddle value has been doubled, so theta should be double likewise.

Hence at 32% volatility, the gamma will be half the 1,000 from the example mentioned before, at 500. At the same time the theta would double from $90 to $180. The ratio $\frac{1,000}{90}$ changes into $\frac{500}{180}$ or $\frac{1,000}{360}$. In other words; gamma has become four times as expensive. So, in relation to volatility it has a squared relationship, being that when volatility increases the cost of one unit of gamma will increase by the squared volatility ratio. So when volatility goes from 10 to 15%, the cost of a unit of gamma will be 2.25 as much at 15% volatility compared to the cost at 10% volatility, which is 1.5 times 1.5.

With regards to different Future/ATM levels, Chart 10.8 made clear that when the underlying ATM level doubles; the theta would double as well (here also the straddle value doubled). The gamma however would halve, as depicted below in Charts 10.10 and 10.11. So here as well, the ratio $\frac{1,000}{90}$ changed into $\frac{500}{180}$ or $\frac{1,000}{360}$.

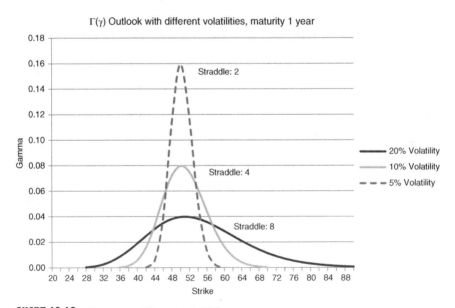

CHART 10.10   Gamma at different volatilities

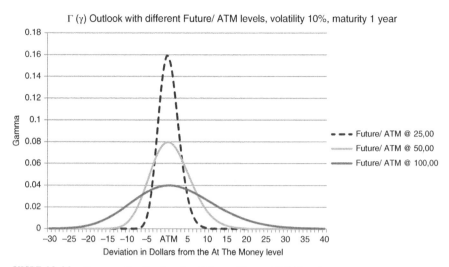

CHART 10.11 Gamma distribution for different Future/ATM levels

In other words, gamma became four times as expensive. So, in relation to Future/ATM level it has a squared relationship as well.

Now looking at time to maturity; when time to maturity doubles, the gamma will decrease by a factor $\sqrt{2}$, as shown in Chart 10.12, and the theta would also decrease by the same factor, so in relation to maturity the gamma theta ratio will remain the same.

The initial ratio of $\frac{1,000}{90}$ will change in $\frac{707}{64}$, which is equivalent to the former ratio. This is a very important feature to remember: the gamma theta ratio does not change when volatility and Future/ATM level are stable.

Looking further ahead in time: the gamma for an at the money option increases with time, but the theta will be doing the same in such a way that the gamma theta ratio will remain stable.

When comparing the formulas for gamma and theta: $\gamma = \frac{\varphi(d1)}{F\sigma\sqrt{T}}$ and $\Theta = -\frac{F\varphi(d1)\sigma}{730\sqrt{T}}$, the gamma theta ratio ($\frac{\gamma}{\Theta}$), also called α (alpha), can be computed as follows:

$$\frac{\dfrac{\varphi(d1)}{F\sigma\sqrt{T}}}{-\dfrac{F\varphi(d1)\sigma}{730\sqrt{T}}} = \frac{\varphi(d1)}{F\sigma\sqrt{T}} \times -\frac{730\sqrt{T}}{F\varphi(d1)\sigma} = -\frac{730}{F^2\sigma^2} \text{ (dividing by a fraction is the}$$

same as multiplying by the reciprocal).

It is absolutely unnecessary to reproduce the ratios off the top of the head; the importance is knowing that gamma is at a cost, the theta, and knowing that this cost per unit of gamma is stable over time. A 1,000 gamma position will all the way (towards maturity) have the same cost when volatility and Future levels remain stable. Obviously, as time proceeds the gamma will increase, but so will theta. When trying to keep gamma stable at 1,000 the option position will have to be decreased in volume and hence theta will be reduced as well. Table 10.4 shows gamma and its theta for an ATM option, volatility at 20%, Future at 50, resulting in the ratio α.

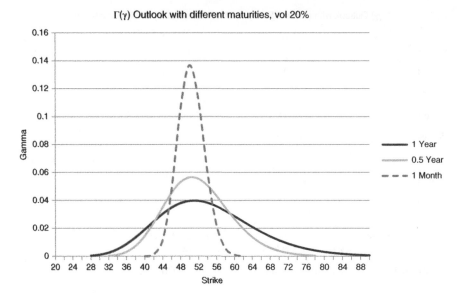

CHART 10.12.   Gamma at different maturities.

TABLE 10.4

Time to Maturity	2 Year	1 Year	9 Months	6 Months	3 Months	1 Month
Gamma	0.028	0.040	0.046	0.057	0.079	0.139
Theta	−0.00383	−0.00544	−0.00630	−0.00774	−0.01087	−0.01905
Ratio $\left(\dfrac{\gamma}{\Theta}\right)$	−7.3	−7.3	−7.3	−7.3	−7.3	−7.3

In the gamma theta ratio $(\frac{\gamma}{\Theta}) = -\frac{730}{F^2\sigma^2}$; there is no strike component. The ratio will hence be indifferent to the strike. Any strike in a distribution (at equal volatility) will have the same ratio. For a distribution with volatility at 20% and maturity at 1 year the ratio for different strikes will look as follows:

TABLE 10.5

Strike	35	40	45	50	55	60
Gamma	0.007	0.019	0.033	0.040	0.037	0.027
Theta	−0.0009	−0.0026	−0.0045	−0.0054	−0.0051	−0.0039
Ratio $\left(\dfrac{\gamma}{\Theta}\right)$	−7.3	−7.3	−7.3	−7.3	−7.3	−7.3

When halving the volatility to 10%, the ratio should quadruple (gamma doubles while theta halves). The Black Scholes model comes up with the following values:

TABLE 10.6

Strike	35	40	45	50	55	60
Gamma	0.000	0.006	0.043	0.080	0.053	0.017
Theta	−0.0000	−0.0002	−0.0015	−0.0027	−0.0018	−0.0006
Ratio $\left(\dfrac{\gamma}{\Theta}\right)$	−29.2	−29.2	−29.2	−29.2	−29.2	−29.2

Having a stable relationship over the whole distribution of strikes between gamma and theta, this could be shown by drawing the chart of both at the same time, as shown in Chart 10.13. As the boundaries are at the same levels and the gamma theta ratio $(\frac{\gamma}{\Theta})$ (with volatility, Future and maturity stable) is a fixed ratio they should be identical, albeit that the theta has a negative value. When applying 10% volatility, maturity 1 year and Future/ATM level at 50.00, it looks as shown in Chart 10.14:

The relationship depicted as shown in Chart 10.14 could be made clear when giving them both the same magnitude. This could be done by multiplying the theta by 29.2:

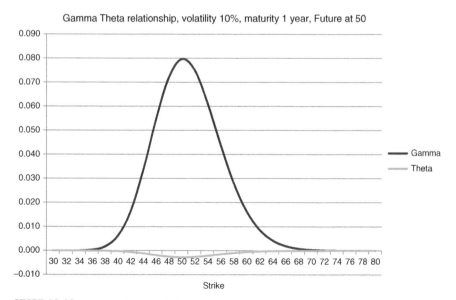

CHART 10.13 Gamma Theta relationship

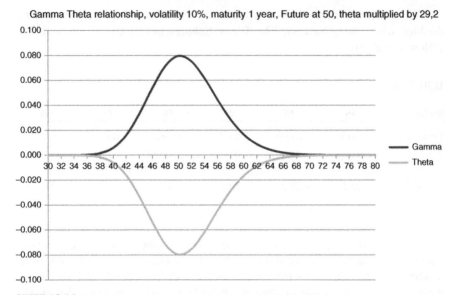

CHART 10.14   Gamma Theta relationship, theta multiplied by 29.2

One more step could be made by mirroring the theta, making it a positive value by multiplying it by −1, as shown in Chart 10.15:

Theta has exactly the same distribution, boundaries and outlook as gamma. Vega also had this feature, so as a conclusion it could be said that gamma = vega = −theta The vega/theta ratio should be evident now. It doesn't serve any purpose; the main importance is to know that the distribution of these three Greeks have exactly the same characteristics (be it in ratio and mirrored for the theta).

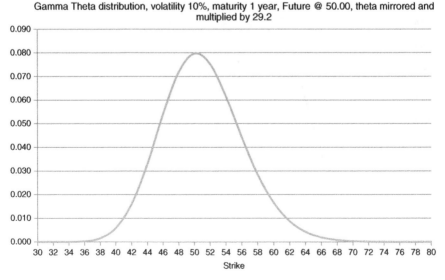

CHART 10.15   Gamma Theta relationship, theta multiplied by - 29.2

THETA ON A 3-DIMENSIONAL SCALE, THETA VS MATURITY AND THETA VS VOLATILITY

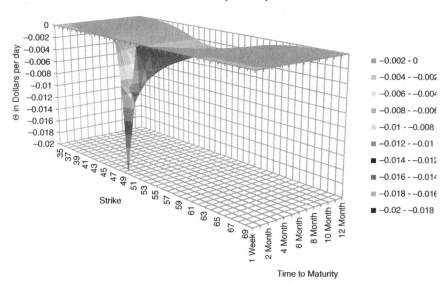

Theta distribution versus time to maturity, volatility 10%, Future at 50

CHART 10.16 Theta distribution compared to time to maturity, volatility 10%, Future/ATM level at 50.00

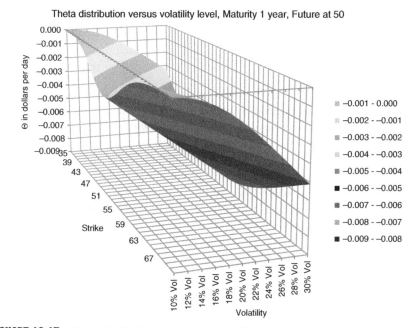

Theta distribution versus volatility level, Maturity 1 year, Future at 50

CHART 10.17 Theta distribution compared to volatility, Maturity 1 year, Future at 50

DETERMINING THE THETA VALUE OF AN AT THE MONEY STRADDLE

Applying the formula for pricing an at the money straddle, $0.8\sigma\sqrt{TF}$, it is fairly easy to come up with the theta.

Assuming 20% volatility and 1 year to maturity and Future at 50 the straddle will have a value of \$8. This is when maturity is 365 days. To know the theta, one should know the value of the straddle when time to maturity is 364 days. When dividing the straddle value by $\sqrt{365}$ and then multiplying it with $\sqrt{364}$ the difference between the two values is the theta. Applying this rule will result in the following values:

TABLE 10.7

Time to Maturity	1 Year	9 Months	6 Months	3 Months	2 Months	1 Month
Days	365	274	183	92	61	31
Straddle	8	6.931	5.665	4.016	3.270	2.331
New Straddle D + 1 Ratio	$\dfrac{\sqrt{364}}{\sqrt{365}}$	$\dfrac{\sqrt{273}}{\sqrt{274}}$	$\dfrac{\sqrt{182}}{\sqrt{183}}$	$\dfrac{\sqrt{91}}{\sqrt{92}}$	$\dfrac{\sqrt{60}}{\sqrt{61}}$	$\dfrac{\sqrt{30}}{\sqrt{31}}$
Ratio	0.9986292	0.9981735	0.997264	0.9945504	0.9917694	0.9837388
New Straddle	7.989	6.919	5.649	3.995	3.244	2.294
Computed Θ	−0.011	−0.012	−0.016	−0.021	−0.026	−0.037
B & S Θ	−0.011	−0.013	−0.015	−0.022	−0.027	−0.037

The way the theta has been estimated is very accurate compared to the values given by the Black Scholes model and could thus be applied for estimating the time decay. It is, however, quite impossible to divide a straddle by, for instance, $\sqrt{274}$ and then multiply it by $\sqrt{273}$ off the top of the head. Luckily there's a nice trick to do this, which is quite simple.

The ratio $\frac{\sqrt{273}}{\sqrt{274}}$ is very very close to $\frac{1}{548}$, being 1 divided by twice the amount of days to maturity, as shown in Chart 10.18. This works very well up to 5 days to maturity: the two different ratios have a correlation of 99.99%. Up to 2 days before maturity the correlation slightly decreases to 99.85%, so it's a bit more unreliable when really close to expiry.

So when using this trick one can compute for instance the theta of the at the money straddle with volatility at 20%, Future at 50.00 and maturity 1 year: it is \$8 times $\frac{1}{730}$, which makes around 1.1¢. In formula $\Theta(Straddle) = \frac{Straddle}{2T(days)}$ for the at the money options, as shown in Table 10.8.

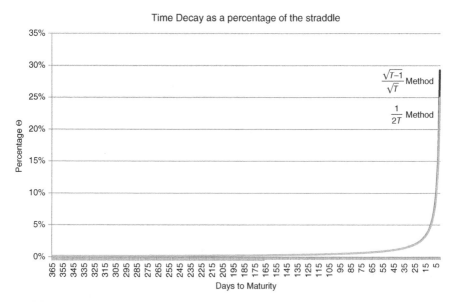

CHART 10.18

TABLE 10.8

Time to Maturity	1 Year	9 Months	6 Months	3 Months	2 Months	1 Month
$\dfrac{\sqrt{T-1}}{\sqrt{T}}$ Method	−0.011	−0.012	−0.016	−0.021	−0.026	−0.037
$\dfrac{1}{2T}$ Method	−0.011	−0.013	−0.015	−0.022	−0.027	−0.038
B & S Θ	−0.011	−0.013	−0.015	−0.022	−0.027	−0.037

When the volatility is at 10%, Future at 50 and maturity 3 months, the straddle will be valued at 2$, theta (of the straddle) will thus be $\frac{2}{184}$ making it approximately 1.1¢. With 10% volatility, Future at 50 and maturity 50 days, the theta will be: $1.48 (straddle) divided by $100\left(\frac{1}{2x50}\right)$, making it 1.5¢.

DETERMINING THETA VALUES OF OUT OF THE MONEY OPTIONS

Just like determining gamma and vega for out of the money options, the same assumptions will be applied again; 3½ straddles for the way up, 2½ straddles for the way down. So with an at the money 50 straddle of $4 (10% volatility, 1 year maturity), the boundaries for theta will be (artificially) set at 64 for the upside and 40 for the downside.

When drawing a straight line from the top to 64 for the upside and drawing a line from the top to 40 for the downside, it will be easy to compute the theta, as shown in Chart 10.19. The theta for the 50 strike is known ($\frac{4\$}{730} = 0.0055$, divided by 2 for determining call/put being 0.00274) and thus it is simple to derive theta levels for a linear relation, for the downside: $10 range for $0.00274 making $\frac{0.00274}{10} = \$0.000274$ decrease in theta per dollar change in the strike.

For the upside: $14 range for $0.00274, making $\frac{0.00274}{14} = \$0.0002$ decrease in vega per dollar change in the strike, as shown in Table 10.9.

TABLE 10.9

Parameters:	Strike	Computed Θ Call/Put	Black Scholes Θ
	38	0	−0.0001
Future @50,00	42	−0.0005	−0.0005
Volatility @ 10%	46	−0.0016	−0.0018
Maturity: 1 Year	50	−0.0027	−0.0027
50 Straddle: $4.00	54	−0.0020	−0.0021
	58	−0.0012	−0.0010
	62	−0.0004	−0.0003
	66	0	−0.0001

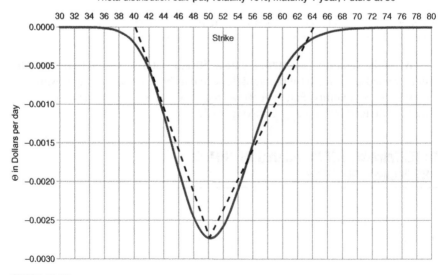

Theta distribution call/ put, volatility 10%, maturity 1 year, Future at 50

CHART 10.19   Linearisation of the Theta distribution

CHAPTER 11

Skew

So far all strikes of a range of options, with the same maturity date, have been treated as all having the same volatility, but in reality one could find differences in volatility between or around at the money options and out of the money options. One could also find discrepancies in volatility among different maturities, as discussed with relation to vega bucketing in the chapter on vega. The combination of these discrepancies is one of the shortcomings of the model, as mentioned in the introduction: the model assumes a stable volatility over different maturities and different strikes.

The difference in volatility in a range of strikes of options with the same maturity on the same underlying is called vertical skew, or volatility surface. The difference in volatility with regards to options with different maturities is called the term structure of volatility.

An example of the term structure has been shown in the chapter on vega, as shown below in Table 11.1:

TABLE 11.1

Maturity	Initial Volatility	Vega Position (total 8,000)	New volatility	Change in vol × Vega position	P&L
Up to 3 months	23%	−$5,000	20%	−3 × −$5,000	$15,000
3–6 months	23%	$3,000	21%	−2 × $3,000	−$6,000
6–12 months	23%	$1,000	22%	−1 × $1,000	−$1,000
More than 12 months	23%	$9,000	23%	0 × $9,000	$0
Total		$8,000			$8,000

As shown for the different buckets, volatility can behave differently per period of time to maturity. There are no fixed rules for how different buckets should relate to each other. It is all about the assessment of the market participants where volatility should be trading. The changes in volatility, or the vol of vol, will usually be the highest in the front months. Any change in market circumstances or certain expectations of future behaviour will be reflected at first in the short-term options. Longer term options quite often lag behind; a structural change in volatility is quite often the result of short-term events and/or expectations: it may not be justified to infer that this change will persist in the longer term. Therefore the vol of vol for longer-term options is much lower. Obviously, large volatility differences for different maturities in the volatility term structure might activate or increase the volume in trading of time spreads.

The vertical skew can have very different shapes, as shown in Chart 11.1 on the following page. These shapes depend on the market assessment of risk, opportunities and simply on demand and supply.

A smile, for instance, where the out of the money options are trading at a higher volatility and positive skew, than the around the at the money options, could be the result of the market trading around the mean with fairly low daily standard deviations. People don't want to own around the at the money strikes (for fear of heavy bleeding), but would like to have out of the money options for when the market starts moving again.

In the equity options trading business, many owners of equities try to increase their returns somewhat by entering into a covered call writing; hence, a large supply of short-term out of the money calls. At the same time drops in the market have a tendency to have a higher velocity than increases in the market; hence, there is more risk on the downside, and consequently out of the money puts are in demand for reasons of protection. Equity markets are thus often characterised by negative (lower volatility level) skew for out of the money calls and positive skew for out of the money puts – so-called reverse skew. Sometimes, when a certain stock is exploding, the negative skew for out of the money calls can obviously become positive.

Some markets might be characterised by negative skew for the out of the money puts and positive skew for out of the money calls, so-called forward skew. One might think, for instance, that when the price of a commodity drops below the marginal cost of production, a facility might decide to stop producing, thus creating an imbalance in supply versus demand and as a result supporting price levels. On the other hand, when demand is increasing or if there is a supply disruption and supply cannot meet the demand as a result prices could go sky-high.

So there are many occasions on which a skew shape can be seen in the market. Also, the steepness of the shape can differ immensely: some are flattish, only a few tenths of a per cent per dollar strike difference; some very steep, a few percentage points per dollar strike difference. There is no fixed rule; in principle, anything can happen. It is all about market perception, risk assessment, risk appetite and supply and demand.

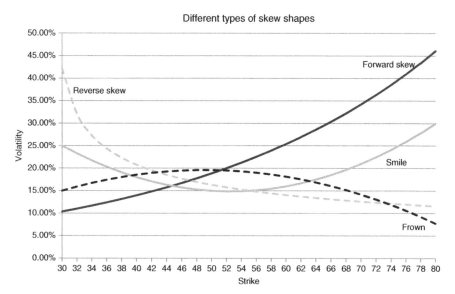

CHART 11.1 Different types of skew shapes

VOLATILITY SMILES WITH DIFFERENT TIMES TO MATURITY

When looking at options on a Future with three different maturities, each of which displays a smile shape in their vertical skew and a flat shape in their horizontal skew (i.e. same volatility for the at the money) it is possible to detect various degrees of steepness in the skew shapes. The options with the shortest time to maturity will have the steepest skew, the one with the longest time to maturity will have the flattest shape.

In Chart 11.2, the dark grey line represents the skew shape of a short maturity term, the light grey line the mid term and the dashed line a long term to expiry.

With the Future trading at 50, a short term to expiry 40 put will hardly have any value. However, there are some people who will want to own the 40 puts in case of extreme events. They will have to bid up the volatility of the strike before anyone will agree with selling it. No one would be willing to run the risk of being short an out of the money put for just a few cents. The same will happen with out of the money calls: initially there are no sellers, but when the options are bid up someone might see a good risk return rate. Consequently, an equilibrium is reached where supply meets demand. As soon as there is consensus in the market the shape is created. The shape can be very steep or much more flat, depending on the level where the supply and demand are in equilibrium. One will have to understand that far out of the money options with a short time to maturity are almost impossible to hedge.

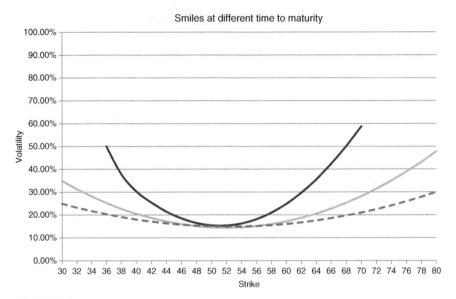

CHART 11.2   Smiles at different times to maturity

For the mid term and long term to expiry, the 40 and 65 strike are, due to the longer time to maturity, more "around the at the money level". They are easier to hedge and they carry a much higher vega. Therefore the skew shape should be much less pronounced.

Quite often the differences in shape are modelled on the back of the "moneyness" (logarithm) of the strike in relation to the Future level divided by the square root of the time to maturity. In some other markets people assign additional volatility to the specific delta of a strike. For instance, the 30 delta strike will get an additional vol point, the 20 delta strike two vol points, etc.

With regards to the first example one could say that, if the at the money 50 straddle has a value of $5, a maturity of 3 months and a 55 call with a positive skew of 1 vol point, then, with a maturity of 1 year (4 times as long as the former maturity), the 55 call should have half of that skew. This is the result of the initial skew, divided by the square root of the 3 months ratio, as opposed to 1 year. Another way to say it is that you can apply 1 vol point skew for an out of the money option which matures in 3 months, which is 1 straddle out of the money and hence the 55 call. When maturity is four times as long, according to the $0.8 \times \sigma \times \sqrt{T} \times F$ rule for determining the straddle value, its straddle should now be $10. Applying 1 point vol skew for 1 straddle out of the money, would now result in a 1 point skew for the 60 call. Unfortunately, this is a bit too simplistic, as a skew curve mostly resembles an exponential formula, rather than a linear one. However, this shows that one should be able to find some relationship between different skew shapes.

When assigning a skew to an option with a specific delta, something similar will apply. Bearing in mind the 30%/15% rule for delta calculation, one could say that an out of the money call which is $\frac{2}{3}$ of the straddle value out of the money would have a 30% delta; a call which is 1 straddle out of the money would have a 20% delta. So, it all comes back to the straddle value.

STICKY AT THE MONEY VOLATILITY

Usually volatility is assigned to the at the money strike: skew will be calculated in relation to that point. When the Future, for instance, moves from 50 to 55, the 55 strike is an at the money strike. When applying the same volatility to the new at the money strike, it is called sticky at the money volatility; this is a tendency which can be found in most markets. Next to that, because of the log normality, skew is also based on the moneyness. Moneyness implies that a move from 40 to 44 is equivalent to a move from 60 to 66; $\ln \frac{44}{40} = \ln \frac{66}{60}$, as shown in Chart 11.3. The result of the moneyness is that the skew shape for options which have a low level for the at the money strike is much steeper compared to options which have a high level for the at the money strike.

When continuously delta hedging, the sticky at the money volatility can raise some difficulties. Due to changing volatility levels in different strikes, the vega position could result in a change in P&L. When long the at the money strike and the Future will trade towards a new level: the former at the money strike will increase in volatility level, so the owner has an advantage due to his vega long position. The owner of out of the money puts will have a disadvantage when the Future goes down, but will profit from an increase of the Future. The owner of out of the money calls will profit from a decrease in the Future, but will lose on vega when the Future is trading up. When running large portfolios of options it is well advised to check on the consequences of sticky at the money volatility.

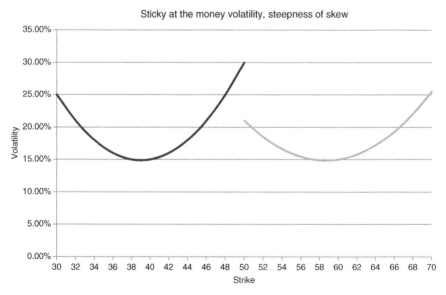

CHART 11.3

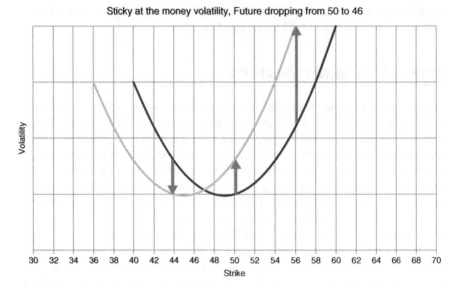

CHART 11.4   Sticky at the money volatility, Future decreasing

Chart 11.4 shows that, with a decreasing Future (from 50 to 46), the former at the money strike will increase in volatility level; so will the out of the money calls. When coming off out of the money puts will decrease in volatility level.

With an increasing Future, as shown in Chart 11.5, at the money options and out of the money puts will increase in volatility level, the out of the money calls will decrease in volatility level.

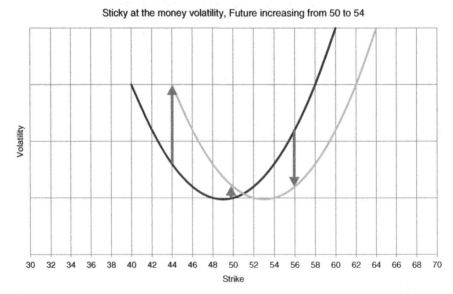

CHART 11.5   Sticky at the money volatility, Future increasing

CHAPTER 12

Spreads

Plainly buying a call or a put could become very costly when the market is slow/ not going the right way. Losses can arise quite quickly and time decay can be painful. In order to mitigate these losses or to create the most optimal P&L distribution according to the assessment of the Future towards maturity, a trader can enter into a spread strategy. It consists of one long call or put and another short: the short option will partly offset the investment of the long option.

When the long and short strikes have the same maturity one usually speaks of a "call spread" or "put spread", "horizontal call/put spread" or "bull/bear spread". With different maturities, the strikes being the same, one speaks of "time call/put spread" or "vertical spread". When maturities as well as strikes differ, these strategies are called "diagonal spreads".

When the long and short strikes are set up with differing volumes for each strike, quite often the further out of the money strike in a higher volume than the more at the money, the combination is called a "ratio spread".

CALL SPREAD (HORIZONTAL)

When entering a (long) call spread, one buys one strike and sells a higher strike. For the put spread it's the other way around – buy a higher strike and sell a lower strike. The initial investment is obviously lower than just buying the call option at the lower strike. When the Future is trading at 50, a trader could buy the 50–55 call spread, buying the 50 call, selling the 55 call. His P&L at expiry would look as follows (not taking initial investment into account):

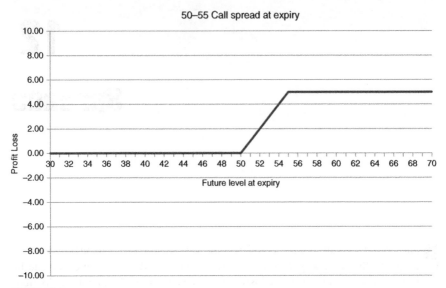

CHART 12.1 50–55 Call spread at expiry

The maximum profit of this call spread is $5 at the 55 level or higher; hence the name bull spread. At 55 the long 50 call option has a value of $5 where the short 55 call has no value at expiry. Any level above 55, for each dollar higher the 50 call will be worth one dollar more. However, this will be fully offset by the short position in

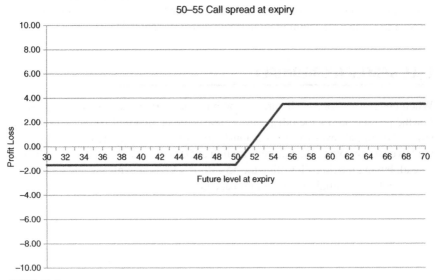

CHART 12.2 50–55 Call spread at expiry minus investment of $1.50

the 55 strike and thus the value of the spread remains at $5. Anything below 50 will result in a zero P&L – both the 50 and the 55 call have no value at expiry. In this example no initial investment has been taken into account, but certainly one should have paid upfront in order to create this opportunity. When deducting the initial premium, for instance $1.5, the P&L distribution will look as shown in Chart 12.2.

Having paid $1.50 for the 50–55 call spread, the P&L distribution will show a loss of $1.50 at any level below 50. Above 50, the 50 call will first have to make up for the investment; hence, at 51.50 the breakeven point of the strategy will have been reached. The maximum profit will be at 55 or higher: it will be $5 minus the initial investment of $1.50 resulting in a $3.5 profit.

PUT SPREAD (HORIZONTAL)

For the 50–45 put spread the strategy will yield a profit when the market comes off: hence the name bear spread. The maximum profit will be reached at a level of 45 or lower; the put spread will be worth $5, creating a profit of $5 minus the initial investment, as shown in Chart 12.3.

A spread can be set up in many ways: deep in the money call/put spreads, far out of the money or all close to the prevailing at the money level.

If the spreads are really deep in the money, they will approach their full value. If they are very far out of the money they will tend to go to zero value. So when looking at the 30–35 call spread with the Future trading at 50 and expiry very close; the call spread is worth $5, a one dollar move up or down in the Future will not have any impact on the value of the call spread. Next to that, the 35–30 put

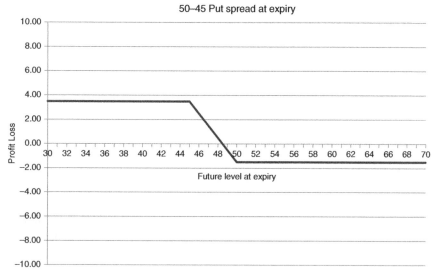

CHART 12.3   50–45 Put spread at expiry

spread will remain worthless: only below 35 will it start to gain in value; but with this short time to expiry in a normal volatility environment, these moves are not anticipated.

BOXES

When looking at the combination of the 30–35 call spread and the 35–30 put spread together, it can be said that they always have an aggregate value of $5, as shown below. Any deviation from that can be arbitraged.

Future at expiry	30–35 Call spread	35–30 Put spread	Aggregate Value
20	0	5	5
25	0	5	5
31	1	4	5
32.50	2.50	2.50	5
34	4	1	5
35	5	0	5
45	5	0	5

TABLE 12.1   In other words a formula could be formed (in this case 30 and 35 strike with the same maturity):

Calls	Strike	Puts	
+	30	−	= 5
−	35	+	

or

Calls	Strike	Puts	
+	X	−	= Strike Differential
−	Y	+	

This holds for any combination. The sum of the call spread and put spread of strikes X and Y is equivalent to the strike differential (Y - X), as shown in Table 12.1. This sum is called the "Box".

The Box could be viewed as a combination of a reversal and a conversion (C – P in combination with P – C). At any level for the Future (as shown in the table above) the combination has a value which is equivalent to the strike differential. When regarding a conversion as being short a reversal (which it actually is: P – C = – (C – P)), the trader is spreading here two reversals where he knows that the difference in value is the strike differential.

From the perspective of trading synthetics: when buying a call with strike X and combining it with selling a Future one creates a long position in the put with strike X; when selling a call with strike Y and buying a Future one creates a short position in the put with strike Y. So, buying call (X) – F and at the same time selling call (Y) + F is equivalent to buying put (X) and selling put (Y): the Futures will offset each other. As a result, one will end up being short the Y – X put spread (in a very direct way call = put has been applied here). In order to flatten the position one could sell the (X – Y) call spread, but another way to flatten it is to buy the (Y – X) put spread, where the (X – Y) call spread and the (Y – X) put spread together have a value of the strike differential; namely Y – X.

As an example, one buys the 50–55 call spread at $1.75 (Future at 50, volatility at 15%, maturity 1 year). Offsetting the position could be done by selling the call spread again at 1.75 or buying the put spread at 3.25 (no interest applied). In both cases the trader wouldn't lose any money while having a flat book. When selling the call spread he had a negative cashflow of 1.75 and later a positive one of 1.75 as well, and no position in the call spread anymore. By buying the put spread he has a negative cashflow of $5 in a combination which is always worth $5 at expiry (the cash will be returned at settlement at expiry).

A trader trying to have a flat position all the time could maybe acquire this call spread at 1.70 and the put spread at $3.20, buying a $5 box at 4.90 will yield a profit of 10 cents without any risk. Therefore, he should always keep in mind that if he can't sell the 50–55 call spread (at a higher level in the Future and thus at a profit) he could buy the put spread instead. Buying the call spread at 1.70 (long 50 strike, short 55 strike) would imply selling the put spread at 3.30 (long 50 strike, short 55 strike), being the value of the box minus the initial investment. So, acquiring the put spread at any level below 3.30 would generate a profit for the trader.

APPLYING BOXES IN THE REAL MARKET

Working with Boxes can prove to be very important when having a portfolio of options. Assume a trader is bullish on the market and has therefore bought the 50–55 call spread at 1.75. When the market goes to 60 in a short time, the call spread increases in value towards $4. When trying to sell it back into the market he will face difficulties in selling the 50 strike and buying back the 55 strike, since in the money calls are less liquid (the bulk of trading is concentrated in at and out of the money options) and the bid ask spread is much wider. Next to that, not many

TABLE 12.2

Strike (Future at 60)	Call bid	Call ask	Put bid	Put ask
50	10.20	10.70	0.40	0.50
55	6.25	6.75	1.35	1.55
60	3.40	3.65	3.40	3.65
65	1.60	1.80	6.50	7.00

market makers are willing to make markets for in the money calls, because of the high delta for each call option and the chance of an adverse move in the Future. In many markets a wide bid ask spread is applied to in the money options while out of the money options are often characterised by tight bid ask spreads. As an example the market could look as shown in Table 12.2.

When the call spread has a theoretical value of $4, the put spread should be worth $1. In a worst case scenario, the trader, trying to sell his callspread by separately selling the 50 call and buying the 55 call, will only receive $3.45 for his combination (selling at 10.20, the bid price, and buying at 6.75, the offer price), leaving him with a 1.70 profit, 55 cents worse than the $2.25 he had anticipated as his profit (4 as fair value minus 1.75 as initial investment). When buying the put spread instead (buying the 55 put at 1.55, offer price and selling the 50 put at 0.40, bid price) he will be able to close the deal at 1.15. As a result he invested 1.75 in the call spread and 1.15 in the put spread, being 2.90 in a combination which is worth $5, making his profit $2.10, being 15 cents worse than the anticipated fair value. In the end, by trading the box rather than selling his call spread in the market, the trader has saved himself 40 cents and only given away 15 cents as a margin for the market makers.

THE GREEKS FOR HORIZONTAL SPREADS

Delta

As discussed in the chapter on delta, delta differentials for different strikes are related to the value of the straddle. When, for instance (Future at 50, volatility at 25% and maturity 1 year) the at the money straddle is worth $10, the delta of the 45–50 call spread is around 15% (this will be the same for the put spread) and the delta for the 50–55 spread is also around 15%. At lower strikes, as well as higher strikes, this delta differential will diminish to end at zero difference when the boundaries for the distribution have been reached, as shown in Table 12.3. The value of the spread will change according to its delta per dollar move in the Future.

The delta of the put spread is the same as the delta of the call spread. So, when a long 40–45 call spread has a delta of 14%, the 40–45 put spread, long the 40 put, short the 45 put, should also have a 14% delta (the 45–40 put spread, thus being long the 45 strike, will yield a delta of –14%).

TABLE 12.3

Strike Call	Delta Call	Call spread strikes	Delta Call spread	Puts spread strikes	Delta Put spread
30	99				
35	94	30–35	5	35–30	−5
40	85	35–40	9	40–35	−9
45	71	40–45	14	45–40	−14
50	55	45–50	16	50–45	−16
55	40	50–55	15	55–50	−15
60	27	55–60	13	60–55	−13
65	18	60–65	9	65–60	−9
70	11	65–70	7	70–65	−7
75	7	70–75	4	75–70	−4
80	4	75–80	3	80–75	−3

The shorter the time to maturity, or the lower the volatility, the earlier the boundaries will be reached in the delta distribution. The distribution will steepen, resulting in a larger delta for at the money call/put spreads. Also, when taking into consideration that the value of the straddle will decrease if time to maturity is shortening or volatility is lower, the 30%/15% rule of thumb will apply for a much smaller range. With longer time to maturity or higher volatility the

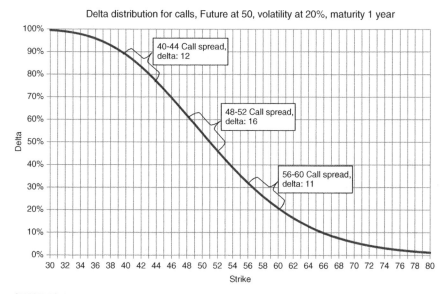

CHART 12.4 Delta of spreads, longer time to maturity

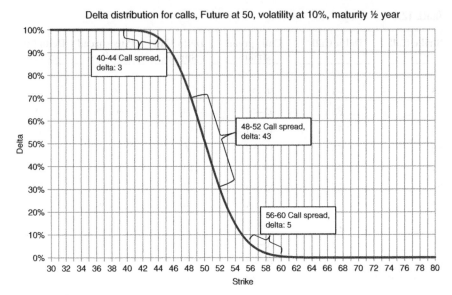

CHART 12.5   Delta of spreads, short time to maturity

probability distribution will increase, the delta curve will flatten and as a result the delta for at the money spreads will decrease, but will increase for out of the money spreads.

Chart 12.4 displays how the delta of a $4 call spread decreases when more out of the money. Whenever the delta of both legs of the spread has reached a value of zero or 100 %, the spread has obviously no delta anymore. The in the money call spread will then have maximum value, and thus the put spread will have no value anymore. The out of the money call spread will have no value anymore and the put spread will have maximum value.

Chart 12.5 shows that, at a lower volatility and/or shorter time to maturity, the at the money delta curve is much steeper, while at the same time the boundaries are much earlier reached, resulting in no delta for the further out of the money spreads. (The 36–40 call spread has hardly any delta; both strikes have 100% delta, as well as the 60–64 call spread where both strikes have a zero delta.)

Gamma

Taking another look at the table shown before, Table 12.4, it shows that the delta of the spreads are changing. The further out of the money (or in the money) the lower the delta will be. Whenever the delta is changing it should have gamma.

When looking at the 45–50 call spread at different levels in the Future, as shown in Table 12.5, the delta will look as follows (volatility at 25%, maturity 1 year).

TABLE 12.4

Strike Call	Delta Call	Call spread strikes	Delta Call spread	Put spread strikes	Delta Put spread
30	99				
35	94	30–35	5	35–30	–5
40	85	35–40	9	40–35	–9
45	71	40–45	14	45–40	–14
50	55	45–50	16	50–45	–16
55	40	50–55	15	55–50	–15
60	27	55–60	13	60–55	–13
65	18	60–65	9	65–60	–9
70	11	65–70	7	70–65	–7
75	7	70–75	4	75–70	–4
80	4	75–80	3	80–75	–3

TABLE 12.5

Future level	Delta 45 call	Delta 50 call	Delta call spread
30	7%	3%	4%
35	19%	10%	9%
40	36%	22%	14%
45	55%	38%	17%
50	71%	55%	16%
55	82%	69%	13%
60	90%	80%	10%
65	95%	88%	7%
70	97%	93%	4%
75	99%	96%	3%

As shown in Table 12.5, with 30 in the Future, the delta of the 45–50 call spread is 4%, which is increasing towards 17% when the Future trades at 45 and decreasing towards 3% when the Future trades up towards 75. In other words, below 45 in the Future the spread has a positive gamma (increasing when the Future is going up, decreasing when the Future is trading down) and somewhere between 45 and 50 the gamma will turn negative. This is actually a logical consequence because of the different strikes. As explained in the chapter on gamma, the more a strike is at the money the more gamma it has:

Calls	Strike	Puts
+	45	
−	50	

So, when long the 45 strike and short the 50 strike, the 45 strike generates a gamma long position where the 50 strike generates a gamma short position. At any level in the Future around 45 or lower, the gamma of the 45 call will be more positive than the gamma of the 50 call is negative; hence, the spread has a positive gamma. At any level around 50 or higher in the Future the gamma of the 50 strike will dominate and hence the spread has a negative gamma. Around 46 (with this specific volatility) the change from gamma long to gamma short will occur.

Chart 12.6 displays the gamma distribution of the 45–50 call spread at different underlying levels. Any level below 46 will have a positive gamma; a Future level above 46 will make the spread become gamma negative. The positive gamma in absolute terms is larger than the negative gamma because at lower levels in the Future, the gamma of an at the money option is larger than the gamma at higher levels (an at the money 45 straddle generates more gamma than an at the money 50 straddle, see the chapter on Gamma)

Vega

The vega outlook is comparable to the gamma distribution (gamma = vega = −theta). However, below 46 the vega will be smaller than above 46 (an at the money 45 straddle generates less vega than an at the money 50 straddle, see chapter on vega), as shown in Chart 12.7.

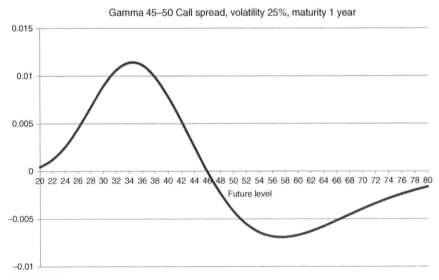

Gamma 45–50 Call spread, volatility 25%, maturity 1 year

CHART 12.6   Gamma distribution of the 45–50 call spread

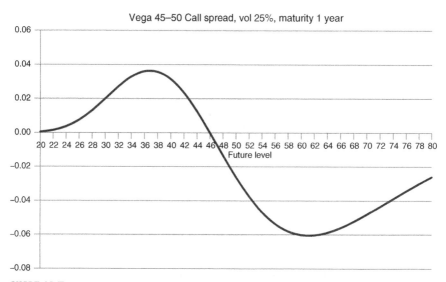

CHART 12.7   Vega distribution of the 45–50 call spread

Theta

The distribution of theta will be negative below 46; the negative theta of the long 45 call outweighs the positive theta of the short 50 call. Above 46 the theta will be positive: the positive theta above 46 is larger in absolute terms than the negative theta below 46 (an at the money 45 straddle generates less theta than an at the money 50 straddle, see chapter on theta), as shown in Chart 12.8.

When comparing Chart 12.8 with Chart 12.6, the chart on gamma, it looks like a remarkable feature has been shown. Below 46, the absolute gamma is larger than

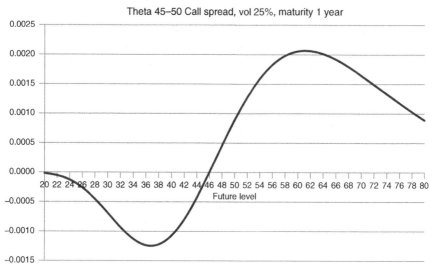

CHART 12.8   Theta distribution of the 45-50 call spread

above 46, but at the same time below 46 the absolute theta is smaller than above 46. This seems a bit contradictory because of the gamma/theta relationship, α (alpha), which dictates the ratio to be constant and thus a higher theta at higher gamma levels. The point is that the relationship is changing with regards to the Future level. So, at a much higher level (60 compared to 36) the gamma is decreasing, while at the same time the theta is increasing (higher value in the at the money straddle); consequently, the gamma theta ratio will be subject to change.

In most cases the buyer of a call or put spread has a directional view on the market and is not hedging his deltas and is not bothered with the other Greeks of the spread. It is, however, good to know how it all behaves. Especially in the case of ratio spreads things can unexpectedly change and hedges might become necessary.

TIME SPREAD

When buying a time spread, the trader sells an option with a short time to maturity and buys one (with the same strike) with a longer time to maturity. The combination will slowly become worth more towards expiry of the short option with a short time to maturity. The positive theta of the short option will outweigh the negative theta of the long option, and when the market does not move too much it is a fairly safe strategy. The worst case is when the market makes a large move. Either way, the spread will be deep in the money or far out of the money. In the first case they both purely exist out of intrinsic value: neither option has extrinsic value, and as a result the initial investment has been lost. The same would happen if they end up being far out of the money, neither has further value and the initial investment has been lost as well.

When hedging the time spread one could prevent or mitigate the loss of the initial premium, but the trader should certainly take his Greeks into account now. He's short gamma (the shorter the time to maturity the more gamma an at the money option generates) and thus long theta and he has a long vega position.

Obviously the best scenario is when the market remains trading around the strike of the timespread: the most theta profit will be incurred and the spread increases to maximum value. However, when the position would benefit most from a sideways market, the strategy is long vega. It is likely that in this scenario the volatility would drop somewhat and hence some anticipated profit would not kick in. When selling a 3 month 50 call and buying the 6 month 50 call, with the Future trading at 50, at expiry of the short option the P&L will be distributed as shown in Table 12.6 (keeping volatility constant at 15%):

It's not a fantastic result, only being "spot on" is rewarded. For calculating the vega of the position; the original 6 month option now became a 3 month option. The vega of a 3 month at the money 50 call is $0.10, maybe also the vol came off when the market remained so stable that it expired after 3 months at the same level as it was at before, hence reducing the P&L. But this structure is still favoured by many traders.

TABLE 12.6

	Value short call	Value long call	Value spread	P&L
Investment	−1.49	2.10	0.61	
Future level				
40	0	0	0	−0.61
42.5	0	0.02	0.02	−0.59
45	0	0.13	0.13	−0.48
47.50	0	0.53	0.53	−0.08
50	0	1.49	1.49	0.88
52.50	−2.50	3.09	0.59	−0.02
55	−5.00	5.19	0.19	−0.42
57.5	−7.50	7.55	0.05	−0.56
60	−10.00	10.01	0.01	−0.60

Obviously with a higher volatility, the structure should give more room for the Future to move in a certain direction and still generate a positive result. The table below shows the P&L distribution of a time spread with a volatility of 25%. The same maturities and underlying levels as in the former example are applied.

TABLE 12.7

	Value short call	Value long call	Value spread	P&L
Investment	2.50	3.54	1.04	
Future level				
40	0	0.09	0.09	−0.95
42.5	0	0.27	0.27	−0.77
45	0	0.67	0.67	−0.37
47.50	0	1.39	1.39	0.35
50	0	2.50	2.50	1.46
52.50	2.50	4.01	1.51	0.47
55	5.00	5.85	0.85	−0.19
57.5	7.50	7.95	0.45	−0.59
60	10.00	10.22	0.22	−0.82

In Table 12.6, the 47.50 and 52.50 levels already resulted in a small loss. Now, at a volatility of 25%, the structure will start losing money around 46.50 and 54.

APPROXIMATION OF THE VALUE OF
AT THE MONEY SPREADS

When using 10% volatility for options maturing in 1 year and the Future and the at the money level at 50, according to the straddle formula $(0.8 \times \sigma \times \sqrt{T} \times F)$ the 50 straddle should be worth around $4 being $2 for the 50 call and $2 for the 50 put, the delta for the 50 call is 52%. When having a look at the 48–52 call spread, 50 being exactly in the middle, $2 value should be taken into account as a fair mid price. It should however be corrected for the additional delta of 2 (52% delta for the at the money instead of 50%) over a $4 range. The model values the call spread at 1.92; the put spread will thus be valued at 2.08 (applying box value) when the Future is at 50.

The call spread thus has a smaller value, depending on the additional delta, compared to 50% of the at the money strike. So, the higher the volatility, the smaller the at the money call spread. This is a logical consequence of the lognormal distribution. The smaller the at the money and out of the money call spreads the longer it takes for the call options to end at zero value, the put options tend to have reached zero earlier.

When, for instance, the vol is at 25%, the at the money call delta is 55%, resulting in 48–52 call spread, which is worth $2 minus 4 times 5 deltas: 2 minus 0.20 resulting in a value of 1.80 for the call spread and 2.20 for the put spread (resulting in $4 for the box).

With different volatilities and the Future trading at 50, the 48–52 spreads will look as follows

TABLE 12.8

Volatility level	Delta 50 call	Additional delta x spread range	48–52 Call spr (2–delta reduction)	48–52 Put spr (put call parity)
10%	52	8¢	1.92	2.08
15%	53	12¢	1.88	2.12
20%	54	16¢	1.84	2.16
25%	55	20¢	1.80	2.20
30%	56	24¢	1.76	2.24

Breaking the 48–52 spread into two, 48–50 and 50–52, at each volatility level the aggregate value of the two spreads will be known. When looking at the call spreads, the 48–50 should be bigger than the 50–52 (it's more in the money). The 48–50 call spread relates to 50 in the Future as the 50–52 call spread would relate to 52 in the Future. In other words, the 50–52 call spread will have approximately the same value when the Future trades at 52 as the 48–50 call spread when the Future is at 50. Since the Future is trading at 50 instead of 52 in reality, the 50–52 call spread will have a value which is 2 times its delta lower (the Future is $2 lower compared to 52) than compared to the 48–50 call spread.

When the straddle is trading at $8, the delta of the 48–50 and the 50–52 spreads would be according to the 30%/15% rule 7.5%; so, the difference in the call spreads is 15 cents, 48–50 being 15 cents more expensive than the 50–52. The 48–50 and 50–52 call spreads together are worth 1.84 and combining this with 48–50 call spread being 0.15 more expensive than the 50–52 call spread, the first one needs to have a value of $1 while the 50–52 will have a value of $0.85 ($0.85 has been used in order to simplify: estimating spread values is not an exact science – only a rough approximation).

The 46–48 spread also has a 7.5% delta (according to the 30%/15% rule), so this call spread could be valued at 1.15, even so for the 44–46 call spread, at 1.30. The 52–54 has 7.5% deltas so it will be worth around 0.70: 0.84 for the 50–52 call spread minus a $2 move times a delta of 7.5% and the 54–56 also with a 7.5% delta $0.56. So, each calculation of the delta of the spread times the $2 change for the spread will result in the value of the difference of the respective spreads (as with the butterfly, which is characterised by delta differential x strike differential), as shown in Table 12.9.

TABLE 12.9

Strike	Call	Put (via put call parity)	Model, Call	Model, Put
44	7.45	1.45	7.49	1.49
46	6.15	2.15	6.17	2.17
48	5.00	3.00	5.00	3.00
50	4.00	4.00	4.00	4.00
52	3.15	5.15	3.16	5.16
54	2.45	6.45	2.46	6.46
56	1.90	7.90	1.89	7.89

Actually, the approximation for the at the money options is quite accurate; only accurate, though, when the at the money straddle is big enough to create a large enough area where the delta distribution is linear. For further out of the money options the estimation method proves not to be very precise; the 44 strike already shows a deviation of 4 cents.

RATIO SPREAD

A ratio spread means that the two "legs" of a spread are not of equal volume. One can set up any kind of ratio. A few examples of options are laid out in Table 12.10 (Future at 50, volatility at 10%, maturity 1 year). Quite often ratio spreads are set up in order to lower or minimise the initial investment.

TABLE 12.10

Calls	Strike	Puts
10.02	40	0.02
9.04	41	0.04
8.08	42	0.08
7.14	43	0.14
6.23	44	0.23
5.36	45	0.36
4.55	46	0.55
3.80	47	0.80
3.12	48	1.12
2.52	49	1.52
2.00	50	2.00
1.56	51	2.56
1.19	52	3.19
0.90	53	3.90
0.66	54	4.66
0.48	55	5.48
0.34	56	6.34
0.24	57	7.24
0.17	58	8.17
0.11	59	9.11
0.08	60	10.08
0.05	61	11.05
0.03	62	12.03

A trader buying the 50–52 call spread, 1 by 2, is buying the 50 call once and selling the 52 call twice. With values of $2 and $1.19 respectively, he receives $0.38 for the structure at inception. At expiry at 52 the structure will have its best performance – the trader earns $2 on the 50 call; but the 52 calls are worthless, so he will not lose anything on those and will receive $0.38 when setting up his strategy initially. In total his profit is $2.38. His breakeven point is $54.38, earning $4.38 on the 50 call, losing two times $2.38 on the 52 calls, making $4.76 and receiving 38 cents when setting up the strategy. Any dollar higher compared to the 54.38 level he will lose 1 dollar (he will earn 1 dollar per dollar uptick in the Future on the 50 call, but will lose 2 dollars on the short 52 calls), as shown in Table 12.11.

TABLE 12.11

Future at expiry	50 Call	52 Calls	Initial cashflow	P&L
50	0	0	0.38	0.38
51	1.00	0	0.38	1.38
52	2.00	0	0.38	2.38
53	3.00	−2.00	0.38	1.38
54	4.00	−4.00	0.38	0.38
54.38	4.38	−4.76	0.38	0.00
55	5.00	−6.00	0.38	−0.62
56	6.00	−8.00	0.38	−1.62
57	7.00	−10.00	0.38	−2.68

For the 50–47 put spread in a 1 by 2.5 ratio, setting it up at price levels according to the table with the option prices above, the trader will have to pay $2.00 for the 50 put while selling the 47 put 2.5 times at $0.80, receiving $2 and hence resulting in a cash flow neutral strategy.

The payoff of the structure will be zero above 50, but will start to generate a P&L below 50, with a profit of $3.00 at 47. Below 47, one will start losing profit because of the short position in the 47 puts. At 45, the owner of the strategy makes $5.00 on the long 50 put but will have lost $5 on the 47 put (2.5 times the volume) and hence will have his breakeven point there. Any dollar below 45 the owner of the strategy will lose an additional $1.50 per dollar down move in the Future. So $5 lower, at 40, he should have lost $7.50. To check: at 40 the 50 put will have a value of $10.00 where the 47 put will have a value of $7: this put is 2.5 times short compared to the long 50 put. Hence the trader will have made $10.00 on the 50 put and would have lost $17.50 on the 47 put, resulting in a $7.50 loss in the strategy.

In order to find a way for calculating breakeven points and profit levels one should first value the profit of the structure when the market is trading at the level of the short options. Then afterwards the net option position should be calculated.

So for instance, for a 50–47 ratio put spread 1 by 2.5 with a Future trading at 47, a profit of $3 will be made; then, below 47 the trader will have a net short position of 1.5 put (1 put long, 2.5 puts short), losing $1.5 for every dollar downtick in the Future. To know the breakeven point, the trader should divide the $3 profit (he made by reaching the 47 level) by the net short position of 1.5, making it $2; hence, the breakeven point is 45, being $2 lower compared to the 47 level.

For the 50–52 1 by 2 ratio spread, the trader initially received 38 cents and at 52 his position is worth $2. So at 52 his profit is $2.38 and he will be net short one call above 52 (1 call long, 2 calls short). So when moving up this $2.38 towards

54.38 in the Future he will have reached the breakeven point. In this way one can easily calculate any ratio spread. For instance, for the 50–54 2 by 7 ratio call spread he pays $4 for the 50 strike (two times $2) and receives $4.60 (seven times $0.66, ignoring the last 2 cents) for the 54 calls it would look as follows:

TABLE 12.12

Future	Cashflow	Value 50 Call (2x)	Value 54 Call (7x)	P&L
50	0.60	0.00	0.00	0.60
54	0.60	8.00	0.00	8.60

So when having made $8.60 at the 54 level, he is short net 5 calls above that level. When dividing 8.60 by 5, being 1.72 the breakeven level can be set at 55.72, as shown in Table 12.13.

TABLE 12.13

Future	Cashflow	Value 50 Call (2x)	Value 54 Call (7x)	P&L
54	0.60	8.00	0.00	8.60
55.72	0.60	11.44	−12.04	0.00

For each dollar higher than 55.72 in the Future the trader would lose $5.

By setting up ratio spreads one can quite easily determine in what ratio one should make a certain spread when having a preferred/anticipated scenario in mind, and also a worst case scenario. So, when a trader is very bearish and expects the market to drop to a level around 46, but no further down than 44, he could think of several ratio put spreads to set up. He could enter into a 50–46 1 by 4, receiving initially $0.20, worth $4.20 when the market is at 46, while maintaining a breakeven point at 44.70. As a result, he could lose money when the market hits his worst case scenario. Another strategy will be necessary.

A 48–46 1 by 2 put spread, with best performance at 46 and breakeven level at 44.02, will suit better in his scenario forecast. The profit however, if the market expires at 46, will be half the profit of the 50–46 1 by 4. A trader should not just blindly set up a ratio spread, he should have the scenarios in mind, but also will have to think about his risk appetite, best performance, break even point and also the potential losses when hitting the worst case scenario.

In the above ratio spreads the maturity of the options has been set at 1 year. Another very important issue is the Greeks of the options during the lifetime of the ratio. For instance, the 50–46 1 by 4 ratio put spread will generate a large gamma short, vega short position when the market goes towards 46 shortly after initiating the trade. It will probably generate a large market to market loss, at the prevailing volatility level of 10%, the loss already mounts up to $2.80. If the market stays at 46 all this money will come back, and even more (being the 4 dollar profit at expiry) in the form of theta. He will, however, still have a large exposure caused by a short vega position (for the 46 strike, which is at the money and thus generating the most vega) and a short gamma position. Quite often with these sudden drops one can expect higher volatility in the market and thus the trader will even lose more. He might have to adjust his scenarios when his first interpretation of the market proves wrong.

As a conclusion one could say that ratio spreads are a very nice way to structure (low cost) strategies around certain market expectations, but one has to be extremely careful of sudden unexpected moves. They can be very destructive, but also very very rewarding when hitting the right scenario and all moving slowly towards the short strike towards expiry (being the best case). As said before, the option trader hopes that the market will move away from his long strike towards his short strike.

CHAPTER 13

Butterfly

A butterfly is a structure where one buys the wings of an option combination once and sells the middle twice: for instance, a 46–50–54 put butterfly can be set up by buying the 46 and 54 put once and selling the 50 put twice. This specific structure is defined as a long butterfly.

The maximum payoff at expiry will be when the underlying is exactly in the middle at the short strike. Obviously, when the butterfly is short, it will be the maximum loss level.

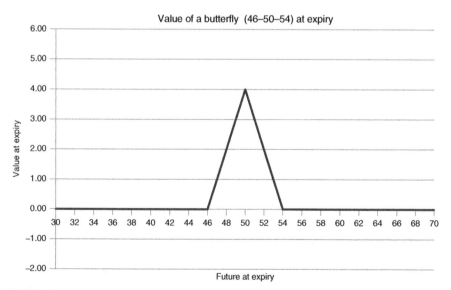

CHART 13.1 Profit Loss distribution of a 46–50–54 butterfly

In Chart 13.1 the 46–50–54 butterfly at expiry is depicted, the strategy will be set up by:

TABLE 13.1

Buying	46 Strike	Once
Selling	50 Strike	Twice
Buying	54 Strike	Once

The butterfly, set up with calls, will be the same as a butterfly set up with puts: the P&L distribution will be exactly the same.

When set up with put options, as shown in Table 13.2, at any level above 54, no put has any value and thus the value of the butterfly is zero. When expiring between 54 and 50 the 54 put will generate a profit, maximised at $4 when the market expires at 50. Below 50 the owner of the butterfly will be net short one put (long 54 once, short 50 twice) and up to the 46 level the $4 value will have decreased to zero again. Below 46 the owner of the butterfly has a balanced portfolio in long/short strikes and hence the value cannot decrease further.

TABLE 13.2

	Value 54 Put (1 long)	Value 50 Put (2 short)	Value 46 Put (1 long)	Total P&L
At or above 54	0	0	0	0
53	1	0	0	1
52	2	0	0	2
51	3	0	0	3
50	4	0	0	4
49	5	−2	0	3
48	6	−4	0	2
47	7	−6	0	1
46	8	−8	0	0
45	9	−10	1	0
40	14	−20	6	0

When being set up with call options, as shown in Table 13.3, it will result in the following P&L at expiry. At or below 46, no option has any value and the value of the butterfly will be zero, but anything between 46 and 50 the 46 call will generate the profit up to $4 when the market expires at 50. From 50 to 54 the owner of the butterfly will be net short one option (long 46 once, short 50 twice) above 50, so each dollar above 50 he will lose one dollar up to 54 level where his P&L has dropped to zero. At 54 the 46 call is worth $8, the 50 call is worth $4, being it short twice, so also $8, the 54 call still has no value, resulting in zero value. When above 54, the owner of the butterfly has a balanced portfolio in long/short options; he has a flat position. When long one 46 call and short two 50 calls, for each dollar above 54 (where the P&L is zero) he loses a dollar. But because he's long one 54 call he will earn that dollar back and hence will end up with a zero P&L above 54.

TABLE 13.3

	Value 46 Call (1 long)	Value 50 Call (2 short)	Value 54 Call (1 long)	Total P&L
At or below 46	0	0	0	0
47	1	0	0	1
48	2	0	0	2
49	3	0	0	3
50	4	0	0	4
51	5	−2	0	3
52	6	−4	0	2
53	7	−6	0	1
54	8	−8	0	0
55	9	−10	1	0
60	14	−20	6	0

When a butterfly is purchased (with long wings) it comes at a cost: there is no free lunch. The initial investment should be deducted from the P&L distribution, as shown below.

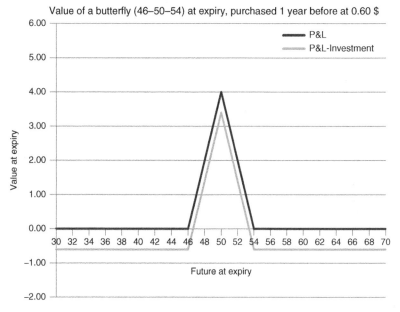

CHART 13.2 Profit Loss distribution of a 46–50–54 butterfly minus initial investment

PUT CALL PARITY

As stated before, the value of the put butterfly is exactly the same as the call butterfly (when strikes and maturity are the same). When there are different values for the two, there would be an arbitrage possibility. Assuming that the put butterfly would be more expensive than the call butterfly, one could arbitrage it by buying the call butterfly cheaper and selling the put butterfly more expensively, resulting in the following position:

Calls	Strike	Puts
+	46	−
− −	50	+ +
+	54	−

So, the trader ends up with two reversals (C – P: 46 and 54 strike) and two conversions (P – C: 50 strike, see chapter on put call parity). With the Future trading at 50, the 46 reversal will have a value of $4, which will have to be paid; the 54 reversal will also have a $4 value, but it will be a cashflow to be received when setting it up (put being $4 more expensive than the call); and the 50 conversion should have a zero value. Setting up this combination will result in an arbitrage profit when there is a positive cashflow; at the same time these positions bear no risk. In order to have no possibility of arbitrage, the combination should have a zero value.

Hence, put call parity dictates that the call and put butterflies have the same value (irrespective of the interest rate level).

A butterfly is actually a spread of two call spreads for a call butterfly or a spread of two put spreads for a put butterfly, as shown in Chart 13.3.

With regard to a call butterfly, when purchasing it in order to make the butterfly long one will have to buy the 46–50 call spread and at the same time sell the 50–54 call spread. Obviously, the 46–50 call spread will have a higher value than the 50–54 (it is more in the money). To set up a long put butterfly at these strikes one will have to buy the 54–50 put spread, selling the 50–46 put spread.

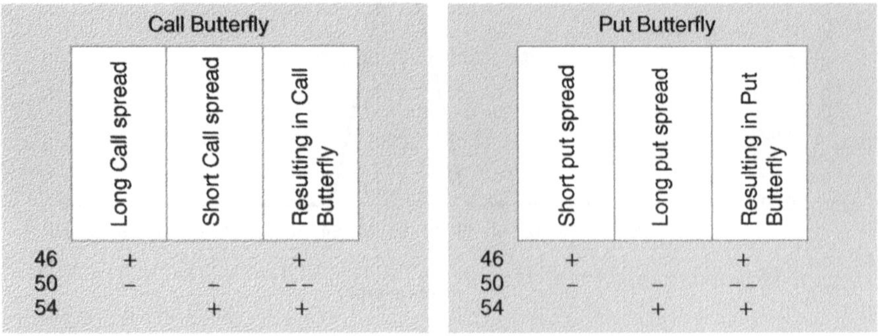

CHART 13.3   A butterfly is the combination of two spreads

The valuation of butterflies will be discussed at a later stage in this paragraph, but by trying to estimate the value, which is in fact the difference between the two call spreads, one can make fairly good estimations when knowing the delta of one put or call spread. It is precisely as explained in the chapter on spreads; it's about how the 46–50 spread relates to the 50–54 spread. So, for instance, when the delta of the 50–54 call spread is 15%, this call spread would be worth $0.60 more than when the Future is $4 higher at 54. When assuming a 46–50 call spread with the Future trading at 50 to have the same value as the 50–54 call spread when the Future is trading at 54, the value being X (There is a slight difference due to the higher at the money level and hence higher straddle value. We will ignore this, however, to keep things simple.), one can deduct that the 50–54 call spread will be $0.60 lower when the Future trades at 50. From this reasoning one could conclude that the fair value for the butterfly here is $0.60. The 46–50 call spread has its value X, the 50–54 call spread will have a value of X minus $4 times 15%, which is X minus $0.60. The secret lies in the delta determination of the respective spreads. From the chapter on delta we know that when the Future is trading at 50, the volatility is 20%, maturity is 1 year, and the at the money straddle has a value of $8. With these parameters, the delta of the 46–50 spread and the 50–54 spread will also be around 15%; thus, the butterfly will have a value of approximately $0.60.

DISTRIBUTION OF THE BUTTERFLY

So far some at the money butterflies have been mentioned, but there will be more butterfly combinations possible which are within the distribution range of the Future towards maturity.

So when, for instance, volatility is 20% for a Future trading at 50 and the maturity 1 year, a 34–36–38 butterfly will have a potential to generate a profit, much less though than the 48–50–52. However, because the first butterfly will fall within the probability distribution, it will accordingly have a value as well.

There are many possible butterflies which have a value, but the maximum value of all the butterflies together is limited. When applying a $2 spread in the strikes for the butterflies and assuming that 30 and 70 are far away from the probability distribution for the Future to end at expiry (a Future trading at 50, volatility at 10% and maturity ¼ year will result in boundaries at 60 and $41\frac{2}{3}$) buying all the butterflies available will result in the following position, as shown in Chart 13.4.

So one starts by buying the 30–32–34 butterfly, then the 32–34–36, and later the 34–36–38 … up to the 66–68–70. The trader accumulating all these butterflies will end up being long a deep in the money call spread (30–32) and being short a far out of the money call spread (68–70). For put butterflies, the trader will end up with a long position in a deep in the money put spread (70–68) and a short position in a far out of the money put spread (32–30). For the call spreads, both the 30 and the 32 strikes fall out of the probability distribution (the lower boundary is $41\frac{2}{3}$) and hence both strikes will have a delta of 100%. As a result, both strikes will only have intrinsic value (no value in the puts of the respective strikes) and thus the trader

Strike

```
30  +                                                              +    long
32  -- +                                                           -    short
34  +  -- +                                                        flat
36     +  -- +                                                     flat
38        +  -- +                                                  flat
40           +  -- +                                               flat
42              +  -- +                                            flat
44                 +  -- +                                         flat
46                    +  -- +                                      flat
48                       +  -- +                                   flat
50                          +  -- +                                flat
52                             +  -- +                             flat
54                                +  -- +                          flat
56                                   +  -- +                       flat
58                                      +  -- +                    flat
60                                         +  -- +                 flat
62                                            +  -- +              flat
64                                               +  -- +           flat
66                                                  +  -- + flat
68                                                     +  -- -    short
70                                                        +  +    long
```

CHART 13.4   All the butterflies from 30 to 70

Strike

```
0    +                                                             +    long
2    -- +                                                          -    short
..   +  -- +                                                       flat
..      +  -- +                                                    flat
..         +  -- +                                                 flat
40            +  -- +                                              flat

42               +  -- +                                           flat
44                  +  -- +                                        flat
46                     +  -- +                                     flat
48                        +  -- +                                  flat
50                           +  -- +                               flat
52                              +  -- +                            flat
54                                 +  -- +                         flat
56                                    +  -- +                      flat
58                                       +  -- +                   flat
60                                          +  -- +                flat
..                                             +  -- +             flat
..                                                +  -- +          flat
..                                                   +  -- +       flat
∞-2                                                     +  --  -   short
∞                                                          +  +    long
```

CHART 13.5   All the butterflies from 0 to infinity

will be long a spread which has a value of $2. The 68 and 70 calls are beyond the upper boundary of $60 and will thus both have a delta of 0% and zero value. The 68–70 spread will as a result have no value. For the put butterfly it will be obviously the other way around, the 70 and 68 puts will both have a delta of 100% and thus the spread a value of $2 and both the 32 and 30 put have no delta and no value: consequently, the out of the money put spread will have no value.

Even when one accumulates all the butterflies from 0 to infinity, as shown in Chart 13.5, where the owner of all the call butterflies has a long 0–2 call spread position and a short infinity–2–infinity call spread position, where the owner of the put butterflies will have a long infinity–infinity–2 put spread position and a short 2–0 put spread, the value of all butterflies together in a distribution is the strike differential (in these cases $2).

So, no matter how many butterflies one takes, the maximum value of them all together is the strike differential as applied in the strategy, as shown in Chart 13.6.

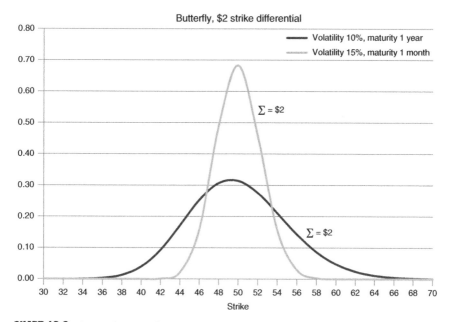

CHART 13.6 Butterflies with $2 strike differential

BOUNDARIES OF THE BUTTERFLY

Whenever a call option has reached a delta of 100%, its value is only intrinsic. Combining that with the fact that a butterfly is the structuring of two call spreads, it will be clear where the boundaries of the butterfly are. With a Future at 50, volatility at 10% and maturity 3 months, the 40 call (the lower boundary is $41\frac{1}{2}$) will have a 100% delta. So any strike which is $41\frac{2}{3}$ or lower will have 100% delta for the calls (0% delta for the puts). So, when looking at a 36–38 call spread, at these parameters, it is clear that it should trade at $2 (put spread at zero, box being worth $2); the same can be said for the 38–40 call spread: both strikes at intrinsic value will generate a value of the call spread at $2. When setting up a 36–38–40 call butterfly, one buys the 36–38 call spread at $2 and sells the 38–40 call spread at $2 – a zero value butterfly.

When setting up this butterfly with puts, one buys the 40–38 put spread at zero (theoretical value). The calls in both strikes have a delta of 100%, implying that the puts have a zero delta and hence no value anymore. And next one sells the 38–36 put spread at zero (theoretical value) – also a zero value butterfly.

As a conclusion it can be said that whenever the delta of an option has reached 100%/–100% or 0% the value of the butterfly has reached the zero level – it simply has become worthless. Since the boundaries for the delta are the boundaries for the gamma, vega and theta, it also applies for the butterfly. When comparing a distribution of butterflies with, for instance, the vega it will look as follows:

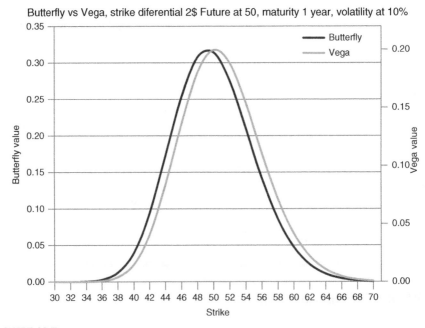

CHART 13.7   Butterfly versus vega

Chart 13.7 is slightly skewed on the downside; this has to do with the uneven distribution for the at the money delta (call has a higher delta than 50%), which will even have a bigger impact for the value of the butterflies when the volatility is higher (or time to maturity is longer, see the chapter on Delta). However, when the delta for the calls has reached 100% or 0% and –100% or 0% for the puts, the butterfly will have no value anymore, just like the other Greeks.

METHOD FOR ESTIMATING AT THE MONEY BUTTERFLY VALUES

It has been mentioned that the value of the butterfly could be calculated by comparing the two different spreads at different Future levels and then applying the delta for the spread for calculating how the value would have been at the actual Future level. This approach is equivalent to multiplying the delta of one of the two call or put spreads by the strike differential of the butterfly. So, for at the money butterflies the following could be computed according to this calculation method:

TABLE 13.4

48–50–52 Butterfly	Vol 10%, maturity 1 year	Vol 20%, maturity 1 year	Vol 10%, maturity 3 months	Vol 20%, maturity 3 months
ATM straddle	$4	$8	$2	$4
Delta differential per call spread	15%	7.5%	30%	15%
Strike differential	2	2	2	2
Butterfly value	$0.30	$0.15	$0.60	$0.30

Please note that if the strike differential doubles, the delta differential will also double, resulting in a butterfly which is four times as big as the former one, as shown below in Table 13.5.

TABLE 13.5

46–50–54 Butterfly	Vol 10%, maturity 1 year	Vol 20%, maturity 1 year	Vol 10%, maturity 3 months	Vol 20%, maturity 3 months
ATM straddle	$4	$8	$2	$4
Delta differential per call spread	30%	15%	NA	30%
Strike differential	4	4	4	4
Butterfly value	$1.20	$0.6	NA	$1.20

This method will only be applicable for at the money options, up to 1 straddle in or out of the money. Therefore, this method cannot result in a fair estimate where the at the money straddle has a value of $2 and the strike differential for the butterfly is $4 (as shown in Table 13.5).

ESTIMATING OUT OF THE MONEY BUTTERFLY VALUES

Having shown in Chart 13.7 that the butterfly has a distribution comparable to that of vega (and thus gamma and theta) some more information can be derived from its distribution. Just like the linearisation of the charts of the Greeks, one could also linearise the butterfly chart in the same way: it will, however, be much less precise, as shown in Chart 13.8. When applying 3½ straddles for the way up and 2½ straddles for the way down a $2 strike differential butterfly distribution, with the Future trading at 50, volatility at 10% and maturity 1 year, will look as follows:

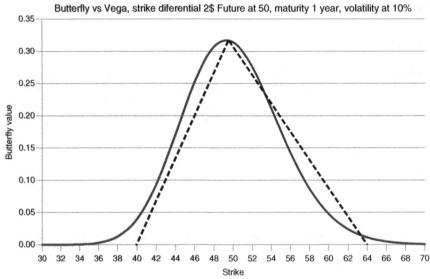

CHART 13.8 Linearisation of the butterfly distribution

TABLE 13.6

Butterfly	Linearisation method	Black Scholes model
38–40–42	0.00	0.04
40–42–44	0.06	0.09
42–44–46	0.12	0.17
44–46–48	0.18	0.25
46–48–50	0.24	0.31
48–50–52	0.30	0.31
50–52–54	0.26	0.28
52–54–56	0.21	0.21
54–56–58	0.17	0.14
56–58–60	0.13	0.09
58–60–62	0.09	0.05
60–62–64	0.04	0.02
62–64–66	0.00	0.01

Linearisation in the same way as the Greeks will generate the butterfly values of Table 13.6. The outcomes are not very reliable, mainly caused by the fact that the butterfly distribution is "somewhat" skewed on the way down (especially at high volatility levels and longer term maturities); they can merely be used as a very rough indication.

BUTTERFLY IN RELATION TO VOLATILITY

As shown in the paragraph on estimating at the money butterflies, the ATM butterfly will have a linear relationship with volatility and a square root relationship compared to time to maturity, which all has to do with the value of the straddle. This way makes it quite easy to compute the at the money butterflies: however, due to the earlier mentioned uneven delta distribution, the butterfly is fairly skewed on the way down when applying high volatility levels. In a normal market scenario, up to 30% volatility, it will be quite easy to understand the distribution of the butterfly.

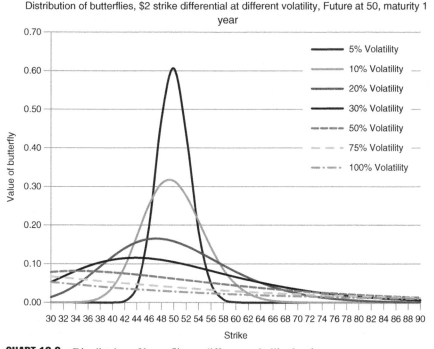

CHART 13.9 Distribution of butterflies at different volatility levels

Chart 13.9 clearly shows that, when at a normal market volatility scenario, when volatility quadruples from for instance 5% to 20%, the butterfly will be four times less valuable. The straddle value will be 4 times as big, causing the delta of the at the money call spreads to be 4 times smaller. With volatilities at 50% and higher the distribution seems to be irrational and makes no sense anymore to come up with any rule of thumb. A simple constitution that the at the money butterfly should be the most expensive butterfly simply doesn't hold anymore.

BUTTERFLY IN RELATION TO TIME TO MATURITY

Where the butterfly has a linear relation compared to volatility level, the relation in terms of time to maturity is a square root function. As discussed previously, the straddle value is the one determining the delta of the two at the money call spreads (together forming the butterfly): when the straddle value doubles the delta of the respective call spread will halve. When taking into account that the value of a straddle will only double when time to maturity is 4 times as big, the square root function should be obvious.

Value of butterfly, $2 strike difference, different maturities, Future at 50, volatility 20%

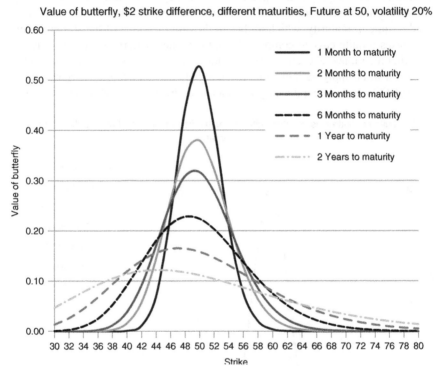

CHART 13.10   Price evolution of a butterfly

Chart 13.10 displays the square root function: the 1 year at the money butterfly, for instance, is two times cheaper than the 3 month butterfly. The fact that at longer time to maturity the butterflies are somewhat skewed for the downside will again have to do with the uneven distribution of the ATM delta. The longer the time to maturity the higher the difference between the ATM call delta compared to the delta of the ATM put.

BUTTERFLY AS A STRATEGIC PLAY

When entering into a butterfly position, it is possible to create great potential with (when long enough before maturity) a small investment. When you own an at the money butterfly you can afford to sit back, relax and wait. In a rangebound market – i.e. one staying close to the initial level where the position was set up – the butterfly will keep increasing in value. This is a great play: where traders may have set up positions that will start bleeding when nothing happens, the butterfly owner will have time on his side.

However, the value of the butterfly increases in value very very slowly. The 48–50–52 butterfly, bought at $0,15, one year before expiry at 20% vol and Future at 50, will have a value of $0.30 at 3 months before expiry. So in 9 months the owner has only earned $0.15 and that will only be the case when the market is still at or around 50. To make real money with a butterfly, one should have a very good view of how the market will develop in the coming year, and a great portion of luck.

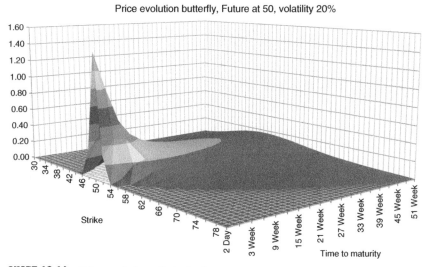

CHART 13.11   Price evolution of a butterfly

Chart 13.11 reflects how slow the price evolution is at an unchanged volatility. Seen from 1 year to maturity, It literally takes months to substantially increase in value. In the last weeks towards expiry the value increase will be much faster. However, when setting up a butterfly strategy at that time, the initial investment is much larger.

THE GREEKS OF A BUTTERFLY

Delta

In principle, a butterfly has hardly any delta when being set up/structured. When the delta distribution looks like the trendline (see Chart 13.12) then any butterfly would have no delta: it has a small delta, but almost negligible. When the market starts to move, a butterfly will gain or lose deltas: for instance, when the market moves away from the strikes, the butterfly will lose in value: hence it must have a delta (being the first derivative of the value).

When coming very close to expiry (a few days) and the strikes being around the Future level, the butterfly will gain or lose deltas rapidly. At expiry the legs for the call butterfly obviously have a delta of 0 or 100% and for the put butterfly 0 or −100% and the aggregate delta of the butterfly can become very large (up to 100% or −100%).

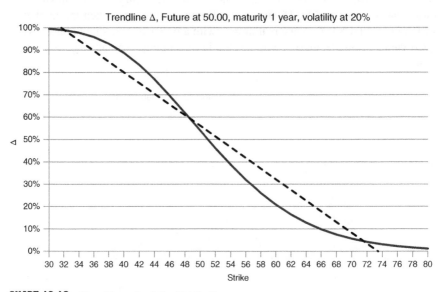

CHART 13.12   Trendline of a delta distribution

Gamma

When setting up a butterfly, initially there is no delta position. However, when the market starts moving the delta suddenly starts to change. Without a delta position, a butterfly cannot increase or decrease in value. At inception the butterfly hardly has a delta, but in order to be able to change in value it must have a dynamic delta position when the market changes. Hence the butterfly must have gamma, visualised:

The gamma of every butterfly will have the same shape as that depicted in Chart 13.13. (Obviously the Future level can have completely different levels, depending on the strikes of course, but also on the volatility and the time to maturity: it is only useful to remember the shape.) The 40–50–60 butterfly below has a short gamma at around the 50 level. When entering in a 40–50 call spread or put spread, it creates a gamma short position when short the 50 strike with the market in that area. The same counts for the 50–60 spread. So, around the 50 level for the Future the owner of the butterfly will be double gamma short compared to being gamma long around the 40 and the 60 level for the Future.

It might look odd to see the gamma around 40 being quite a bit higher than the gamma around 60; but, as explained in the chapter on gamma, if the atm level is low an option creates more gamma (when being at the money a 50 call or put with the

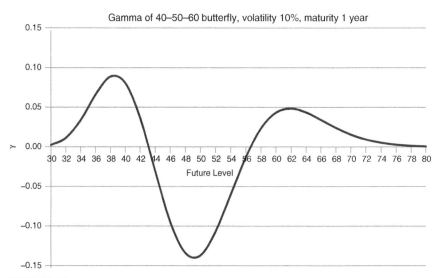

CHART 13.13 Gamma distribution of the 40–50–60 butterfly

Future at 50 will have twice as much gamma as the 100 call or put with the Future at 100, all with the same volatility).

When volatility changes, all will change accordingly; lower volatility results in higher gamma and vice versa. It's the same with time to maturity: the shorter time to maturity the more gamma an option will generate.

When entering into a long butterfly position, it is extremely important to know: be careful with gamma hedging when exactly in the middle towards expiry (hence large gamma short position). When the market is fairly volatile many people have lost money through hedging a negative gamma, whilst being exactly right (when being close to expiry) in picking the right strikes when setting up the butterfly strategy.

Vega

When volatility changes, the value of the butterfly will change accordingly, as shown in Chart 13.14. When at the money, the owner of the butterfly is short vega. So if the volatility increases the strategy loses value: the butterfly gets cheaper. With increasing volatility the probability range will increase and thus (far) out of the money butterflies, initially being worthless, will suddenly generate a value. Since all the butterflies together have a value equivalent to the strike differential, the more at the money butterflies will have to decrease in value.

With volatility decreasing, the probability distribution will narrow and out of the money butterflies, initially with a (small) value will now become worthless. For all the remaining butterflies, that still have value, the value should increase to a level where all of them together have the value of the strike differential again.

In time the vega of the strategy will decrease, according to the vega time relationship for an option in general.

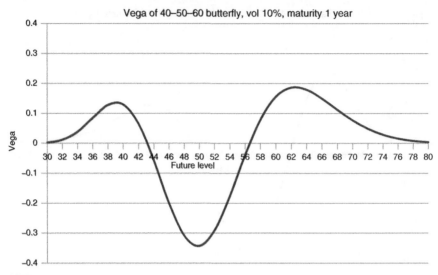

CHART 13.14 Vega distribution of a 40–50–60 butterfly

Theta

The price evolution of a butterfly is a direct result of the theta of the short options minus the theta of the long options. As shown in the 3d Chart 13.11 it starts with a slow evolution in price, which accelerates towards expiry.

In Chart 13.15, it is shown that the theta at the money (around 50 level) is positive, creating the increase in value in time. With a changing market towards one of the two long strikes theta will become negative, the butterfly is losing its value.

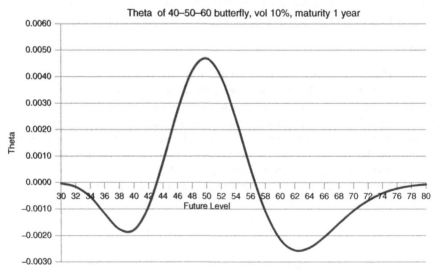

CHART 13.15 Theta distribution of a 40–50–60 butterfly

The theta around 40 is slightly smaller than the theta around the 60 level. As explained in the chapter on theta, an option which is at the money, with volatility and time to expiry being the same, has a higher theta when having a higher strike price. A 30 call or put (being at the money and other parameters being the same) will have half the theta of the 60 strike.

STRADDLE–STRANGLE OR THE "IRON FLY"

The 45–50–55 call butterfly will have the same value as the 45–50–55 put butterfly. As mentioned earlier in this chapter, where there is a difference in value there is an arbitrage opportunity.

Calls	Strike	Puts		Calls	Strike	Puts
+	45				45	+
− −	50		is equivalent to		50	− −
+	55				55	+

Also when buying the Future (100%) with it, according to put/call parity the 45 put will be equivalent to the 45 call, hence:

Calls	Strike	Puts		Calls	Strike	Puts
+	45				45	+
− −	50		is equivalent to	− −	50	
+	55			+	55	
					+1 Future	

The 45 put + 1 Future is the same as the 45 call in terms of Greeks, in terms of value it has a value which is $5 less than the 45 call (which had a $5, or strike differential, intrinsic value), with the Future trading at 50.

In order to create one short 50 put option from one short 50 call option one will need to sell 1 Future, according to put/call parity. When doing so, the initial 45–50–55 butterfly will look as follows:

Calls	Strike	Puts		Calls	Strike	Puts
	45	+			45	+
−	50	−	is equivalent to	−	50	−
+	55			+	55	
	+1 Future				~~+1 Future~~	
	−1 Future				~~−1 Future~~	

As a conclusion, the call or put butterfly is the same as selling the straddle and buying the strangle:

Calls	Strike	Puts		Calls	Strike	Puts
+	45				45	+
$--$	50		is equivalent to	$-$	50	$-$
+	55			+	55	
					$-$ Strike Difference	

As mentioned above when comparing straddle strangle with the butterfly, straddle/strangle $-$ \$5 is equivalent to the butterfly.

When the 50 call is worth \$5 (\$10 in the straddle, around 25% vol when maturity is 1 year), the delta of a 45–50 spread is around 15%; hence the butterfly could be valued around \$0.75. The option values are approximately:

Calls	Strike	Puts
7.65	45	2.65
5.00	50	5.00
3.10	55	8.10

When looking at the call butterfly, the value is: $7.65 + 3.10 - 2 \times 5.00 = 10.75 - 10.00 = 0.75$.

The put butterfly will/must have the same value: $2.65 + 8.10 - 2 \times 5.00 = 10.75 - 10.00 = 0.75$.

When converting the 50 call into a 50 put, the value will not change. However, when converting the 45 call into the 45 put, \$5 (7.65–2.65) will be "lost". So, when calculating the straddle/strangle (45 put, 55 call) firstly one has to deduct \$5 (being the strike differential) and then to add the butterfly a value of 0.75 to come up with a value of 5.75 for the strangle.

For the "other" strangle (45 call 55 put), \$5 will need to be added plus the butterfly of 0.75 making it \$15.75.

This method could make it quite easy to come up with strangle values. When the straddle (atm) is known, one could estimate the value of the butterfly, then valuing the strangle (otm put, otm call) by just deducting the strike differential from the straddle and adding the butterfly value.

So, when at unknown volatility and unknown maturity, the 50 straddle is quoted \$7.50, the 45 (put)/55 (call) strangle could be set at \$7.50–\$5 strike differential, being \$2.50 plus the butterfly value. When at this straddle value the 45–50 call spread (or put spread) delta will be estimated at 20%, thus creating a \$1 butterfly: the strangle should have a value of \$3.50 then.

Just for a double check on the model; when applying 18.75% volatility and a maturity of 1 year, the straddle has a value of 7.47 where the 45–55 strangle has a value of 3.50. Another strong tool!

CHAPTER 14

Strategies

CALL

The buyer of the 50 call is aiming for the market to increase in order to generate a profit. For each dollar higher than 50 at expiry he will earn $1, as shown below in Chart 14.1. The initial investment will need to be deducted. He is long gamma and vega, losing value because of the time decay. However, he is not bothered by the Greeks. His sheer interest is the Future moving up to higher levels. Obviously,

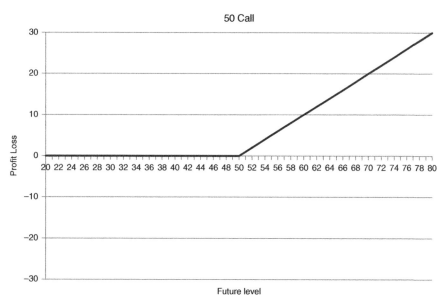

CHART 14.1 50 Call at expiry

when selling it without a hedge the trader must have a strong view on the market,
The Future will have to trade either sideways or towards lower levels.

When the delta of the option is hedged, it is a completely different story. The
buyer, when being long the option, has an exposure in gamma, vega and theta. He
must have the conviction that volatility is too low valued or he believes in a trend
(in either direction) in which he applies a wide hedging strategy on the back of his
gamma. He will be bleeding when the market is sideways. The seller must see the
volatility as being overprized and at the same time believe that the market is sideways.
When the market is trending he will have difficulties in preventing losses on his position. The safest thing for him will be to apply a tight(-ish) gamma hedging strategy.

One should be aware that when the call is hedged for a delta of 50% one actually buys a straddle. When owning 10,000 calls and having hedged them with 5,000
Futures (selling the Futures), the following position has been created:

5,000 calls

5,000 calls – 5,000 Futures = 5,000 puts (a synthetic put has been created)

A portfolio consisting out of 5,000 straddles

PUT

For the put, as shown in Chart 14.2, obviously resulting in a profit when the market
would drop, everything is kind of similar as for the call. When hedged, it will also
result in a straddle position.

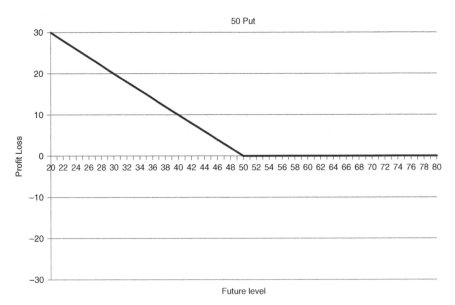

CHART 14.2   50 Put at expiry

CALL SPREAD

The call spread consists of two legs, one strike being long and another strike being short. The two options will have the same maturity and their volumes are equal. Chart 14.3 depicts the 50–55 call spread. At expiry the structure starts to generate a profit above 50 up to the 55 level. At 55, the maximum profit of the structure will be reached. At any level above 55 the net option position will be flat. The initial investment will need to be deducted.

The buyer of the call spread could be mildly bullish and therefore selling the 55 call, but quite often a spread is being set up to mitigate the initial investment. When the market makes a modest move up, the call spread performs, percentagewise, much better than just buying the 50 call. Obviously when there is a large move, just buying the 50 call will be the better performer.

When not being hedged, the buyer is indifferent with regards to the Greeks. He is purely aiming for a profit when the market goes up. When hedged he will be gamma and vega long from below 50 up to around 52 and he will be vega short and gamma short at any level higher than approximately 52. When a market is characterised by lower volatility levels when it goes up, this is a logical position. The danger is only there when the market is sideways: the trader will be bleeding on the time decay and will probably lose as well on volatility, which is under pressure.

Some markets however are characterised by increasing volatilty when the market moves up. If that is the case, the trader will either be bleeding on time decay, when the market is rangebound, and will probably lose as well on volatility, which

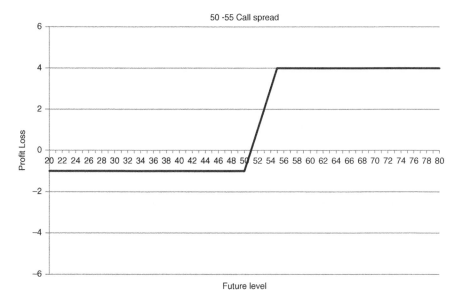

CHART 14.3 50–55 Call spread at expiry

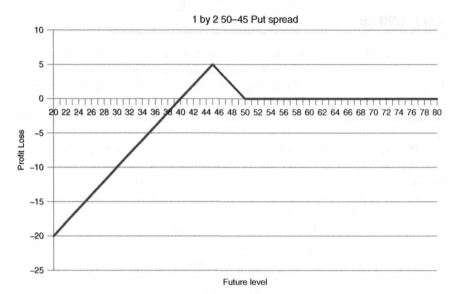

CHART 14.4 1 by 2 50-45 ratio put spread at expiry

is under pressure, or will lose when the market will go up in combination with higher volatility and larger intraday moves (i.e. he will get hurt by short gamma and short vega). When the market experiences a sharp drop, the position will generate a modest profit on the back of gamma and vega. The point, however, is that the market ran away from his strike. Therefore his gamma and vega positions are already heavily reduced.

Another reason for trading spreads is trading the skew. As shown in the chapter on skew, skew is the application of different volatility levels for different strikes. For reasons of protection traders could bid up prices (and thus pay a higher volatility) for out of the money options – calls as well as puts (volatility smile). The buyer of the call spread might expect the steepness of the skew to flatten; this is a way to structure a short position in skew.

When setting up call spreads or put spreads one will have to consider first what the impact of the Greeks will be and how the characteristics of the market, in terms of volatility, are at higher and lower levels.

RATIO SPREAD

A ratio spread is a spread where the volume of the two legs are different, the ratio can vary. The call spread or put spread, when the market is trading at the short strike, will result in a net flat option position and therefore, at higher levels for the call and lower levels for the put, the profit will remain stable. With ratio spreads, the profit being generated at a certain level can quickly evaporate and turn into a large loss. Chart 14.4 depicts a 1 by 2, 50–45 put spread, being long once the 50 put and short twice the 45 put. At 45 the 50 put has a value of $5, below 45 the position is net short one put option resulting in a zero profit at the 40 level turning into a loss below 40. In the chapter on spreads an easy way to determine breakeven levels for ratio spreads was discussed. The ratio spread is quite often applied to mitigate the initial investment, but also, when having market scenarios in mind, it can be a perfect instrument for maximising profit towards predetermined/anticipated levels in the market.

When not being hedged, the structure works beautifully when the market, towards expiry, would slowly move from the long strike towards the short strike; the trader is not being bothered by the Greeks. When the move is swift and there is still a long time to maturity this position can become nerve-wracking. Firstly, the market is trading around the short strike: it could easily move further and therefore cause losses. Secondly the combination entails a vega short position (the bigger the ratio, the larger the vega short position), when the first move is violent, there's a good chance that the volatility will increase as well.

STRADDLE

The straddle is the combination of trading the call and put together, as shown in Chart 14.5 (or a hedged call option or a hedged put option as shown before). Straddles are expensive and heavyweight: they generate the most gamma, vega and theta. When trying to buy Greeks, straddles could be ideal: however, one should be careful and consider what would happen with his option position when the market is rangebound. The heavy time decay can become quite costly. An alternative could be buying strangles instead, being out of the money calls in combination with out of the money puts.

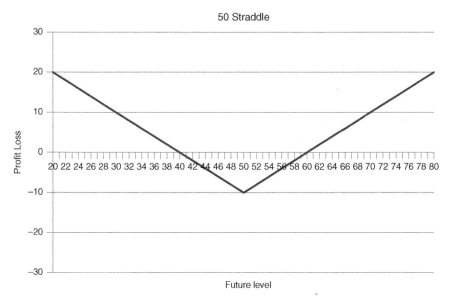

CHART 14.5   50 Straddle at expiry

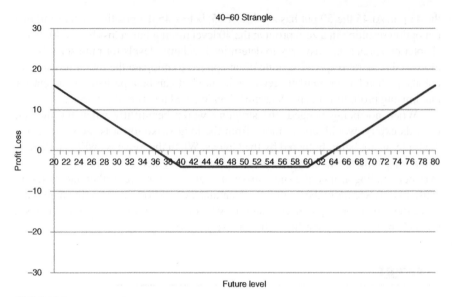

CHART 14.6   40–60 Strangle at expiry

STRANGLE

A strangle is a combination of an out of the money call and an out of the money put (when one of the legs is at the money it is also called a strangle). Chart 14.6 depicts the combination of a 60 call and a 40 put. The strangle is obviously much cheaper than the straddle and it generates less gamma and vega and hence theta. If the market is rangebound there will be less bleeding on time decay and when the market starts moving (in any direction) the position's gamma and vega will start increasing; as opposed to the straddle, where the Greeks will decrease when the market moves away from the strike.

A strangle is also a typical instrument for trading the skew.

COLLAR (RISK REVERSAL, FENCE)

The collar, sometimes called risk reversal or fence, is a combination where one buys a put and sells a call at a higher strike (or selling a put and buying a call). Quite often collars (buying the puts selling the calls) are traded by natural longs: for instance, producers, protecting their output against losses when prices are going down. Producers are net long and hence entering in such a structure makes sense. Setting up collars, being long the calls and short the puts, is often done by the natural shorts: for instance, aviation companies which are net short of fuel. Many collars are structured in such a way that there is no initial cost, prices of calls equal to those of the puts – so-called zero cost collars.

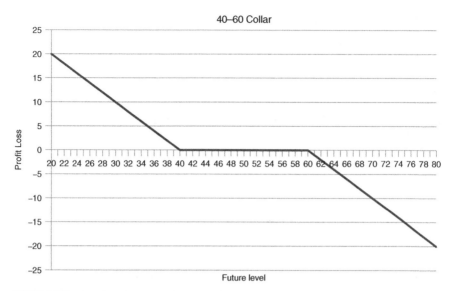

CHART 14.7 40-60 Collar at expiry

A trader running an unhedged collar position is actually betting on a move in a certain direction; he is not bothered by the Greeks.

The trader hedging the collar should again be aware how the characteristics of the market are. When setting up the structure depicted in Chart 14.7, he is long out of the money puts and short out of the money calls. Do the specific market conditions justify such a position?

A collar is very useful for setting up skew spreads.

GAMMA PORTFOLIO

When running a gamma long position, the most complicated thing is to apply the right hedging strategy which will optimise the profit through the scalps and hedges on the back of the gamma portfolio. According to market expectation, its volatility and intraday behaviour … a strategy is set up somewhere between the tight and the wide hedging strategy, as briefly discussed in the chapter on gamma.

In the following examples we will discuss how different hedging strategies could be applied and also what the implications with regards to the P&L will be. 3 Monte Carlo (simulation method) scenarios are created at 20% volatility: a Future which initially trades at 50 will enter into a trend in scenario 1; it will come up and then retrace sharply in scenario 2 and it will be sideways trading in scenario 3. Further, the cost of theta will be added in order to make it comparable with the real trading world.

GAMMA HEDGING STRATEGIES BASED ON MONTE CARLO SCENARIOS

In these examples 45 trading days – i.e., 9 weeks – are computed (5 trading days per week). The trader will have a flat delta position at the start of the trading horizon and a gamma of 2,000 (deltas) per dollar (which is evenly distributed over the whole trading area). The cost of Theta for his gamma is $275 per day, totalling $17,325 for 63 days (i.e. 9 weeks times 7 days).

There are 5 different hedging strategies:

Each 50 cents up or down, the trader will be long or short 1,000 deltas, he will hedge all of these deltas instantly and will wait for the next level 50 cents higher or lower and will hedge again all of his deltas. This trader will do an awful lot of hedging (with associated costs, which are not taken into account here).

The trader will wait with hedging until he is at least 2,000 deltas long or short (being 1 time his gamma). He will then hedge by the full dollar. So if the market starts at 50 he will buy 2,000 deltas at 48, or will sell 2,000 deltas at 52. If the market trades at 53, he has sold 2,000 at 52 and 2,000 at 53, still 2,000 delta long in his overall delta position. If the market then retraces, at 52 he will have a flat delta position, at 51 he's 2,000 short (so no hedging yet) and at 50 he will start buying again 2,000 deltas. So each time the market is in an up trend he will remain at least 2,000 deltas long; when the trend is down he will remain at least 2,000 deltas short. His maximum long or short position is 4,000 deltas, which is his basis position, combined with the deltas he gained or lost after an additional $1 move (so 2,000 deltas added).

The trader will have the same hedging strategy as under 2, waiting to go long or short 1 times his gamma. However, afterwards he will be hedging his delta exposure each 50 cents instead of $1. His maximum long or short position is 3,000 deltas. His basis position combined with the deltas he gained or lost after an additional half dollar move (so 1,000 deltas added).

The trader will apply a strategy where he remains long or short 2 times his gamma and then will apply a strategy where he hedges every full dollar again as under 2. It might be clear that with this scenario he will not be able to profit from a small retracement. He will need a large retracement in order to reverse the trades he did before.

The trader will let the position run, but every time there is a retracement of 1 dollar, compared to a round dollar level reached, he will sell all his length or will buy back his full short position. So if the market drops 3 dollars to 47 he will be 6,000 deltas short, still not hedging. As soon as the market hits 48, he will buy back his short position at that level, being 4,000 deltas. If the market had gone to 46 first, he would have committed in his strategy to buy back 6,000 deltas at 47. This trader will profit from large retracements or long trends. If the market is sideways trading (e.g. 1 dollar up and then 1 dollar down again, etc) he would perform no hedges and will end up with a losing strategy.

The trader performing strategy 1 is called a tight hedger, and traders at strategy 4 and, especially, 5 are called wide hedgers.

Scenario I

All the hedging done will look as shown in Table 14.1 on the next two pages:

Scenario I was a trending Future, as shown in Chart 14.8, so Strategy 4 and/or 5 were expected to be the winning strategies. This is exactly what happened: strategy 5 made around $17,500 with only two hedges, while at the same time strategy 1 lost around $8,500 (not taking hedging costs into account).

Clearly the tight hedging strategy is performing the worst; it is actually showing a loss. In this specific scenario the tight hedging strategy doesn't look appropriate, it seems to be eligible for the trader who would have been short gamma. When being short gamma, the trader still would have made money (the loss of the gamma long trader is the profit of the gamma short trader), even when the market entered into a trend.

There is one feature which has not been taken into account, and that is the intraday swings. If there are many intraday moves (between 50 cents and $1), the tight hedger, being long gamma, will clearly earn some additional P&L (the gamma short trader will have to give up some P&L), he will have several positive intraday scalps. But it is very unlikely that he will be able to capture 17 scalps of $500 each (being 34 intraday trades in total; buy and sell) in order to bring his P&L at the zero level.

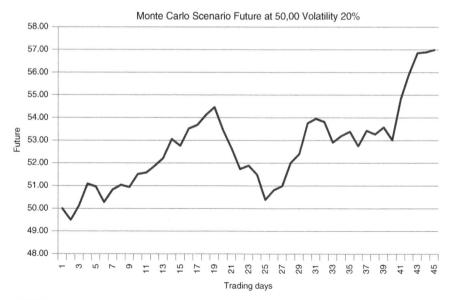

CHART 14.8 Trending Future market

TABLE 14.1

Day	Future	Strategy 1			Strategy 2			Strategy 3			Strategy 4			Strategy 5		
		Hedges	Level	P&L	Hedges	Level	P&L	Hedges	Level	P&L	Hedges	Level	P&L	Hedges	Level	P&L
1	50,00															
2	49,49	1.000	49,50	7.500												
3	50,14	-1.000	50,00	-7.000												
4	51,09	-1.000	50,50	-6.500												
5	50,96	-1.000	51,00	-6.000												
6	50,28	1.000	50,50	6.500												
7	50,83															
8	51,04	-1.000	51,00	-6.000												
9	50,94															
10	51,51	-1.000	51,50	-5.500				-1.000	51,50	-5.500						
11	51,58															
12	51,88															
13	52,21	-1.000	52,00	-5.000	-2.000	52,00	-10.000	-1.000	52,00	-5.000						
14	53,06	-1.000	52,50	-4.500	-2.000	53,00	-8.000	-1.000	52,50	-4.500	-2.000	53,00	-8.000			
15	52,77	-1.000	53,00	-4.000				-1.000	53,00	-4.000						
16	53,53	-1.000	53,50	-3.500				-1.000	53,50	-3.500						
17	53,69															
18	54,12	-1.000	54,00	-3.000	-2.000	54,00	-6.000	-1.000	54,00	-3.000	-2.000	54,00	-6.000			
19	54,47															
20	53,46	1.000	53,50	3.500										-6.000	53,00	-24.000
21	52,65	1.000	53,00	4.000												
22	51,74	1.000	52,50	4.500												
23	51,89	1.000	52,00	5.000												
24	51,49	1.000	51,50	5.500	2.000	51,00	12.000	1.000	51,50	5.500						
25	50,39	1.000	51,00	6.000				1.000	51,00	6.000						

Step	Underlying	Block A qty	Block A strike	Block A P&L	Block B qty	Block B strike	Block B P&L	Block C qty	Block C strike	Block C P&L	Block D qty	Block D strike	Block D P&L	Block E qty	Block E strike	Block E P&L
26	50,81															
27	50,99	1.000	50,50	6.500										2.000	52,00	10.000
28	52,02	−1.000	51,00	−6.000												
29	52,39	−1.000	51,50	−5.500												
30	53,76	−1.000	52,00	−5.000				−1.000	53,50	−3.500				−1.000	53,50	−3.500
31	53,96	−1.000	52,50	−4.500												
32	53,82	−1.000	53,00	−4.000												
33	52,92	−1.000	53,50	−3.500												
34	53,21	1.000	53,00	4.000												
35	53,39															
36	52,75	−1.000	53,50	−3.500												
37	53,44	1.000	53,00	4.000												
38	53,28	−1.000	53,50	−3.500												
39	53,58	−1.000	54,00	−3.000				−1.000	54,00	−3.000						
40	53,02	−1.000	54,50	−2.500				−1.000	54,50	−2.500						
41	54,83	−1.000	55,00	−2.000	−2.000	54,00	−6.000	−1.000	55,00	−2.000						
42	55,95	−1.000	55,50	−1.500	−2.000	55,00	−4.000	−1.000	55,50	−1.500	−2.000	55,00	−4.000			
43	56,86	−1.000	56,00	−1.000	−2.000	56,00	−2.000	−1.000	56,00	−1.000	−2.000	56,00	−2.000			
44	56,90	−1.000	56,50	−500				−1.000	56,50	−500	−2.000	57,00	0			
45	57,00	−1.000	57,00	0	−2.000	57,00	0	−1.000	57,00	0						
	P&L Hedges			**−40.000**			**−24.000**			**−28.000**			**−20.000**			**−14.000**
	P&L Position			**49.000**			**49.000**			**49.000**			**49.000**			**49.000**
	Theta			**−17.325**			**−17.325**			**−17.325**			**−17.325**			**−17.325**
	Total P&L			**−8.325**			**7.675**			**−3.675**			**11.675**			**17.675**

TABLE 14.2

Day	Future	Strategy 1			Strategy 2			Strategy 3			Strategy 4			Strategy 5		
		Hedges	Level	P&L	Hedges	Level	P&L	Hedges	Level	P&L	Hedges	Level	P&L	Hedges	Level	P&L
1	50,00															
2	49,66															
3	50,75	–1.000	50,50	.500												
4	51,20	–1.000	51,00	1.000												
5	51,47															
6	50,74															
7	50,61															
8	50,03	1.000	50,50	.500												
9	51,17	–1.000	51,00	1.000												
10	52,40	–1.000	51,50	1.500	2.000	52,00	4.000	–1.000	51,50	1.500						
11	52,58	–1.000	52,00	2.000				–1.000	52,00	2.000						
12	51,75	–1.000	52,50	2.500												
13	51,74	1.000	52,00	–2.000												
14	52,25															
15	51,84															
16	52,92	–1.000	52,50	2.500				–1.000	52,50	2.500						
17	52,41															
18	52,67															
19	52,23	–1.000	53,00	3.000	–2.000	53,00	6.000	–1.000	53,00	3.000	–2.000	53,00	6.000			
20	53,88	–1.000	53,50	3.500				–1.000	53,50	3.500						
21	53,81															
22	53,85															
23	54,69	–1.000	54,00	4.000	–2.000	54,00	8.000	–1.000	54,00	4.000	–2.000	54,00	8.000			
24	53,84	–1.000	54,50	4.500				–1.000	54,50	4.500						

#	Price	Qty	Px	P&L	Qty	Px	P&L	Qty	Px	P&L	Qty	Px	P&L
25	53,57	1.000	54,00	−4.000									
26	53,03	1.000	53,50	−3.500									
27	53,24	1.000	53,00	−3.000									
28	52,24	1.000	52,50	−2.500							18.000	53,00	−6.000
29	51,25	1.000	52,00	−2.000				1.000	52,00	2.000			
30	52,32	1.000	51,50	−1.500				1.000	51,50	1.500			
31	51,30	1.000	52,00	2.000									
32	51,07	1.000	51,50	−1.500									
33	51,57												
34	52,18	−1.000	52,00	2.000									
35	51,47	1.000	51,50	−1.500									
36	50,88	1.000	51,00	−1.000	2.000	51,00	−2.000	1.000	51,00	−1.000			
37	51,09	1.000	50,50	−500									
38	50,18							1.000	50,50	−500			
39	50,02												
40	49,54	1.000	50,00	0	2.000	50,00	0	1.000	50,00	0			
41	50,08												
42	50,27												
43	49,89												
44	49,73												
45	50,00												

P&L Hedges	**6.500**	**16.000**	**16.000**	**16.000**	**−14.000**	**18.000**
Theta	−17.325	−17.325	−17.325	−17.325	−17.325	−17.325
Total P&L	−10.825	−1.325	−1.325	−1.325	−3.325	675

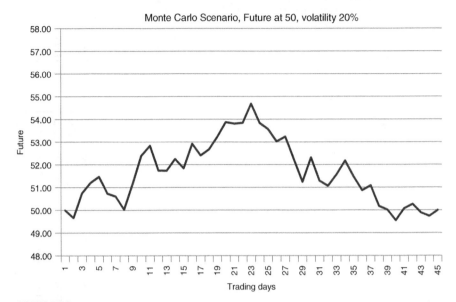

CHART 14.9   Retracing Future market

Scenario II

All the hedging done will look as shown in Table 14.2 on the two previous pages:

Hedging strategy 1 performs the worst (a loss of nearly $11,000); however, there is actually no strategy which is generating a (noticeable) positive P&L. Even though the market had a fairly large move up followed by a "sharp" retracement, as shown in Chart 14.9, it still didn't suffice for any hedging strategy to generate a decent P&L.

Scenario III

All the hedging done will look as shown in Table 14.3 on the next two pages:

A sideways market, as shown in Chart 14.10, has a devastating effect on the P&L for every strategy. Although there might be another hedging strategy which could earn some profits, in principle these kinds of market are absolutely not eligible for running a gamma long portfolio.

As a conclusion, after having studied these 5 hedging strategies in 3 market scenarios, the following could be said with regards to these specific market environments:

Strategy 1 performs badly under all circumstances. There is no winning market scenario for this strategy. Although the trader performing this strategy will be able to scalp some intraday moves, he'll never be able to recoup the time decay. In fact this hedging strategy is more applicable to the gamma short trader. Even with a fairly large trend he will make some money by hedging his gamma short position in a tight way.

Strategy 2 is performing quite ok, in the trending market its quite easy to make money. However, when the market behaves in a sideways manner, it is more

TABLE 14.3

Day	Future	Strategy 1 Hedges	Level	P&L	Strategy 2 Hedges	Level	P&L	Strategy 3 Hedges	Level	P&L	Strategy 4 Hedges	Level	P&L	Strategy 5 Hedges	Level	P&L
1	50,00															
2	49,71															
3	48,53	1,000	49,50	500												
4	49,87	1,000	49,00	1,000												
5	49,79	−1,000	49,50	−500												
6	49,31															
7	49,32															
8	50,12	−1,000	50,00	0												
9	51,16															
10	50,04															
11	51,23	−1,000	50,50	500												
12	51,42	−1,000	51,00	1000												
13	50,90															
14	50,62															
15	50,47	1,000	50,50	−500												
16	50,95															
17	51,24	−1,000	51,00	1000												
18	51,46															
19	52,12	−1,000	51,50	1,500	−2,000	52,00	4,000	−1,000	51,50	1,500						
20	51,67	−1,000	52,00	2,000				−1,000	52,00	2,000				−2000	51,00	2,000
21	50,66	1,000	51,50	−1,500												
22	50,20	1,000	51,00	−1000												
23	50,53	−1,000	50,50	−500												
24	51,04	−1,000	51,00	−1,000												
25	50,47	1,000	50,50	−500												
26	50,05															

(Continued)

TABLE 14.3 (Continued)

Day	Future	Strategy 1	P&L	Strategy 2	P&L	Strategy 3	P&L	Strategy 4	P&L	Strategy 5	P&L
27	50,44										
28	49,73	50,00 1,000	0								
29	49,79										
30	50,00										
31	49,33	49,50 1,000	500			1,000 49,50	500		500		
32	49,05										
33	49,68										
34	48,07	49,00 1,000	1,000	2,000 49,00	2,000	1,000 49,00	1,000		1,000		
35	48,51	48,50 1,000	1,500			1,000 48,50	1,000		1,500		
36	48,07										
37	47,93	48,00 1,000	2,000	2,000 48,00	4,000	1,000 48,00	1,000		2,000		
38	48,01	48,50 −1,000	−1,500								
39	48,66	49,00 −1,000	1,000								
40	49,31	49,50 −1,000	−500							4000 49,00	4.000
41	50,10	50,00 −1,000	0								
42	50,08	50,50 −1,000	500								
43	50,86	51,00 −1,000	1,000			−1,000 50,50	−1,000		500		
44	51,02	50,50 1,000	−500	51,00 −2,000	2,000	−1,000 51,00	−1,000		1,000	−2000 50,00	
45	50,00	50,00 1,000	0							50,00	0
		P&L Hedges	7.000	P&L Hedges	12.000	P&L Hedges	10.000	P&L Hedges	0	P&L Hedges	6.000
		Theta	−17.325	Theta	−17.325	Theta	−17.325	Theta	−17.325	Theta	−17.325
		Total P&L	−10.325	Total P&L	−5.325	Total P&L	−7.325	Total P&L	−17.325	Total P&L	−11.325

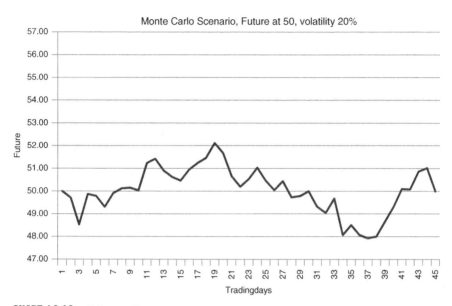

CHART 14.10   Sideways Future market

and more difficult to earn back the time decay, though it is still the best performer in such a market (be it with a loss).

Strategy 3 is based on strategy 2, because it has a slightly tighter hedging strategy it actually generates less P&L than strategy 2.

Strategy 4 is a big winner in a trending market, but will lose a bit when the market is characterised by retracements and/or mean reversion and is actually a big loser when the market is in a real sideways state.

Strategy 5 is a very good performer when the market is in a trend, will also generate some P&L when the market shows (rather large) retracements but will lose quite a bit in a real sideways market.

Obviously there are many more hedging strategies and also many more market scenarios, but already a fairly large array of possible hedging strategies has been discussed. A gamma long book can truly be a winner when the market is trending. Sideways markets however are actually not eligible for (large) gamma long positions. In the end it is very hard, if not impossible, to recoup the time decay.

Another problem arises, especially for the tight hedgers, when the market makes a sharp move during the day. The tight hedgers will far too early start hedging their gamma; just think of the example that was mentioned under paragraph hedging the gamma in the chapter on gamma. The gamma long trader not doing anything from 50 to 54 in the Future will realise a $20,000 profit during that day (no theta taken into account) while the tight hedger will only make $5,000 when hedging every full dollar and only $2,500 when hedging every 50¢. When compared with the applied theta, this is a substantial difference in P&L.

Another practical disaster is "missing the trade". The wide hedger could have missed selling his deltas at 54 and is now facing 50 in the Future again without any hedges.

A tight hedging strategy could be advised for gamma short plays; entering a gamma long position could be best done when expecting a fairly large move. The most applicable hedging strategy there is the wide hedging strategy.

The only way to generate a good P&L with a long gamma position and a tight hedging strategy is when the Future moves much more than the implied volatility would justify: the intraday moves become bigger and bigger (think of the Parkinson volatility and the stretch as explained in the Volatility chapter) and the trader can perform more intraday scalps on his gamma. In essence this means that the trader is actually profiting from the fact that volatility is increasing.

If that were the case, it actually means that it would not have been necessary to set up a gamma long position. The trader could have set up a position which generates money when the volatility rises. One could enter into a vega long position which generates a P&L when the (implied) volatility increases. This is much better and easier than being right in the direction of the volatility when entering in a gamma long position but not making money with the gamma because of applying the wrong hedging strategy.

SETTING UP A GAMMA POSITION ON THE BACK OF PREVAILING KURTOSIS IN THE MARKET

As mentioned in the introduction, the Black and Scholes model assumes a normal distribution of the (logarithmic) daily returns of the Future. Very often this is not the case. Kurtosis is the measure of the "peakedness" of the distribution in comparison to the normal distribution. The main characteristics for departure from the normal distribution are formed by the height, tails and shoulders of the distribution.

In a formula:

$$Kurtosis = \sum_{i=1}^{n} \frac{(xi - \mu)^4}{(n-1)\sigma^4}$$

where:

- xi stands for the daily logarithmic return of each trading day
- xi = Logarithm (ln) of the Future value on day i divided by the Future value of the day prior to day $xi = \ln\left(\frac{Future\,Value\,on\,day\,i}{Future\,Value\,on\,day\,i-1}\right)$

- μ stands for the average of the daily logarithmic returns and n for the amount of trading days
- σ stands for the standard deviation (and not for volatility)
- $\sum$ is the symbol for Sum, just adding up all the values there are (in this case 1st to the nth value)

EXCESS KURTOSIS

The kurtosis value for the normal distribution is 3 and is corrected by -3 to make the kurtosis of this distribution equal to zero. As a result any deviation from 0 is called excess kurtosis. Distributions with excess kurtosis higher than 0 are called supergaussian distributions (for instance Laplace and Cauchy distribution); they display fat tails. Distributions with excess kurtosis lower than 0 are called subgaussian distributions (for instance Uniform distribution); the distribution is more concentrated around the mean and it doesn't display real tails (returns which are larger than 2 standard deviations).

Distributions with zero excess kurtosis are called mesokurtic, those with positive excess kurtosis are called leptokurtic and those with negative excess kurtosis are called platykurtic.

In Chart 14.11 some distributions are depicted. The kurtosis of the uniform distribution has a kurtosis of -1.2 (platykurtic); the normal distribution is 0 (mesokurtic); Laplace has a kurtosis of 3 and the Cauchy distribution has a kurtosis which is going towards ∞/undefined (both leptokurtic).

Studying the kurtosis helps the trader to get a rough feeling about the market and to see whether the returns of the Future are not normally distributed. When not being normally distributed, there might be a way to benefit from the market situation.

When studying the distributions there may be periods where the underlying is somewhat static: the daily moves, measured in standard deviations, are not that big.

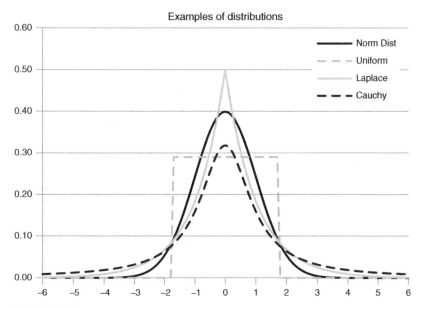

CHART 14.11 Different types of distribution

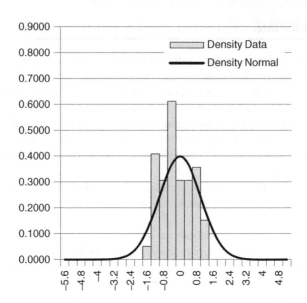

CHART 14.12   Platykurtic distribution

The distribution of the asset looks as if it has a negative kurtosis, it has no fat tails. When it has a platykurtic distribution, one might be able to profit from it.

Chart 14.12 is an example of a platykurtic distribution of the daily returns: it looks a bit like a uniform distribution. All the returns stay within 2 standard deviations and they are centred around the mean, while the normal distribution dictates a few events (5% of all occurrences) where the returns will be more than 2 standard deviations.

BENEFITTING FROM A PLATYKURTIC ENVIRONMENT

The strategy that will benefit from the limitation of (fat) tails is the gamma short strategy. When being gamma short and hedging on a daily basis, one large move could already be very costly. However, when the daily returns stay within certain limits and show no magnitude larger than two standard deviations, the positive theta will outweigh the cost of the negative scalps from the hedges on the gamma short position.

When for instance, with the Future trading at 50, the standard deviation of the daily returns is one dollar (i.e. vol is 32% according to the 16% rule) and the logarithms of the daily returns are normally distributed, one could expect in a year's time a few days where the underlying will shift $3 – i.e. 3 standard deviations – and some days $4 – 4 standard deviations (albeit very rarely). Those days will be very costly for the gamma short trader. One move of three dollars in the Future (three standard deviations) will cost a trader with a 2,500 gamma short position $11,250–9

TABLE 14.4

	Gamma position	Delta new level	Average Delta over range	Amount of Standard deviations	P&L
50–51	−2,500	−2,500	−1,250	1	−1,250
50–52	−2,500	−5,000	−2,500	2	−5,000
50–53	−2,500	−7,500	−3,750	3	−11,250
50–54	−2,500	−10,000	−5,000	4	−20,000

times as much as just one dollar move – and a move of $4 in the Future will cost 16 times as much as just one dollar move in the underlying, as shown in Table 14.4.

These few large shifts in the underlying are incorporated in the distribution and a trader who is short gamma will need to expect and anticipate them. When these moves don't occur the trader will save a considerable amount of money on negative hedging costs and he will have statistically a much higher chance to end up with a positive P&L.

A simplified example might clarify this: suppose that instead of 10 days of a shift of 3 standard deviations and 20 days where the Future doesn't move at all, the gamma short trader experiences 30 days where the Future shifts one standard deviation: in both cases the Future showed 30 returns adding up to 30 standard deviations. Instead of $112,500 (10 times $11,250) the traders hedging costs will be limited to $37,500 (30 times $1,250).

So, as a result, the gamma short trader has benefitted from the fact that the market has shown a platykurtic distribution. Options in these kinds of markets are overprized/too expensive and selling them will increase expected profits.

THE MESOKURTIC MARKET

When the market behaves as in a mesokurtic environment, the trader's cost of hedging should equal his theta. Options are reasonably prized and at maturity his P&L should be zero (in the long run as a statistical average).

THE LEPTOKURTIC MARKET

Obviously when the market is leptokurtic, there will be some extreme shifts in the market in combination with more days when nothing would happen, as shown in Chart 14.13. The extreme shifts will outweigh the days where there is a low volatility environment. There will be more days where the underlying is around the mean, however, a few days showing large shifts in the Future will contribute to the gamma long strategy. The profit of one 6 standard deviation move ($45,000) equals 36 days of theta and will very much contribute to the P&L of the gamma long trader.

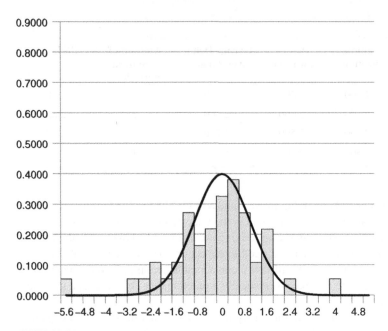

CHART 14.13   Leptokurtic distribution

In other words, one would prefer being short gamma when being in a platykurtic environment and being long gamma when being in a leptokurtic environment. When studying historical data of the distribution of the daily returns of several assets one could find some which have a platykurtic distribution and others having a leptokurtic distribution.

TRANSITION FROM A PLATYKURTIC ENVIRONMENT TOWARDS A LEPTOKURTIC ENVIRONMENT

A platykurtic environment could also apply for a market being stable where traders/investors don't have a real edge. People are less interested in the asset, liquidity/trading volumes are decreasing and therefore the assets kurtosis might become negative. Until it all starts moving again, more and more people will step into the market, trading volumes will explode etc. The distribution will become leptokurtic and gamma long players will be the winners in the market.

One could set up a position, being short gamma at the current stage, creating a gamma long position at the levels where he would anticipate the market to become leptokurtic again. This could be done by setting up spreads.

Chart 14.14 displays a potential scenario for the transition of a platykurtic distribution of a Future towards a mesokurtic and a leptokurtic distribution. Futures within different asset classes might show very different distributions and different

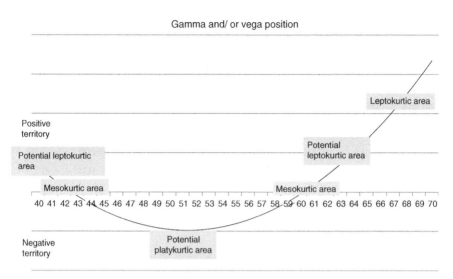

CHART 14.14 Transition from a platykurtic environment towards a leptokurtic environment

transition areas. The trader setting up a kurtosis strategy shall obviously perform a market assessment and consequently will have to estimate where to position the transition from a gamma short position into a gamma long position. In this specific example the trader could for instance sell the 50 strike and buy the 40 and 64 strike.

WRONG HEDGING STRATEGY: KILLERGAMMA

The last topic on gamma hedging will be the killergamma. When a trader has a portfolio of long out of the money options and time to maturity is decreasing he could run into some serious problems/costs due to the gamma hedging of his portfolio. When he is long out of the money calls and the market, coming closer towards maturity, will slowly go towards the strike which he is long, he will hedge his delta according to the Black Scholes model on the way up. At expiry the market is exactly trading at the strike which he is long. In the past weeks he has been selling Futures, in order to create a delta neutral portfolio, on the back of the gamma from the calls, however now, at expiry, the calls no longer generate any delta and every delta he sold on the way up he will have to buy back, resulting in the following P&L as shown in Table 14.5.

So when the trader would have bought 100,000 55 Calls at 10¢ each, his investment will add up to $10,000 plus hedging costs of $71,800 making $81,800 in total, what he would lose in the end, as shown in Table 14.5. He would have been much better off by not performing any delta hedges and so now and then sell some calls on the way up, or just do nothing. Having a long position in out of the money puts and the market going towards the strike when time to maturity narrows will create a similar negative P&L when hedging according to the book/model.

TABLE 14.5

Week	Future	Amount of 55 Calls	Δ of 55 Call	Future/Δ Hedge (vs hedge week before)	Cost of Δ Hedge (vs 55 level)	Value of the 55 Call
1	50	100,000	6.6%	−6,600	−33,000	0.09
2	51	100,000	9.1%	−2,500	−10,000	0.12
3	52	100,000	12.6%	−3,500	−10,500	0.15
4	53	100,000	17.7%	−5,100	−10,200	0.20
5	54	100,000	25.8%	−8,100	−8,100	0.23
6 (expiry)	55	100,000	0	25,800	0	0
Total					−71,800	

The trader having sold these options made quite some money by simply hedging according to the Black Scholes model. It is especially this feature that is responsible for the saying that an option trader wants the market to run away from his long strike going towards his short strike.

In this particular case, the call options all the time had a value, but when being long out of the money options that are outside the distribution, i.e. which have no value anymore, it might be smart to book them out of the portfolio for not performing loss making hedges when going towards the strike. In any case, when the market really starts to trend they can generate a profit without having hedged them too early. When they are part of a combination trade/position and are in the portfolio for reasons of protection, obviously: they shouldn't be taken out of the position.

VEGA CONVEXITY/VOMMA

The following strategy is a complex strategy. It is not easy to set up for the private investor; costs and the need for continuous monitoring of the position might make it unattractive. It is good though to study this strategy for it shows how volatility can heavily impact a vega neutral position and also what the consequences are, with regards to vega, for the different strikes in relation to each other when volatility starts to move.

It is called a vega convexity- or vomma strategy because one could scalp the changes in volatility, just as with gamma, which is sometimes called convexity because of the convex value development of an option, where one scalps the changes in delta on the back of the moves in the Future.

In this strategy the position will become short vega when the volatility drops and will become long vega when the volatility will go up. The trader is scalping volatility by buying vega (through options) at lower levels and selling vega at higher levels.

The structure is based on the fact that (when time to maturity doesn't change) the vega for an at the money option is a stable one (see chapter vega) when volatility

TABLE 14.6

	Vol 10%	Vol 15%	Vol 20%	Vol 25%	Vol 30%
50 Call vega	0.20	0.20	0.20	0.20	0.20
60 Call vega	0.04	0.10	0.14	0.17	0.18
40 Put vega	0.01	0.06	0.10	0.12	0.13

TABLE 14.7

	Vol 30%	Vol 35%	Vol 40%	Vol 45%	Vol 50%
50 Call vega	0.20	0.20	0.20	0.20	0.20
70 Call vega	0.12	0.15	0.16	0.17	0.18
40 Put vega	0.13	0.14	0.15	0.16	0.16

would change, while the vega for out of the money options (and thus also in the money options) is changing when volatility would change. The change in vega for options is being called vomma.

With a maturity of 1 year and the Future at 50, the vega of the 50 and 60 call and the 40 put at different volatilities will look as follows:

Table 14.6 shows how the vega of out of the money options, as opposed to the at the money options, increase along with an increase in volatility.

At higher volatilities (around 45%) the vega for the 60 call will not increase much more. The probability distribution/range for the Future to trade at maturity is so large (see chapter on volatility) that the 60 call is considered as being fairly at the money and hence will end up having a vega of around 0.20 as well. As a result the call will have no vomma anymore. At higher volatility levels, obviously a higher strike (for instance the 70 call) will have to be chosen for displaying changes in vega with increasing volatility. The same applies to the 40 put: the higher the volatility, the closer to 0.20 the vega of the strike is, as shown in Table 14.7.

Chart 14.15 depicts the vega distribution at 20% volatility, maturity at 1 year and the Future at 50. To set up a vega convexity position, one will have to trade out of the money options because they are the ones having vomma. As shown in the tables before, the 60 call (and also 70 call) and the 40 put will have a higher vega at higher volatility levels and their vega will decrease when the volatility will drop, their vomma will thus be positive.

By just buying the 40 puts or 60 calls (or both) in order to have a positive vomma position, one would initially set up a vega long position, this vega position will have to be hedged by selling vega (thus selling options) preferably options without vomma in order to create a vega neutral position with a positive vomma at inception. There is no directional view on the volatility so the trader doesn't want to run the risk of an adverse move in the volatility and hence enters into a vega neutral

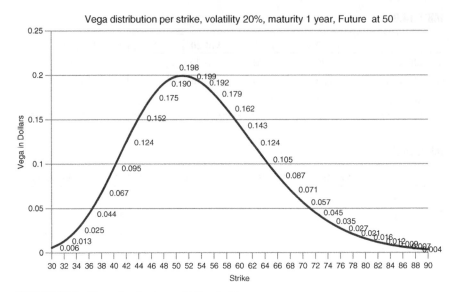

CHART 14.15   Vega distribution at 20% volatility

position. The options to be sold are the at the money options which are in this case the 50 calls and puts. No matter what happens in the volatility (within certain limits) they will not generate vomma.

Let's assume a trader who sells 10,000 50 calls in order to buy the 60 calls twice as much (he will hedge his delta), with a volatility of 15%, maturity at 1 year and the Future trading at 50. Table 14.6 shows that this is a vega neutral trade; being short 10,000 50 calls with a vega of 0.20 and long 20,000 60 calls with a vega of 0.10. When the volatility would move to 20%, the Future still at 50, he will lose 10,000 × 0.20 × 5 (% points) being $10,000 on the 50 strike, but he will earn 20,000 × 0.12 (average vega over the range) × 5 (% points) being $12,000 on the 60 call, making a total profit of 2,000 dollars. Now, at a volatility level of 20%, the trader is long 800 vega (short 10,000 calls at 0.20, long 20,000 calls at 0.14); he could decide to sell 4,000 50 calls additionally in order to have a flat vega position again (Future at 50).

Following on that move the volatility drops 5 points again. The trader is short 14,000 50 calls, generating a $14,000 profit (14,000 × 0,20 × 5 vol points) where he loses 20,000 × 0.12 × 5 being 12,000 on the 60 calls. Back at 15% volatility he is now short vega because he sold too many 50 calls and he will have to buy back 4,000 50 calls. As a result he sold 4,000 calls at 20% volatility and bought them back at 15% volatility, so actually one dollar lower (selling 4,000 at $4, buying them back at $3). So he scalped 4,000 calls with a dollar.

Having sold the 50 calls when volatility had been gone up (no vomma) he could have decided to buy the vega back by buying additional 60 calls when the volatility would have come off again. That is increasing the position in size, but his P&L has grown and he will have a vega neutral position again.

The same would have worked with the 40 puts, he actually would have made slightly more because he had to buy more options to create the vega neutral position. The vega was on average a bit smaller but the volume outweighted that. The 60 calls increased by 40% in vega (from 0.10 to 0.14) where the 40 puts increased by 66% in vega (from 0.06 to 0.10).

When setting up this strategy one needs to choose the right strikes, when being too close to the at the moneys, the vomma of the option is too small to make a good profit. The 54 call for instance would only change from 0.18 vega at 15% to 0.19 vega at 20% volatility. Far out of the money options generate a high vomma, however for other considerations in the position, like adjusting the strikes or having protective options, a strike which is around 1.75 straddles out of the money could work quite well for the upside. The strategy will hence be set up in a 1 by 2 ratio where, as explained in the chapter on vega, options with half the vega of the at the money are approximately 1.75 straddles away for the out of the money calls and 1.25 straddles away for the out of the money puts. So when the straddle is worth 8 dollars at 20% vol, one would expect the vega of the 64 call being around 0.10 and the vega of the 40 put being 0.10 as well. In the Black & Scholes model it is quite close to that:

Chart 14.16 depicts that when setting up a vega neutral 1 by 2 ratio by selling the 50 strike once, one should either buy the 40 puts twice or the 64 calls twice. Bear in mind that one trader sets up a ratio call spread or ratio put spread while his counterparty is actually setting up a vomma strategy. It all depends on expectations of the market which definitely differ per market participant. In this perspective both are reasonable strategies, it is all about proper market assessment.

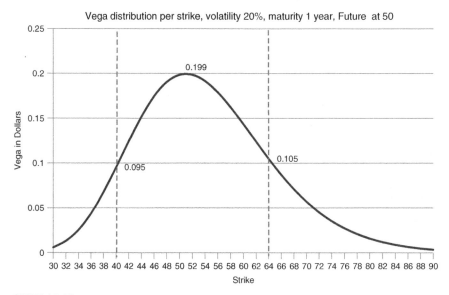

Vega distribution per strike, volatility 20%, maturity 1 year, Future at 50

CHART 14.16 Vega distribution, values for 40, 50 and 64 strike

The vomma buyer is happy when setting up the structure and the market remaining around the 50 level. There is quite a good chance that the volatility would drop. But for the volatility to come up, the market would need a move. If he would have the wrong position he could lose money. For instance, when he sets up the vomma strategy by selling the 50 strike and buying the 64 calls, he is vega short when the market would drop: a good chance that volatility will rise. So when the volatility would have the tendency to come up when the market moves down, one should have actually set up the 50 40 put spread 1 by 2 (selling the 50, buying the 40). But what if the volatility was already at a high level? There are many more scenarios. Each trader should consider these scenarios and set up his strategy accordingly. These scenarios might differ per asset class, it is based on the personal experience of the trader as well.

One could also enter into a position containing as well the (ratio) 1 by 2 call spread as the (ratio) 1 by 2 put spread. This is actually the position as discussed in the introduction where the trader sells the 50 puts once and buys the 40 puts twice and sells the 50 call once and buys the 60 (instead of the 64) call twice. Especially when volatility is already low and the market is slow and not moving much, it could have great potential. Any (large) move in the Future either way might cause volatility to move up. The trader is ready for that because at higher levels and at lower levels in the Future he will be vega long, next to that an increase in volatility will increase his vega position even further. When nothing would happen in the market, volatility would have a tendency to move down a bit further, hence a win-win situation.

In Table 14.8 below is shown that the full position is vega flat at 50 (at 20% volatility) and will gain vega when either way the market will start moving or the volatility will move up. At a lower volatility the structure will become vega short.

In Chart 14.17 one can see the effect on the vega of the strikes chosen. With an unchanged level in the Future and the volatility increasing from 20% to 25%, the 40 put will gain 2.4 cents and the 64 call will gain 3.3 cents in vega. The position consists of 20,000 options in each strike resulting in a vega increase through the 40 strike of 480 and a vega increase through the 60 strike of $660 adding up to $1,140 vega position increase (the vega of the 50 strike remains unchanged). At the inception of the trade; Volatility at 20% and the Future trading at 50 the initial vega

TABLE 14.8 Long 20,000 40 puts, short 20,000 50 calls/puts, long 20,000 64 calls, volatility at 20% at inception, Future at 50 at inception, maturity 1 year

Future	Vega at Vol 10%	Vega at Vol 15%	Vega at Vol 20%	Vega at Vol 25%	Vega at Vol 30%	Vega at Vol 35%	Vega at Vol 40%
45	−470	−200	460	1,145	1,705	2,130	2,440
50	−3,475	−1,640	30	1,170	1,910	2,405	2,740
55	−1,130	−185	865	1,700	2,295	2,710	3,005

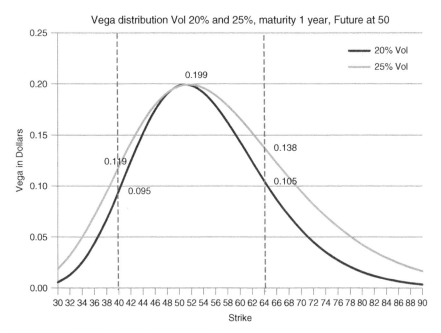

CHART 14.17   Vega distribution at 20% and 25% volatility

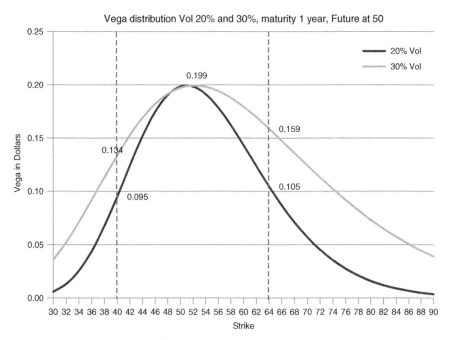

CHART 14.18   Vega distribution at 20% and 30% volatility

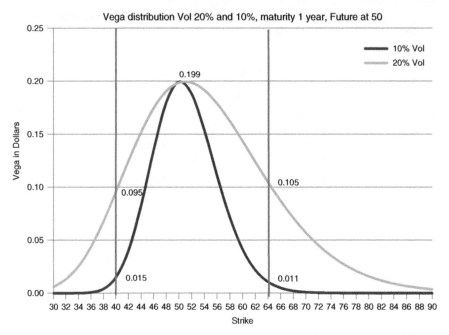

CHART 14.19 Vega distribution at 20% and 10% volatility

position was 30. When adding $1,140 vega, the structure will have an aggregate vega position of $1,170 as shown in the table.

When moving from 20% to 30% volatility, as shown in Chart 14.18, the position will gain 3.9 cents on the 40 strike and 5.4¢ on the 64 strike in vega, being 20,000 times 9.3 cents aggregated, resulting in a vega increase of approximately $1,860.

Chart 14.19 is an example of how the vega distribution narrows extremely from 20% to 10% volatility, resulting in a large profit. Not many traders would let their profits run for 10 points (on the way down) and run the risk of a retracement in volatility. Letting it run would have created a large profit, however the prudent trader will gradually buy back some vega when the volatility will come off.

VEGA CONVEXITY IN RELATION TO TIME/ VETA

A very important feature of the vega-convexity strategy is that it is also much influenced by time. As shown in the chapter on vega, in time the distribution will narrow (when volatility is stable). Out of the money options will quickly lose value and hence vega. The at the money options also lose vega but at a slower pace.

The 40 50 or 50 64 vomma strategy, or a combination of both, will lose vegas in time. The structure with a maturity of 9 months is already vega short, as shown in Chart 14.20. The trader will have to decide to buy some 50s, however not resulting in vomma, or some more out of the money options. This feature will become

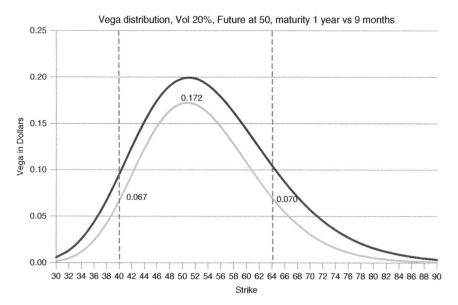

CHART 14.20 Vega distribution, maturity 1 year and 9 months

more pronounced further in time: the change of vega values in time is called veta. At some stage the 64 calls and 40 puts are too far out of the money, or have even lost all their vega value. New strikes, closer to the at the money strike, will have to be considered as a hedge against the resulting short vega position.

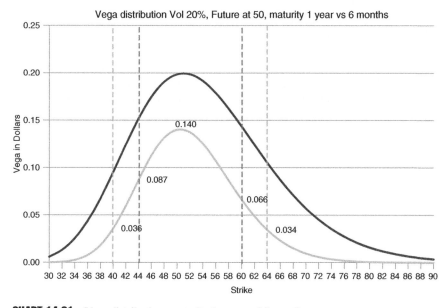

CHART 14.21 Vega distribution, maturity 1 year and 6 months

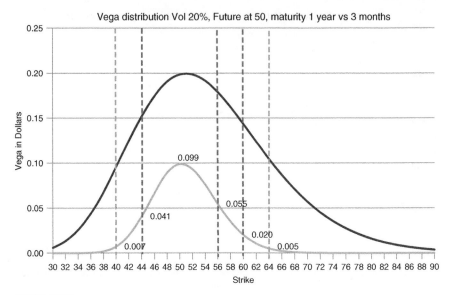

CHART 14.22   Vega distribution, maturity 1 year and 3 months

With 6 months to maturity one might consider buying other strikes. The 64 calls and the 40 puts don't generate any meaningful vega anymore, as shown in Chart 14.21. They might be too far out of the money for protection on the short position in the 50 strike. The trader should consider buying some vega in strikes which are a bit closer at the money.

Chart 14.22 shows that after some time, some long options fall out of the probability distribution. As well the 64 call as the 40 puts have become worthless. They no longer form part of the strategy but it's a free option. When the strategy is vega neutral again one should book his free options out of his position (think of killer-gamma) and continue to "close" the 50 strike in. One day it may start moving again and maybe it will break towards new levels and runs towards strikes which are far out of the money, strikes which are considered being worthless, suddenly creating a large upside.

Index

Printed and bound by CPI Group (UK) Ltd, Croydon, CR0 4YY

16/04/2025

14658499-0002